BRUCE
CHATWIN

"He was looking for stories the world could give him
and that he could embellish. He didn't give a damn whether
they were true or not; only whether they were good."

SALMAN RUSHDIE

The definitive biography
of the most compelling and
the most attractive literary
figure of his generation.

THE HARVILL PRESS
LONDON

NICHOLAS
SHAKESPEARE

GRANTA

GRANTA 66, SUMMER 1999

EDITOR   *Ian Jack*
DEPUTY EDITOR   *Liz Jobey*
MANAGING EDITOR   *Karen Whitfield*
EDITORIAL ASSISTANT   *Sophie Harrison*

CONTRIBUTING EDITORS   *Neil Belton, Pete de Bolla, Frances Coady, Ursula Doyle, Will Hobson, Blake Morrison, Andrew O'Hagan*

ASSOCIATE PUBLISHER   *Sally Lewis*
FINANCE   *Geoffrey Gordon, John Moreira*
SALES   *David Hooper*
PUBLICITY   *Gail Lynch, Louisa Renton*
SUBSCRIPTIONS   *John Kirkby, Darryl Wilks*
PUBLISHING ASSISTANT   *Mark Williams*
TO ADVERTISE CONTACT   *Jenny Shramenko* 0171 274 0600

PUBLISHER   *Rea S. Hederman*

Granta, 2-3 Hanover Yard, Noel Road, London N1 8BE
Tel 0171 704 9776 Fax 0171 704 0474
e-mail for editorial: editorial@grantamag.co.uk

Granta US, 1755 Broadway, 5th Floor, New York, NY 10019-3780, USA
Website: www.granta.com

TO SUBSCRIBE call 0171 704 0470 or e-mail subs@grantamag.co.uk
A one-year subscription (four issues) costs £24.95 (UK), £32.95 (rest of Europe) and £39.95 (rest of the world).

Granta is printed in the United States of America. The paper used in this publication meets the minimum requirements of American National Standard for Information Sciences—Permanence of Paper for Printed Library Materials, ANSI Z39.48-1984. ∞

Design: The Senate
Front cover photograph: Bruno Dössekker © Binjamin Wilkomirski
Back cover photograph: Augustianska orphanage, Cracow, c1946

ISBN 0 903141 28 0

"If you want to get
ahead of the literary game
this year, practise getting your
jaws around the following
syllables: Raj Kamal Jha…
precise yet bewitching prose"

Peter Popham,
Independent on Sunday

Do not miss this year's hottest literary debut

The BLUE BEDSPREAD
RAJ KAMAL JHA

A first novel of
extraordinary power

"An accomplished debut"
Publishing News

PICADOR

DAVID CRANE

LORD BYRON'S JACKAL

A Life of Edward John Trelawny

"There is a mad
chap come here –
whose name is Trelawny...
He comes on the friend of Shelley, great,
glowing, and rich in romance...But tell me
who is this odd fish? They talk on him here
as a camelion who went mad on reading
Lord Byron's 'Corsair'."

JOSEPH SEVERN 1822

'Trelawny emerges from this splendidly readable
account as one of the key makers of the modern celebrity.'

JONATHAN BATE 1998

www.fireandwater.com

flamingo

GRANTA 66

Truth + Lies

Elena Lappin THE MAN WITH TWO HEADS   7

Javier Marías BAD NATURE   67

Jillian Edelstein THE TRUTH COMMISSION   107

Stacey Richter GOAL 666   147

Claire Messud ADULTS   163

Adewale Maja-Pearce HOW PINKIE KILLED A MAN   199

William Fiennes THE SNOW GEESE   207

Jayne Anne Phillips BIG BOY SPORTS   227

NOTES ON CONTRIBUTORS   255

THE BIG ISSUE FOUNDATION

ELIJAH'S STORY

Will you help homeless people to help themselves?

For Elijah, the Big Issue was a godsend. Selling The Big Issue was the first step he took away from the streets. The Big Issue Foundation helped him complete his journey by opening doors to housing, training, education and employment.

"*The Big Issue Foundation really helped me get back on my feet. I was homeless on and off for five years. I couldn't work as I didn't have a stable address. I did a one week decorating course in paint skills through the Big Issue Foundation. Staff spent time with me and provided opportunities for me. They also helped me enrol on a counselling course. I want to help the homeless and old people. I can go to college now without a worry of where I'm going to stay.*"

The Big Issue Foundation gives homeless people real opportunities to help themselves and change their lives for the better. With your support we can help many more people like Elijah move off the streets and into a home and a job or training.

Please give whatever you can afford today. You can see the difference you'll make.

With thanks to Skidmore Turnbull for kind donation of design.

- -

Yes – I want to help people like Elijah.

Please fill in your details using BLOCK CAPITALS

Title

Full name

Address

Postcode

Reg Charity No 1049077   GRAN

I enclose a cheque/postal order made payable to
The Big Issue Foundation for:

☐ £250   ☐ £100   ☐ £50   ☐ £25   ☐ Other £ ....

OR please deduct the amount specified above from my credit card.

Card No ☐☐☐☐☐☐☐☐☐☐☐☐☐☐☐☐

Exp Date ☐☐☐☐

Just call 0171 526 3234 to make an instant credit card donation.

Date   Signature

Please send to: **The Big Issue Foundation, 236-240 Pentonville Road, London N1 9JY**

☐ Please send me further information about The Big Issue Foundation.
☐ Please send me details on how I can help by making regular donations through my bank.

GRANTA

THE MAN WITH TWO HEADS

HEADS

Elena Lappin

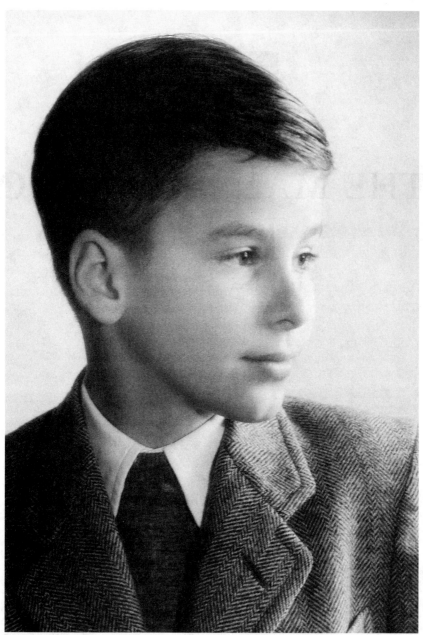

Bruno Dössekker, 1949

In the course of researching the story that follows I talked to Steven Spielberg, who made the film *Schindler's List*. Like the novel, *Schindler's Ark*, on which it is based, the film used fictional devices, invented scenes and dialogue, to dramatize fact. The film was such a popular success that it would be fair to say that many millions of people throughout the world received their primary instruction on the Holocaust through it. Spielberg diverted much of the profits from the film into another of his creations, the Shoah Foundation, which would record and videotape the memories of the Holocaust's real survivors—people as themselves and not played by actors, delivering their witness accounts to camera, the only script their own. The Shoah Foundation has done remarkable work. In Spielberg's words: 'We have collected more than 50,000 testimonies in thirty-one languages across fifty-seven countries. That's more than fourteen years of material [in playing time], enough videotape to circumnavigate the globe.'

The question I wanted to ask Spielberg was an uncomfortable one: would this great archive serve the future as a reliable source of history? 'Absolutely,' said Spielberg. 'Through this material, long after they are gone, survivors can speak to future generations.' It provided, he said, 'an unparalleled means of understanding the experience of the victim... They can teach us about the Holocaust in an educationally compelling and emotionally moving way.'

To break our trust in these memories would be a cruel thing; to question their veracity, equally cruel.

I look at the picture reproduced on the opposite page—that nice-looking, sensitive boy—and wonder, not for the first time, where he thinks he has come from and who he thinks he is.

1.

More than half a century ago, soon after the end of the Second World War, a young boy became the foster child of Dr Kurt and Mrs Martha Dössekker. The Dössekkers were wealthy, German-speaking Swiss citizens who lived in a villa in Zürichberg, the most affluent quarter of Zurich. Dr Dössekker was a well-known dermatologist; his father, Dr Walter Dössekker, had been the country's first specialist in radiology. The couple had no children of their own and no prospect of having any; Mrs Dössekker was nearly fifty, her husband several years older. They had high hopes for their foster son. Perhaps he would become a successful physician and perpetuate the family's name and reputation.

The child arrived, according to all the available documentation, with the name of Bruno Grosjean. He was born in the Swiss town of Biel, and had been taken into care by the town authorities, since his mother was poor and he was illegitimate. The Dössekkers stuck with his Christian name, but in 1947, the year he started school, they changed his last name to Dössekker.

Bruno Dössekker was in some ways a disappointment to his adoptive parents. At school, he took more interest in the arts than in sciences. At university in Geneva, he abandoned a course in medicine and turned instead to history and music. It was music that eventually gave him a living. He became a clarinet player and teacher, and, more extraordinarily, also a clarinet builder, assembling the instruments from scratch in his own workshop.

In 1964, when he was twenty-three, Bruno married a Zurich girl, Annette, from a titled Swiss family, and they had three children, two boys and a girl. But the clarinet proved a hard way to make money and Bruno found it difficult to support his family. The marriage became strained and he and his wife separated. In 1981 he fell seriously ill and had several operations. A year later, he met his new partner, Verena, an opera singer who taught music at the same high school as Bruno near Zurich. Together, they moved to a large farmhouse in the country and slowly Bruno began to regain his health.

It was around this time that he began to write down scenes from his early childhood. These were not scenes from a Christian childhood in Switzerland, but from a Jewish childhood spent in the most terrible time and place to be Jewish in modern history. He remembered being a Jewish child in Poland during the Second World War, and he remembered the horrors he had endured, separated from his parents at the age of three, in the Nazi concentration camps.

He could recall these experiences with such extreme emotional clarity that, encouraged by his partner, he eventually turned them into a book. The book quickly found an agent, the agent found a publisher, and then many publishers. It appeared first in Germany in 1995, and soon after in another dozen countries. The book was widely praised and won literary awards. Publishers and critics talked of it as a 'classic' of Holocaust literature. Its author appeared in several documentary films and began to address conferences and seminars on the Holocaust. In the English translation, its title is *Fragments*, subtitle *Memories of a Childhood, 1939–1948*.

Fragments told the powerful story of how the author was separated from his parents during the massacre of Jews in Riga, how he escaped by boat to Poland, how he was taken to Majdanek concentration camp, and then to another camp, possibly Auschwitz; how at the end of the war he was taken to a Jewish orphanage in Cracow, and then, when he was aged about seven, to Switzerland; and how his adoptive parents and Swiss society in general had repressed these memories by refusing to acknowledge them.

Both his adoptive parents died in 1986, which, given the book's unsympathetic portrayal of them, might have been just as well. In any case, Bruno Dössekker was no longer the author's name. Some years before, in the 1980s, he had begun to call himself Binjamin Wilkomirski as part of his reclaimed identity, and Binjamin Wilkomirski was how he appeared on the title page. The name 'Dössekker' appeared nowhere in the book. By 1998, an Internet search could yield thousands of references to Binjamin Wilkomirski, and not one to Bruno Dössekker.

2.

I first met Binjamin Wilkomirski in the spring of 1997, when he came to London to receive the *Jewish Quarterly* Prize for non-fiction. I was editor of that magazine at the time, and when I met Wilkomirski at the awards ceremony, I thought: Here, for the first time in my life, I see a writer who actually *is* his book. But he hardly seemed old enough or strong enough to have survived the Holocaust. He had a slight body and a soft face which was framed by prominent sideburns and a halo of light-brown curls. He was dressed in a rather theatrical shirt and vest, vaguely reminiscent of Eastern European folklore.

Verena, his partner, accompanied him. She looked taller and stronger; Wilkomirski looked as if he might collapse without her physical support. I tried to congratulate him and to talk a little about

Elena Lappin

Fragments, but he managed only a weak smile. When he did speak, he wept. He was visibly moved by everyone's response to what he had written. In fact, he seemed as moved by the reaction to his book as others had been by the book itself.

Not since Anne Frank's diaries had a child's view of the Holocaust touched so many readers. *Fragments* is a slim book, about 150 pages. I had read it as the terrifyingly stark testimony of a man whose identity had been shattered even before he had a chance to become a child. 'I have no mother tongue, nor a father tongue either,' the book begins. 'My language has its roots in the Yiddish of my eldest brother, Mordechai, overlaid with the Babel-babble of an assortment of children's barracks in the Nazis' death camps in Poland. It was a small vocabulary; it reduced itself to the bare essentials required to say and to understand whatever would ensure survival. At some point during this time, speech left me altogether and it was a long time before I found it again.'

I hadn't been a judge for the prize, but I never doubted that Wilkomirski's book deserved it. As one of a small number of child survivors of the Holocaust, he had written from a rare perspective. It's as if the little girl in the red dress in Spielberg's *Schindler's List* had survived the extermination camps and written about her experience.

The original German version, published by the Frankfurt house, Suhrkamp Verlag, had been quickly followed by translations in English (Schocken Books in the US, Picador in Britain), French (Calmann-Lévy), Italian (Mondadori), Dutch (Bert Bakker) and Hebrew (Yediot Aharonot in Israel), among others. Critics called the book 'morally important', 'fine art', 'brave' and 'profoundly moving'. According to Daniel Goldhagen, the author of *Hitler's Willing Executioners*, 'Even those conversant with the literature of the Holocaust will be educated by this arresting book. All will be deeply moved.' The novelist Paul Bailey, in the London *Daily Telegraph*, wrote: 'I had to read it slowly, taking silent walks between chapters, so raw and powerful are the feelings it contains and inspires... The bravery of this undertaking cannot be exaggerated, nor the sense of human dignity it leaves with the reader.' In America, Binjamin Wilkomirski won the National Jewish Book Award in the autobiography/memoir category from a shortlist which included Elie

Wiesel and Alfred Kazin. It seemed that no one—no prize judge, publisher, critic, scholar or reader—was troubled by the author's two-page afterword in which he shyly introduced the idea to his readers that Binjamin Wilkomirski was not his only identity.

Like many child survivors of the Holocaust, he wrote, he had received a new identity, 'another name, another date and place of birth'. But it was merely a piece of paper—'a makeshift summary, no actual birth certificate'—which gave the date of his birth as 12 February 1941. 'But this date has nothing to do with either the history of this century or my personal history. I have now taken legal steps to have this imposed identity annulled.' He went on: 'Legally accredited truth is one thing—the truth of a life another. Years of research, many journeys back to the places where I remember things happened, and countless conversations with specialists and historians have helped me to clarify many previously inexplicable shreds of memory...'

A year passed after our first meeting, and then we met again at a dinner given by Wilkomirski's London publisher during his British publicity tour. Again, he was with Verena, but this time he did not seem quite so frail or melancholy. Clearly, the international success of *Fragments*—now in paperback—had made him more confident. I can't recall much of our conversation that evening, only that it was pleasant and relaxed, and that he told us how important it was for him to find a good patisserie and a good antiques shop in every city he visits.

Looking back, I can't say that my feeling towards his book could be defined as 'suspicion'—I too had read the afterword without a qualm; but I was struck by how well constructed it seemed, that it wasn't fragmented *enough*, despite its author's claim that he had not imposed an adult perspective on his child's view. Also, he had used an image which was out of place in a Jewish book. 'I rode him like King David on his snow-white horse,' he wrote of an incident with a camp guard who sat Wilkomirski briefly on his shoulders. Where did that come from? Jews didn't ride horses, that was a Roman thing; and a white one? Not a Jewish image at all. (The Messiah is supposed to arrive on a white donkey—but that's another story). But these were small things.

The idea that the book could be a confection, that Wilkomirski had been nowhere near the Holocaust, did not occur to me (and seems to have occurred to very few others) until a Swiss weekly, *Weltwoche*, published two pieces in August and September 1998, by Daniel Ganzfried, a young Swiss Jew and, like Wilkomirski, the author of a book set during the Holocaust. Ganzfried denounced *Fragments* as a work of fiction. He wrote that Wilkomirski's true biography would exclude the possibility of his ever having been in a concentration camp, 'except as a tourist'. The facts of his birth and early life, according to Ganzfried, went like this:

> Born Bruno Grosjean 12 February 1941, in Biel, an industrial town in Kanton Bern, Switzerland; mother Yvonne Berthe Grosjean, unmarried; placed in the care of the Biel welfare authority; taken by the Dössekkers as their foster son from a children's home in Adelboden, and brought to Zurich sometime in 1945; adopted by them in 1957; registered as starting primary school in Zurich, 1947.

Ganzfried supplied some documentary evidence for this childhood spent in peaceful, neutral Switzerland—so far removed from Wilkomirski's memories of death camps in Poland—and his exposé was picked up by the international media. Taken at its face value, it seemed to reveal Wilkomirski as a fantasist and his book as a lie. But Wilkomirski's several publishers did not drop the book from their lists; apparently, they were not convinced. As for Wilkomirski, he refused to respond to his accuser, other than to say in an interview soon after Ganzfried's pieces appeared, that his readers had always had the option to understand his book as either fact or fiction. He then withdrew from public life, on his doctor's advice; no more interviews, no more lectures on the publishing and Holocaust circuits, a time for seclusion.

Still, I wondered if he would see me. We had met before, I was hardly an enemy. In fact—a confession—whether or not his book was a lie, I felt sympathy for him. He had seemed so fragile, and why *invent* such a terrible childhood? His faxed reply to my request was filled with rage against journalists: 'They twist everything I say and what they write or say afterwards is the opposite of what I meant!' But he agreed that we could talk. He would pick me up at Weinfelden station, about an hour's train ride from Zurich, and from there drive to his farmhouse.

3.

The early morning train from Zurich moved through hills and fields which were white with snow. In my compartment, a stern old lady stared at me disapprovingly and reprimanded me for putting my feet up on the opposite seat. Young soldiers with heavy-looking guns filled most of the rest of the carriage, solemnly and silently staring out of the windows. The cliché of Switzerland, I thought: white, clean, unruffled, and, in a quite literal way, defensive (even a hundred years ago, Franz Kafka noted the surprising—to him—sight of the Swiss military).

I thought about Wilkomirski. Either he had been born in this country or he hadn't, in which case *Fragments* was a lie—his early lives were mutually exclusive. But 'lie' might be too strong a word, meant for courts of law. Writing has milder terms. In writing, there is fiction and non-fiction. These seem clear divisions, but as any writer knows the boundary can be blurred, and nowhere more so than in this literary form 'the memoir'. Trying to evoke the past the memoirist needs to recreate it, and in doing so he may be tempted to invent—a detail here and there, a scene, a piece of dialogue. In any case, did it matter so much whether *Fragments* was fact or fiction? Wasn't it enough that its prose was so moving and powerful that it made hundreds of thousands of readers think about and perhaps 'feel'—if not understand—the Holocaust?

On the train, I decided that these defences would not do. If Wilkomirski had made it up, his pretence as a genuine survivor, his public speeches in the name of all child survivors, his book's role in the historical record, his claims to be a witness—all these needed to be denounced. If care with the truth does not matter here, then it can matter nowhere. Then again, if Binjamin Wilkomirski had not, as a small boy, lost his entire family to the Nazis; if he had not witnessed unimaginable suffering and survived; if, inside this man, was not the little boy who remembered such horrors that he had to forget them before he could remember them again—then another question of truth arose: what had happened to him, who was he?

When I walked from the platform I saw him across the tiny station parking lot. He stood leaning against his car, looking slightly lost or abstracted. His distinctive head of curls seemed even bigger than before—but this turned out to be an illusion: he was just much thinner than I had remembered him. As I approached him, I realized that I had kept only a blurred picture of him in my memory. Now I saw a face I would no longer describe as soft. It was a busy, attractive face.

He barely smiled as we shook hands. I worried about his nervous state, but he was a determined, confident driver, negotiating the icy roads at higher speed than I thought necessary. He talked in a low voice in slightly Yiddish-sounding German about the friendliness of his village, and about how fortunate he and Verena had felt when they found their house. 'When we saw it, it was love at first sight,' he said, and finally smiled.

I had imagined a lonely farmhouse in the countryside, but it stood, majestically, on a main road in the centre of the village. I liked it; it was inviting, unpretentious, full of books, papers, photos, paintings. There was a profusion of rather touristy Jewish memorabilia. Verena greeted me warmly, remembering our meeting a year before in London. She, too, looked much thinner now, and I thought of her sustaining presence everywhere he went—all his journeys, interviews, parties, public events. I knew that she had a handicapped son, and that her life had not been easy, even before she met Wilkomirski. In one of the documentary films made about her husband, she says: 'I call him Bruno. "Binjamin" has something diminutive about it, you know, like being the youngest son, and I don't want to see him in that way. In spite of all the suffering, life has moved on, even his life.'

It was ten in the morning. We sat down in the living room and had tea and Swiss pastries, and soon the room filled with cigarette smoke; my hosts were committed smokers. We started talking, and didn't finish till almost six in the evening. Wilkomirski didn't want me to use my tape recorder or my camera. 'There have been too many pictures of him already,' Verena said. 'Every little article comes with a huge portrait of Bruno. It's ridiculous!'

I wondered if I could see his Holocaust library, a personal archive of papers, books (two thousand of them), films and photographs which Daniel Ganzfried had mentioned in his pieces and which has featured in the documentary films. Wilkomirski shook his head: 'I don't have the strength for all that at the moment. Maybe I'll go back to it when I'm better, but now...I'm very weak.' His voice was a young boy's soprano, a little on the feeble side. It occurred to me that it was much easier to tell the story of a traumatic childhood in that delivery, rather than in adult baritone. It was a child's voice—and it was asking for gentle, considerate treatment.

I said that I'd like the interview to begin with his life in the present and then work backwards—a reverse chronology that would, I hoped, prevent his repeating the same story he had told so many times before, and perhaps reveal a little more.

Wilkomirski seemed to like the idea. After a few remarks about the viciousness of the press, he relaxed a little and began to talk about his life and work as a musician. He teaches music at three high schools, and has a workshop where he builds his clarinets. He said he tailored them to a player's anatomy and sometimes their physical handicap. 'I once spent a year putting together a clarinet for a man who was missing a finger. It took me a year and a half to build a special flute for a woman who had cerebral palsy, to make it possible for her to accompany a choir in her home. Her flute contained a tiny mechanism, like a watch.'

Then, although he wouldn't show me the archive, he talked about what it meant to him. He had sophisticated equipment. With the help of a computer technician, he examined documents and photographs which related to children who had been given new identities. 'I have been in contact with many people who are in that situation, from several countries. I try to help them. We have a scanner, which helps us with the analysis of facial features in old photos, and to determine whether a document is genuine or not.'

Where did all these documents come from?

'I actually bought many of them, some of them through "dark", possibly not entirely legal channels...' He mentioned the Nuremberg trials, and three large boxes of papers that he'd received from the daughter of one of the prosecutors.

'I also read the depositions taken as part of Nazi trials, and I always look for anything to do with children,' he said.

Didn't he use the research facilities at universities?

'I don't trust Swiss universities,' he said.

Elena Lappin

'Last time we saw each other you seemed very happy.'

'Happy...that would be the wrong word, but I was pleased that my book had helped people, and that I was receiving so much moral support. I felt that I could come out of my hiding place, and really be myself. For the first time in my life, I felt liberated.'

'And now?'

He fell silent for a moment.

'Now I feel like I'm back in the camps.'

The Holocaust had entered our conversation and now didn't leave it, though we were in the middle of discussing his adult life. He avoided trains, he said, because he could not forget *those* trains. (I apologized for praising the comfort and efficiency of Swiss trains, on our way here in his car, and was rewarded with a benevolent smile.) 'When I was married to my ex-wife and had to commute to Geneva for a while, I pretended to take a train, because she wanted me to, but secretly, I always took the car.'

He had a mortal fear of insects. 'It's quite terrible,' Verena interjected, 'every little bug is a problem. I understand it, but it's really too much! And—can I tell about the feet?' She looked at Wilkomirski, who nodded.

'Bruno moves his feet constantly during his sleep. It's a habit he's had since the camps, to keep the rats away at night.'

'Yes,' Wilkomirski said, 'if you keep moving them, like this'—he demonstrated a waving motion with his feet—'the rats stay away.'

When he talked about the camps, he trembled and cried—a heap of uncontrollable, painful emotions. Sometimes, he couldn't speak and needed to wait quite a while before he caught his breath again. The worst crisis occurred when Verena left us alone for a couple of hours to go shopping. I thought he would have a major breakdown, right there in front of me—and I was afraid. What would I do? Would I be blamed?

But he collected himself after a time and we switched to a less sensitive topic: Switzerland.

'In this country, everything and everyone has to be proper, quiet, bourgeois. Everything must be kept simple, no complicated concepts—otherwise, you are treated with suspicion. That is how I was brought up, and I played along I guess. But in 1981, when I recovered from

18

my illness, which had almost killed me, I said to myself: "I am sick of leading this pretend-Swiss life. Enough of all that." And I decided to be myself, which meant going back to the beginning—my own beginning.'

Ten difficult years followed. He continued to be ill: a disease of the blood cells. He had several serious operations. He lost contact with his children, although one of them, his son Jann, became close to him again, as a teenager. 'I was presented to them as "an idiot", who was too lazy to work, and would soon die anyway.'

It was Verena—after he met her in 1982—who suggested a connection between his recurring physical illness and his mental anguish. 'She was the first person who was willing to listen to me, really listen.' He began telling her what he remembered. Between the early 1980s and 1990 she had heard about two-thirds of the memories which would eventually become his book. She advised him to start writing them down.

Verena said: 'I wanted to lead a normal life, and did not always want to adjust to his fears. He had terrible nightmares.' She recommended a therapist, who was a friend of hers.

Wilkomirski said: 'The idea of the therapy was for me to learn to speak about my past without fear or panic. It also helped me to clarify certain details of my memories.'

I turned to Verena: 'Did you always believe him?'

'Not always. I had my doubts. But the more I listened, the more I was convinced, because his stories were always consistent. And his research, when he travelled to the places in Eastern Europe where he thought his memories belonged, finally confirmed so many things—I have no doubt that he is telling the truth about himself. I checked the papers as well.'

I asked Verena what it was like to live with a man whose past was so traumatic, and so much a part of his present. Did she feel lonely?

'It is a very lonely situation. But he gives me support, as well.'

Wilkomirski added: 'It is good to be able to share all this sadness with someone.'

Remembering those young soldiers on the train, I asked him whether he had done military service. I knew that in Germany the

children of Holocaust survivors—or young survivors themselves—
were automatically exempt from military duty.

'I was drafted, at the age of twenty-seven, for a short while,' he
said; but it had not worked out:

'One day I arrived in the army barracks in Basle. The building,
with its barred windows, confused and frightened me. I was late for
a meal, most soldiers had already finished eating. They laughed at
me, in a vicious, mocking sort of way. There was a tin soup bowl,
but it was quickly taken away. I went looking for some food, and
found a storage room with massive quantities of bread, enough to
feed hundreds of soldiers. I stuffed all my pockets with the bread,
and hid as much of it as I could under my mattress. The next day,
a high officer came to give us a lecture, and I fainted. They had to
call a military doctor.'

The story reminded me of something. In *Fragments*, Wilkomirski
sees cheese rinds left on the table of his Swiss orphanage—
unimaginable waste for a survivor of the camps—and stuffs them into
his pockets. I pointed out the similarity to Wilkomirski.

'Yes,' he nodded. He made no other comment.

Before he drove me to the train, he took me to the barn and
showed me his music room and workshop, where, to my surprise,
he agreed to pose for a picture. On the train back to Zurich, my head
throbbed from all the talk and smoke. We had covered his life—if it
was his life—from his sketchily remembered childhood in Latvia and
Poland to his adolescence and adulthood in Zurich.

I believed him. Whenever he talked about the camps, I believed
him. His anguish was so genuine. It was impossible that someone
could fabricate such suffering simply to justify the claim of a book.
I returned to my hotel exhausted and convinced that I had been in
the presence of a witness to some of the worst horrors of this
century's history.

4.

A few days later after a second meeting with Wilkomirski, this time
at his other home, an apartment in Zurich, I attended a discussion,
also in Zurich, which had been organized by the Swiss branch of the
writers' international organization, PEN. This took the form of a

Binjamin Wilkomirski in his clarinet workshop, 1998.

'tribunal' on the Wilkomirski affair in which Wilkomirski more or less took on the role of 'the accused'. Only Wilkomirski wasn't there—he couldn't be persuaded to appear and face his critics. So instead, in the warm hall of the Neumarkt theatre, its floor scattered with real autumn leaves, we made do with the prosecution minus the defence, and some discussion of literary theory. Actors read excerpts from reviews, interviews, letters and legal documents. A sedate group of specialists in German literature tried to set up Wilkomirski's text as the springboard for a debate about the relationship between literary language and truth. But the audience didn't have much patience for these abstractions, nor did they seem particularly interested in discussing Switzerland's role in the Second World War. They wanted the juice: they wanted to talk about the man who wasn't there. Only one member of the audience seemed anxious to defend the absent author: he stood up and shouted 'Herr Wilkomirski really is ill.' Repeatedly, his book was referred to as 'Holocaust kitsch'.

At the centre of the debate was Wilkomirski's accuser, Daniel Ganzfried, a prematurely white-haired man of about forty, wearing jeans and a white shirt. If there was any passion in this gathering, it surfaced only after Ganzfried made an angry declaration: 'When an author writes about Auschwitz, people don't question the quality of his work. Where did Mr Wilkomirski steal his Holocaust images from?' The audience applauded, but I was torn between endorsing the crucial importance of this question, and resenting Mr Ganzfried for raising it in this hostile forum. I still felt sorry for Wilkomirski and still found it hard to believe his anguish was fake.

But then there is Ganzfried's evidence as published in *Weltwoche* and easily substantiated by the Swiss authorities. According to certificates in the archives of Biel (Kanton Bern), Binjamin Wilkomirski/Bruno Dössekker was born Bruno Grosjean in Biel on 12 February 1941, and placed with his future adoptive parents, the Dössekkers, on 13 October 1945, and finally adopted by them legally on 4 October 1957. The 'makeshift summary' which Wilkomirski refers to in his afterword is one of these documents. Wilkomirski is right—it is 'no birth certificate' in the sense that it wasn't issued at the time of his birth and omits information (the father's name, for example) normally found on birth certificates. It is headed

Abgekürzter Geburtsschein or 'summarized birth certificate'. But it hardly looks 'makeshift'; it contains the names of his mother and his adoptive parents and his place and time of birth, the coat of arms of Kanton Bern, the stamp and signature of Biel's registrar.

Obviously, it was important to meet Ganzfried. I arranged an interview, but he cancelled at the last minute. He was busy, he said, but would talk to me later on the phone. In the meantime I read his book on the Holocaust—a novel—and wondered about his pieces in *Weltwoche*. Their tone was not quite that of judicious, investigative journalism; they seemed suffused with contempt. Already I had heard gossip—Zurich may be a city but it has a small-town society—that Ganzfried had attacked Wilkomirski out of jealousy. Their books on the Holocaust were published in the same year, but it was *Fragments* that achieved international acclaim.

Daniel Ganzfried was born in 1958 in Israel, where his father, a Hungarian Jew and Auschwitz survivor, met his Swiss mother on a kibbutz. Their marriage was not a success and Daniel grew up with his grandparents in Bern. As an adult, he has earned his living in several ways—bookselling, driving taxis and trucks. The idea for his novel came when he and his father spent their first time alone together, in New York. When we talked on the phone, Ganzfried said: 'We were up on the Empire State building, and I asked my father: "Don't you feel that you have wasted your life?" To my enormous surprise, he said not at all, and started telling me all about his life, how full it had been. And I had always thought of him as a victim of Auschwitz, and only that. Now I saw that I had a real father who had lived, really lived, not just suffered.'

Later, in Switzerland, Ganzfried recorded seventy hours of his father's testimony about his life, before and during the war. This material became the basis for his novel. Ganzfried said: 'I know how easy it is to fictionalize real facts; I wrote about the Holocaust as the son of a survivor, but people often thought that I had really been there. That's why I found it so easy to see through Wilkomirski's writing. I didn't like his obsession with brutality, and the confusion between a child's view and that of a grown man. When it comes to Auschwitz, it is essential to tell the truth. I thought about my father, and other survivors: what does this kind of book do to them?'

Elena Lappin

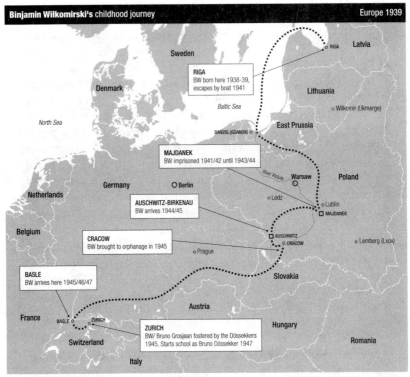

How did Ganzfried come to write about Wilkomirski? In this innocent way. A magazine called *Passages* (published by the Swiss cultural foundation, Pro Helvetia) was putting together an issue devoted to the idea of 'creativity', which in the words of the magazine's editor, Michael Guggenheimer, would feature 'creative people who excelled in an area which was different from their daily job'. Wilkomirski as musician-cum-writer was an ideal subject and Ganzfried seemed an ideal interviewer; they had the Holocaust as their bond. Guggenheimer offered Ganzfried the job. Ganzfried interviewed Wilkomirski, and then told *Passages* that, as he saw it, his account did not seem credible.

He said to me: 'Wilkomirski talked to me about Mengele; he said that his adoptive father wanted to use him for medical experiments. He cried a lot—and always at the right moment. When

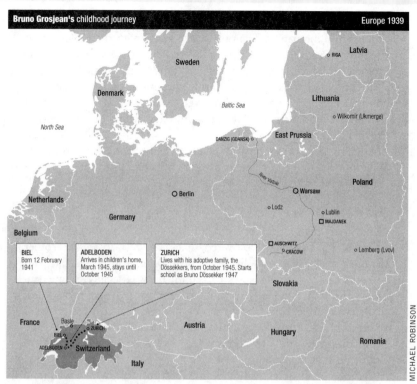

Bruno Grosjean's childhood journey   Europe 1939

BIEL
Born 12 February 1941

ADELBODEN
Arrives in children's home, March 1945, stays until October 1945

ZURICH
Lives with his adoptive family, the Dössekkers, from October 1945. Starts school as Bruno Dössekker 1947

MICHAEL ROBINSON

I asked whether he was circumcised—which is a natural question to ask of a Jewish man—he said yes. At first I thought he was maybe just confused, but when I received a letter from his lawyer forbidding me to look into his official papers, I was pretty convinced that something was not right.'

His story began to turn into a piece of detective-work. The research needed money. *Weltwoche*, which is Switzerland's leading cultural weekly, stepped in as joint funder. Then, when the piece was finished, *Passages* turned it down, because, according to Guggenheimer: 'We had been looking for a sophisticated portrait of the writer Wilkomirski, not a character assassination.'

The people at *Weltwoche*, on the other hand, were delighted. Ludwig Hasler, the paper's literary editor who worked closely with Ganzfried on the piece, said: 'I am not in favour of an emotional

25

approach to the Holocaust. It does not help to respond to it with sadness and mourning. The only way to deal with the Holocaust is to study it, rationally... I despise every sort of exploitation of the Holocaust, which is exactly what Wilkomirski has done.'

The paper feels that publication was more than justified. The consequence for Ganzfried, however, has not been so happy. 'I thought I would publish all the facts, and that would be that. Instead I'm realizing that my article has started a strangely philosophical discussion. So I have now decided to learn something from Mr Wilkomirski—to keep silent, as much as possible... As a writer, I have learned a lot from this dreadful experience.'

5.

Ganzfried's demolition of Wilkomirski relied on more than the archives. He had also discovered that Yvonne Grosjean's brother (Bruno's uncle) was still alive; that Bruno's natural father had paid towards the cost of his son's care until he was legally adopted in 1957; and that Yvonne Grosjean had later got married, though not to Bruno's father, and had no more children. Ganzfried even went so far as to ask Annie Singer, a former girlfriend of Wilkomirski, and his former wife, Annette, about whether or not he was circumcised. Both said that he was not.

None of this changed Wilkomirski's position, which was (and is) that whoever Bruno Grosjean may have been, he, Wilkomirski, was and is not him. He thinks that the Dössekkers must have used Bruno Grosjean's papers in place of his own, possibly non-existent ones. He believes that such cases of false identities were quite common in post-war Switzerland and other countries, and speaks of a 'conspiracy' between 'the Swiss authorities and private individuals'. He has no evidence to support his claims, 'except for my memories'. There is at least one serious problem with his identity-swap hypothesis, however. Binjamin Wilkomirski/Bruno Dössekker accepted a small inheritance from the person his papers describe as his natural mother, Yvonne Grosjean, after she died in 1981.

'My *so-called* natural mother,' he said, when I put this to him. 'I was critically ill at the time, about to undergo a serious operation. I was barely able to support my family. Out of the blue, I received a phone call from a lawyer, informing me that I was to inherit a modest sum of money from my so-called mother. Of course, I told him that I did not accept her as my mother, but the lawyer told me not to worry about it. So I agreed to take the money, after insisting on sharing it with two other persons. It wasn't much, but it actually saved me at that difficult moment in my life.'

Wilkomirski could not show me any documents or legal letters about his inheritance: 'It happened too long ago.' Some time later during this investigation, in Israel, I found an interview with him published in October 1998, in the newspaper *Yediot Aharonot*, in which he declared that he would now pass on some of the money to Yvonne's surviving brother, Max Grosjean (until Ganzfried's article a month or so before he hadn't known of his existence).

Following this up, in a later e-mail to Wilkomirski from London, I got a furious answer in German to my question about whether he had in fact fulfilled his intention to 'repay' Max Grosjean some of his sister's bequest. His reply burst into capital letters. 'I HAVE NOT RECEIVED ANY ILLEGAL MONIES. I HAVE, LEGALLY SPEAKING, NOTHING TO "REPAY"!!!!! Even if the "brother" had been known at the time, HE WOULD NOT HAVE BEEN LEGALLY ENTITLED to receive the inheritance! The officials had made it clear that the inheritance had to go where indicated in the papers. Mr Grosjean would have been entitled to receive it only if I and the corresponding documents had never existed.' He went on to say that he had been considering handing the money over to Mr Grosjean, NOT for legal reasons, but for moral reasons, as compensation for the way Ganzfried had invaded his privacy in the media.

That seemed an elaborate way of saying no, he had not given money to Yvonne's brother. But there was a phrase in his e-mail that struck me: 'if I had never existed' in this context seemed to allow the possibility in his own mind that Bruno Grosjean and Bruno Dössekker/Binjamin Wilkomirski might be one and the same person. I didn't pursue it. I knew by this stage that Wilkomirski could offer an explanation for every appearance of 'Bruno Grosjean' in his life. Again, whoever Bruno Grosjean was, he was only someone whose name and papers Wilkomirski was given, to hide his East European Jewish identity. No external evidence can puncture this approach, though (as I was to discover) much of it can be marshalled against the memories contained in his book. His explanations and denials began to remind me of the two-head theory attributed to the linguist, Paul Postal. It is used to describe an utterly arbitrary and unverifiable hypothesis, and goes something like this: Every person in the world has two heads, one of which is permanently invisible.

So what, in this two-headed world, became of the 'real' Bruno Grosjean? Wilkomirski told me that the Dössekkers took in another child before him. He remembers discovering a storage room full of old toys in their house, which was quickly emptied when he mentioned it to his adoptive mother. The toys, he believes, may have belonged to the real Bruno, whose name and papers Wilkomirski was then given as a young boy. Where did the real Bruno go? Wilkomirski remembers that when he was a teenager in Zurich he once met a boy of around the same age ('His name was Rolf or something like that') who told him that he was pleased to have escaped being raised by the Dössekkers, and that he was emigrating with his family to the United States.

The Dössekkers would know, of course, but they are dead. To judge from *Fragments*, Wilkomirski hated them as cold and unsympathetic despots, especially his adoptive father. But whatever the relations between them, and we have only Wilkomirski's account of it, the Dössekkers' desire, surely, was to make him and themselves happy.

We know from letters that there was opposition to the adoption from within the family, and that the Dössekkers ignored it. Letters dated 1946 and 1951 from Dr Dössekker's father, the radiologist, are fiercely critical, especially of the decision to make Bruno the couples' heir. 'We [wrote the elder Dössekker, meaning he and his wife] cannot bear the thought that, once adopted, Bruno will become the sole legal heir, not only of your entire bequest but also of one half of our joint inheritance, and will thus, without having moved a finger, become a young millionaire.'

Nonetheless, Bruno Dössekker did inherit his adoptive parents' estate when they died in 1986, five years after he inherited the much smaller legacy of Yvonne Grosjean. I do not know the sums, but we must assume that they helped fund his research into the Holocaust and the part he believes he played in it.

6.

Binjamin Wilkomirski is too modest when he declares in the opening pages of *Fragments*: 'I am not a poet or a writer.' His memoir shows a great deal of skill. He writes: 'I can only try to use words to draw as exactly as possible what happened, what I saw, exactly the way my child's memory has held on to it; with no benefit of perspective or vanishing point.' With this introduction, he has established the main character of his book—himself as a young child—whose narrative is not there to be checked for historical veracity. The child's voice is both a shield and a weapon: the author can effectively hide behind its imprecision and its vulnerability, and, at the same time, disarm a potentially sceptical reader with its emotional power.

As non-fiction, it is a tricky book to précis. It does not begin at the beginning and end at the end like old-fashioned biography. It takes episodic jumps back and forth between countries and times: Poland to Switzerland, Switzerland back to Poland. Its tenses slip about. The English version has no helpful chapter titles. It contains very few place names and no dates. The years in its subtitle, 1939–1948, do not appear in the text. The first might be his date of birth or it might be the year his memories start. Its only photograph—of the author 'aged about ten'—is also undated. Many people, including its publishers, have inferred 'facts' from its text which have been left unstated by the writer, or at most are suggestions. Of the city where the book begins: 'It must have been Riga.' Of a train's destination: 'I gather it has something to do with Lemberg (Lvov).'

With those caveats about its 'facts' and chronology, this is the story it seems to tell.

Binjamin is a Latvian Jewish boy born perhaps in 1938 or 1939. At the age of two or three, he witnesses the violent death of a man— 'maybe my father'. (This description lost its tentativeness on most book jackets, which harden it into the statement that he saw his own father die.) During the massacre of Jews in Riga (November 1941), the boy hears frightened cries of *'Achtung! Lettische Miliz!'* ('Watch it: Latvian militia!'). The man who may have been his father is crushed to death by a vehicle against the wall of the building. Binjamin, who was sitting on the ground, remembers: 'No sound comes out of his mouth, but a big stream of something black shoots out of his neck as the transport squashes him with a big crack against the house.' The boy realizes that from now on, he is alone.

He then remembers watching a group of adults poring over what would appear to be a map, in a small, dark room. He escapes from Riga on a boat; arrives at a station in a foreign country; takes two train journeys; then, more clearly remembered, spends an indefinite period hiding in a farmhouse, 'away somewhere amongst the Polish forests', with several older boys whom he describes as his brothers. One day, he is punished for looking out of the window, and is locked in a cellar. While he is there, some sort of battle takes place, and when he finally manages to escape from the cellar, a day or more later, he finds himself all alone in the deserted farmhouse.

Eventually, a truck arrives, full of people, including some older children. There are also grown-ups in uniforms. Binjamin is discovered and told by a woman wearing an impressive grey uniform, a peaked cap and shiny black boots, that they will take him to 'Majdan Lublin—Majdanek'. He is reassured, because he hopes to find his brothers in this place, but when he gets there, he is bitterly disappointed, for 'Majdanek is no playground'. He finds himself in a big barracks 'with a horde of other children'.

Binjamin's memories of Majdanek camp are a series of terrifying tableaux. Rats crawl from the corpses of dead women, lice run over his face in 'racing, ticklish streams', tiny, starving babies chew their own fingers down to the bone. Binjamin is kicked in the back of his head by a guard's black boot, and thrown head-first against a wall by another guard. He hears 'the unmistakable sound of breaking skulls' when babies are killed. At the consequent 'red mess' his stomach heaves with 'horror and disgust'. He also feels guilt. A new boy has come to the barracks. He has diarrhoea. The slop bucket is full. On Binjamin's advice, he relieves himself in his bunk. For this offence, he is taken by the guards and killed out of Binjamin's view ('We waited, motionless. Then there was a crack of bones, then hard footsteps and the sound of something being dragged...').

One day a woman warden comes to the barracks door calling his name. 'Binjamin! Is there a Binjamin here?' She says she has come to take him to see his mother. He does not know what 'mother' means. 'All I understood was that a mother, whether you had one or not, must be something that was worth fighting for, the way you fought over food.' They go to a barrack which is full of sick and dying women. When he reaches the spot indicated by the warden, he can make out 'the shape of a body under a grey cover. The cover moved. A woman's head became visible, then two arms laying themselves slowly on top of the cover.' He wonders whether this is his mother: 'One of the children had once said that if you have a mother, she belongs just to you! So this woman belonged to me, just me?' She beckons him closer. Binjamin sees that she is crying, and that she is trying to put a 'coarse and hard object' in his hand. This turns out to be bread. He never sees his mother—if that is who she was—again.

Now, aged four or five, he is moved to another camp (unidentified in the text, but named as Auschwitz on most book jackets and sometimes by Wilkomirski in interviews) and taken from there when the war ends by a woman who seems to know him, and who eventually brings him to Cracow. They reach a synagogue in Miodowa Street, where the woman introduces him to a man in a long black coat and a big black hat as 'the little Binjamin Wilkomirski'. The sudden acquisition of two names fills Binjamin with pride, and surprise. The man and his colleagues arrange for him to be placed in a Jewish orphanage in Cracow. After some time there, another woman, 'Frau Grosz', takes him to Switzerland (Binjamin remembers post-war pogroms in Cracow and an attack on the orphanage). Frau Grosz disappears once they reach Basle and Binjamin is then placed in a Swiss orphanage, from where he is adopted by an anonymous Swiss family, presumably the Dössekkers.

His new home has a central-heating furnace, 'a huge, black monster', in the basement. Mrs Dössekker (named only as 'the lady') demonstrates it to him one day by opening its cover and shovelling in some coal. 'I could see the flames... So—my suspicions were right. I've fallen into a trap. The oven door is smaller than usual, but it's big enough for children. I know, I've seen, they use children for heating too.'

In Switzerland, the Holocaust is taboo. His adoptive parents say that he must forget it, like a bad dream. Other people say he is making it up. Only when he reaches high school does he have his memories confirmed by the historical record. He sees a documentary about the liberation of a concentration camp by the Americans. Until then, he writes:

'Nobody ever told me the war was over.

'Nobody ever told me that the camp was over, finally, definitely over.'

7.

Wilkomirski has repeatedly stressed that he never intended this story to be read by the wider public, that he had written it for himself, his closest friends and family, especially his children. However, he was persuaded to show the manuscript to Eva Koralnik, of the Zurich-based literary agency, Liepman AG. Koralnik is a well-known agent with distinguished clients, who lives and works in an elegant villa high up in the Zürichberg, the same area where Dössekker/ Wilkomirski grew up. There, when I met her, she told me a little of the manuscript's history. It had come to her because she and Wilkomirski had friends in common: 'And I heard of him as a musician—Zurich is a small town.' But she also pointed out that Liepman AG was a natural destination for Wilkomirski's book because of the agency's record in Holocaust literature; Liepman AG represents Anne Frank's estate and writers such as Norbert Elias and Ida Fink. 'But mostly,' Koralnik said, 'we receive unpublishable, badly written memoirs—we have an archive full of those. We send them to Yad Vashem [the Holocaust memorial museum] in Israel.'

She received Wilkomirski's manuscript in January 1994, and knew immediately that it could be published. 'I was shattered by it, and very impressed by the fragmented nature of his text. In fact, I phoned him and asked—why are there so many dots? He said that he wrote down only what he remembered. And I wanted to know how he could have written such a painful memoir? Talking to his therapist had helped him do it, he told me.'

It never occurred to her, she said, to demand documentation of the author's identity. 'I have never asked any of my authors to prove their identity. And you know, after all, I myself came to Switzerland from Hungary in 1944, as a six-year-old child, with my baby sister.

We were given some protective papers, but I don't have a birth certificate to this day.'

It had taken Eva Koralnik six years to find a publisher for Ida Fink's masterful stories about the Holocaust. By contrast, she had sold Wilkomirski's memoir to Suhrkamp Verlag in Frankfurt by July 1994, no more than six months after it had reached her office.

Suhrkamp made plans to include *Fragments* (or *Bruchstücke* in German) in their spring list for 1995. But in February 1995 the publishing house received a letter from a Swiss journalist, Hanno Helbling. Did they know, Helbling asked, that their author Wilkomirski had been known for years in Zurich as Bruno Dössekker, a Swiss musician, not a Holocaust survivor, and that he was three years younger than his memoir claimed?

The publishers, alarmed enough to halt the printing of their book, got in touch with Wilkomirski and Koralnik. 'I asked Mr Wilkomirski what this was all about,' his agent told me. 'And he said, oh no, now the complicated story with my papers will start all over again. And then he and his lawyer took care of it.' (She added: 'So Mr Ganzfried has not discovered anything new—we already knew that Mr Wilkomirski's birth certificate was somehow incomplete.') This is how the afterword came to be written and included in the book. According to Thomas Sparr, Wilkomirski's editor at Suhrkamp: 'After receiving Mr Helbling's letter, we asked Mr Wilkomirski for legal documents proving his identity. He had, at the time, hired a lawyer, who then provided us with a birth certificate in the name of Bruno Dössekker, date of birth 12 February 1941. It was, as was explained to us, an incomplete version of a typical Swiss birth certificate, because he was an adopted child. The apparent discrepancy between that date and the year 1939, his actual or likely year of birth, was then clarified by Mr Wilkomirski in his afterword.'

But what did Wilkomirski mean when he told Koralnik 'oh, no, the complicated story of my papers will start all over again'? When had it happened before? When—to think of it another way—had Wilkomirski realized that an account of his early life existed which was different to the one which was inside, or may have been inside, his head? That, so far as the Swiss authorities were concerned, he had been born Bruno Grosjean in Biel? According to Wilkomirski he had known this since 1964, when, on the day before his wedding ceremony, he had been told by an official that his birth certificate wasn't a standard one and discovered, for the first time, that 'a Frau Grosjean' was listed as his mother. He wrote to me in an e-mail: 'I had never heard that name until that moment, never read it, it had never been mentioned to me that I had been provided with a "mother"!' After that—between then and 1981, when he inherited her money—he said he had made an attempt to discover more about Frau Grosjean. He had travelled to Biel, 'my so-called birthplace', and had what he considered to be a sinister encounter with an official who refused to give him any information, saying that 'it would hurt or involve too many people'.

And of course the official's refusal would make sense. The rights of the adopted to know their original identities—their biological parents and their social circumstances—is a relatively new idea. Wilkomirski, however, has always chosen a different interpretation. In his afterword, he writes that he was one of 'several hundred children who survived the Shoah, ...lacking any certain information about their origins, with all traces carefully erased, furnished with false names and often with false papers too. They grew up with a pseudo-identity which in Eastern Europe protected them from discrimination, and in Western Europe, from being sent back east as stateless persons. As a child, I also received a new identity, another name, another date and place of birth...'

This is not impossible. A number of Jewish children survived the Second World War in Eastern Europe, hiding with Christian families, or in convents and monasteries. After the war, some of them could not, or did not wish to, find their way back to their origins; others managed to do so with varying degrees of success. In the course of researching this story, I got to know several people of Wilkomirski's age or older with origins in Eastern Europe who have changed their names (or had their names changed for them), sometimes more than once. And it is also true that in Switzerland children have had their identities changed for other reasons, not connected to the Second World War or Jewishness. From the 1920s until the 1970s, a welfare organization called Pro Juventute campaigned to have children of Swiss Roma (Gypsies) removed from the country's roads and streets, which sometimes meant that these children, known as *'Kinder der Landstrasse'* or highway children, were forcibly separated from their parents and given new names.

Wilkomirski did not refer to the fate of Swiss Roma children in his afterword, but he did (as indeed did his lawyer, Rolf Sandberg) mention them to me, as a demonstration of what the Swiss state was once capable of; how it could at least acquiesce in the matter of forged identity. The combination—a secretive state with dubious wartime sympathies, a child victim of the Holocaust in its midst— is plausible and when I talked to Thomas Sparr at Suhrkamp he was happy to take it into account, before offering his own hypothesis: 'Maybe he met young Jewish survivors in his orphanage in Switzerland, and somehow absorbed or was influenced by their stories.'

Sparr said that late in 1998. In 1994, however, he believed Wilkomirski's explanation ('His book had to be true; we would not have published it as fiction.'). The afterword was added and publication went ahead. I asked Sparr if he now thought he should have done more checking, perhaps of the text rather than the author's credentials. He himself, as an editor at Jüdischer Verlag (the Suhrkamp imprint specializing in serious Judaica, which published *Fragments*), is a scholar of Jewish literature and history. Sparr said that he and his colleagues had approached, first and foremost, one other person for her historical authority: Lea Balint, the director of an organization called The Bureau of Children Without Identity, which is located in Israel and has a formal association with The Ghetto Fighters' Kibbutz and its museum. Balint, herself born in Poland, confirmed that there was no doubt whatsoever that Wilkomirski had been a child at the Cracow orphanage, because he had remembered people and details which he could not have known otherwise. Also, Julius Lowinger, a survivor who had been at the same orphanage as a fifteen-year-old boy, and who now lives in Israel, could confirm that Wilkomirski's description of the playground next to the orphanage was correct (and needed to have been written by someone who had been there, because the playground no longer existed). And so the editors at Suhrkamp were satisfied, even though Lea Balint was perhaps not the most neutral authority, having already helped Wilkomirski establish the identity he claimed had been lost.

8.

Lea Balint was keen to speak to me—'anything to help Bruno'—and
served tea and a generous helping of first-class chocolates. Her large
villa in Jerusalem faces the hill which is topped by the Yad Vashem
memorial. She is Wilkomirski's most outspoken defender, and has an
absolute faith in the truth of his story. She is portly and energetic
and refers tenderly to the adults who lost their identities in childhood
as 'my children'. She herself spent the war under an assumed name
in a Polish convent; whatever her qualities as a scholar, her emotional
involvement and compassion are beyond doubt. She keeps her
database—long lists of children, mostly orphans, who were found in
Poland after the war—in her basement and restricts access 'only to
those who are entitled to see it'. (An odd restriction, given that the
same information is publicly available in other archives, including the
original lists in Poland.)

Balint showed me how the database works. She matches the name
of a child on one list with a different name but perhaps similar
information (date and/or place of birth, parents' names and so on) on
another. Clues are yielded. Identities take shape. Her methods have had
only limited success, but with every success story Balint feels almost
as though she has saved a life. It is exciting; she is excited by it.

She met Wilkomirski in October 1993, four months before he
delivered his manuscript. He was introduced to her as 'Bruno', the
name she still calls him, at a conference of child survivors in Israel.
All of them had been together in an orphanage in Lodz after the war.
Balint said: 'I went there to look for my children without identity. A
bearded man went up on the stage, with another man who looked
like a boy, with curly hair, looking completely lost, not knowing a
word of Hebrew. The bearded man said: "This is my friend Bruno
Wilkomirski, does anyone identify him, does anyone know who he
is?" Then he mentioned Cracow.'

'I approached both men afterwards and explained that they were
in the wrong place, because these people were from Lodz, not
Cracow, but that I could try to help them.'

At their first meeting, Wilkomirski told Lea Balint what he
remembered: street names in Cracow, an orphanage there, a few
other details. 'He also told me the name of a woman that he

remembered from this orphanage.'

'A woman?'

'A girl, older than him, who looked after him for a while. Later, we found her name in the lists.'

'Where is she now?'

'I cannot say, because she cannot talk about the past. That is her right. But I wish—we are talking about a person's life here—I mean, it would really help Bruno if she could confirm his memories.'

'Did she remember him?'

'No, she did not remember him.'

Not for the first time during my interviews, I felt like an over-intrusive prosecutor. Here, with Lea Balint, I was reminded of a play by Ida Fink called *The Table* about the trial of a Nazi officer. The characters are a young prosecutor, and four witnesses. The questioning of the witnesses by the prosecutor centres, in an excessively pedantic and often cruel way, on the issue of whether there was or was not a certain table in the square where the selection of Jews for 'work or death' took place. Each witness has a different way of remembering what happened on that winter's day, depending on their character, age and perspective at the time; each witness has a different way of recalling the table in question—one is sure that it was very large, another is convinced that it was tiny, yet another can't remember it at all. All agree that so many people were shot on that day that the colour of the snow was red. As far as the prosecutor is concerned, this is not conclusive evidence; no one actually saw the officer shoot anyone. And so it seems that a conviction will not be possible. The truth—symbolized by the table—proves to be an elusive concept.

Lea Balint, on the other hand, was so convinced by Wilkomirski's scant memories of Cracow that she invited him to join an Israeli television crew, which was researching material for a film about children with lost identities. Balint herself collaborated closely with the research, and travelled to Poland for the shooting. Vered Berman, the Israeli director, was interested in Wilkomirski's story, and it was agreed that it would be a good idea for him to come along for the filming and to meet other survivors, in the hope that this might help him discover his origins. 'He never told us that he had already written his book, or anything about it,' said Vered Berman.

Wilkomirski was not the 'star' of Berman's film. (That role belonged to an Israeli woman, Erela Goldschmidt, who was filmed being reunited with a Polish Christian family which had sheltered her as a child during the war.) But his appearance as a visibly tormented man, searching for his identity in the streets of modern Cracow, attracted some attention when the film, *Wanda's Lists*, was broadcast on Israeli TV in November 1994. In addition to shots of Wilkomirski identifying a building which he believed had been his orphanage (it wasn't), there was amateur video footage (not taken by the film crew) showing him in the Majdanek concentration camp, recognizing the scene of his memories.

Balint told me that Wilkomirski was able to find the real 'Frau Grosz', the woman who took him from Cracow to Switzerland, after the film was shown: 'We were contacted by a woman from New York, who said that she had been at the same orphanage, and that her mother, who was no longer alive, had often been there. Her maiden name—and her mother's last name—was Gross.'

This information has often been cited by Wilkomirski, by Lea Balint, and by Suhrkamp in defence of the book's authenticity. But when I telephoned the woman in New York she told me a less simple version of the story. Mrs Sara Geneslaw was nine years old when she was in the Cracow orphanage. She said that, yes, Wilkomirski's description of 'Frau Grosz' in his book had reminded her of her mother: 'She would have been likely to talk gently to a child, to explain things to him. But I also told him that it would have been utterly impossible for her to leave Poland and travel to Switzerland at the time, for family and other reasons. Nevertheless, he asked me to send him a photo of my mother, which I did—one from the late 1940s. When he received it, he phoned me. He was very excited, and said that he definitely recognized her. He also asked for my permission to keep the photo of my mother beside his bed.'

But Berman's film had another and much more dramatic consequence. A woman who watched the film was struck by Wilkomirski's resemblance to members of her husband's family and alerted her former brother-in-law, Yaakov Maroco, a Polish Jew who had lost his first wife and two-year-old son in Majdanek. The boy who had perished in Majdanek was also called Binjamin.

The Man with Two Heads

Yaakov Maroco was cautious at first, but eventually rejoiced and got ready to welcome Binjamin Wilkomirski into his large family as his long-lost son. They wrote warm letters to each other. Then, before they met, they agreed to have DNA tests which would establish their relationship beyond doubt. In a second television film, also made by Berman, Maroco is to be seen nervously awaiting the doctor's verdict. It was negative. The results of the test were absolutely clear: there was no way that he and Wilkomirski could be a biological father and son.

Maroco was disappointed, but did not give up. Being an orthodox Jew, he consulted his rabbis, who said that despite the DNA results he could continue to think of Wilkomirski as his own son. And so, when Wilkomirski landed at Ben-Gurion airport on 18 April 1995 he was greeted by film crews, reporters and sympathetic spectators, all come to witness the reunion of father and son. Their emotional embrace was a touching sight—reported in the international press—as though love and mutual affection could defy science. Wilkomirski went on to meet all the members of Maroco's extended Hasidic family, and was filmed at family dinners, studying the Torah with his 'father', holding babies.

When I was in Israel—in November 1998—Maroco's widow told me that her husband was well aware that Wilkomirski was not his real son. Wilkomirski confirmed this: he said he simply felt very comfortable with the old man, and was grateful for the warm welcome, and the feeling of having acquired an instant large family.

Other evidence, however, suggests that this isn't the case—that even after the DNA tests Wilkomirski wanted badly to believe that he had found his father. A volume of autobiography which Maroco published before he died contains an affectionate letter from Wilkomirski to Maroco dated 12 February 1995—before they had met. Wilkomirski expresses his joy at receiving a phone call from Maroco, and says: 'I have lived for over fifty years without parents, and now—can it be that I have found you, my father? Has "He" performed a miracle? And think about it: today is February 12th, *the anniversary of my arrival in Switzerland* [my italics], and this day has been made into my official birthday. Is this not a gift?'

He goes on: 'I don't really care about the results of scientific blood tests—there are too many connections... You were also in Majdanek. I have lists of more than a thousand children in Poland, who survived in camps or in hiding, and the name Benjamin does not appear even once. Maybe it was not such a common name in Poland at that time. It is therefore unlikely that there were two different Benjamins in Majdanek in 1943. Also, some things you told Elitsur match my own memories!...'

There are several statements to consider in this letter. First, Wilkomirski says that his 'official' birthday records the day and month he entered Switzerland; in fact it is Bruno Grosjean's birthdate in Biel. Second, in his eagerness to have Maroco as a father he seems willing to deny the record of his memory as presented in his own book. Maroco lived in Poland; Wilkomirski thinks he grew up in Latvia. Wilkomirski thinks he saw his father killed (the blurb on his book jacket has no doubts about it); and Maroco of course was alive.

As to the Benjamin/Binjamin difference...it is hardly worth bothering over. At one point during my sessions with Wilkomirski, I said to him rather impatiently: 'You've invested so much time in trying to trace a boy called Binjamin Wilkomirski—lists of war orphans, people who may have known him—but you must be aware that this is a name you made up.'

To my great surprise, he nodded, and mentioned one or two other names which might have been his. One of them, I remember for no particular reason, was Andrzej.

9.

How did Bruno Dössekker become Binjamin Wilkomirski? What was the process? Perhaps the most important witness to—some might say, agent of—the transformation is Dr Elitsur Bernstein, who is the mysterious 'bearded man' who came on stage with Wilkomirski at the Lodz survivors' meeting in Lea Balint's account. For many years, Bernstein has accompanied Wilkomirski in the latter's search for his Jewish roots. He believes Wilkomirski's story to be true; he privately supported him during his breakdown after Ganzfried's pieces were published ('good but vicious' according to Bernstein); but, unlike Lea Balint, he has not put himself forward in Wilkomirski's public defence. He is a psychologist by profession. Some people referred to him as Wilkomirski's *éminence grise*.

I was curious to see him in person. We met in a stylish Tel Aviv café (his choice), the sort where there is a bell on each table which you can press to call a waitress. He is a large and imposing man; imagining him next to Wilkomirski I thought of a basketball player posed against a jockey. He was courteous if formal. He remembered dates. He had the air of a once-religious man who hadn't quite managed to adjust to the secular world. He said he was the 'black sheep' in an orthodox family. His father, he told me, studied at a *yeshiva* (Jewish religious school) in a place called Wilkomir, in Lithuania. In August and September 1941, nearly 6,000 Jews were massacred in Wilkomir (now Ukmerge), the town's entire Jewish population.

This brought us to—'Bruno,' he said with a quick smile, 'I always call him Bruno. It drives him crazy, but I can't change it—I met him as Bruno, so I can't suddenly start calling him Binjamin. I am talking to you as a friend of Bruno, not of Binjamin.

'I had been living—studying, working—in Switzerland since the early 1960s, but it was only in October 1979 that I met Bruno, when he was recommended to me as a clarinet teacher. He taught in his studio in Zurich. As far as I knew, he was a Swiss man, no Jewish connections whatsoever. After the third lesson, I asked him about an oil painting of an old Jew with a beard on his wall. He said, "Why are you asking?"

'"Because," I said, "maybe I know who he is." He was curious, of course, so I told him that the man was the last rabbi of Wilkomir before the Holocaust.'

To which Bruno, according to Bernstein, replied: 'My name could be Wilkomirski.'

An amazing exchange; but that, according to Bernstein, was the last time they discussed the name until he saw the first pages of the manuscript of *Fragments*.

The clarinet lessons continued, with interruptions when Bruno was ill and in hospital. Bernstein returned to Israel. In 1984, Bruno and his new partner, Verena, visited him there. 'She asked me, out of the blue, whether I believed Bruno's story. I said, "What story?" Apparently, at the beginning of their relationship, Verena had been warned by some of Bruno's family that he pretends to be Jewish.'

'So what did you say?'

'I said, he always behaves like a Jew, when he talks about things to do with Jews, especially Swiss anti-Semitism. That's all I knew at the time.'

But soon, there would be more. 'When Bruno told me, in 1984 or '85, that he had terrible nightmares, about concentration camps, I suggested therapy—not with me, of course, as I am his friend. Please bear this in mind—I am speaking to you as his friend, not as his therapist.'

'Bruno resisted the idea of therapy. But, suddenly, he became interested in the Arab–Israeli conflict, started writing about it, in fact produced a booklet to go with an optional course on the subject—he taught it to students at the same high school he taught music.'

(Later, I obtained a copy from a former pupil of Wilkomirski's. Produced in 1989, by 'BDW Archives' (Bruno Dössekker Wilkomirski), it carries the title *Topics about the History of Palestine and the Middle East Conflict*, and contains anti-Semitic excerpts from the Koran, anti-Semitic cartoons from the Arab press, a chapter on 'The Collaboration between Islam and Fascism after World War II' and a chapter entitled: 'Caution: The Media'. It ends with a quote he attributes to Himmler—though it is usually credited to Goebbels: 'The bigger and more monstrous the lie, the bigger the chance that it will be believed, for it will become unimaginable that anyone would have dared to invent a lie of such proportions.')

In the meantime, his nightmares continued. 'It got worse,' Bernstein said. 'He couldn't sleep and couldn't be touched, especially on the back. If he was touched by accident, he would shiver. Then, one night, in the beginning of the 1990s, he had a particularly bad nightmare. He dreamed that he was asleep; he hears a terrible noise, runs to the window, and sees people being burned. At this point, I said that he must start therapy, because he is obviously having dreams about something that is a part of him. Finally, he agreed.'

The issue of therapy is controversial in Wilkomirski's story. Some reports (and book jackets, in some editions) have referred to it as 'recovered memory', some have mentioned hypnosis. Wilkomirski and Bernstein deny both. Wilkomirski has always stressed that his memories are not 'recovered', that he has had them since his early childhood.

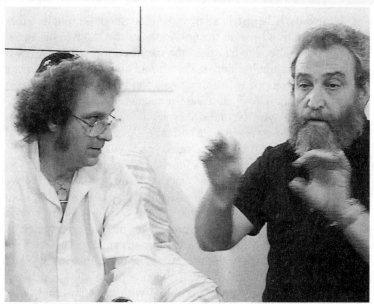

Wilkomirski with Elitsur Bernstein during the filming of the television documentary *Wanda's Lists*, June 1994.

The difference the therapy had made was that he began to write down what he remembered. The therapist had also taught him some 'concentration exercises', to help him remember in greater detail.

Bernstein said: 'One day, I started getting these faxes from him, at two or three in the morning, fifteen or twenty pages. The first one was the story about the mother and the bread. The last one was about the new boy. He wanted to know what I thought of it.'

'Can you remember how he asked you, exactly?'

'Yes. He asked, in German, *"Kann das so gewesen sein?"* Could it have been so? He said, "These are my memories, is there any logic in it? Am I allowed to write this? Would I be considered a murderer, because of the death of the new boy?"'

(This is a sensitive issue with Wilkomirski. He told me that he had asked Yaakov Maroco to take him to see a rabbi about it, and was extremely relieved when the rabbi told him that 'a child cannot be blamed for a crime, because he has not yet learned the commandments, and does not yet know what is right and what is wrong.')

How did Mr Bernstein answer these questions? 'I told him that I didn't know, that I wasn't there. I said the same thing to his agent, Eva Koralnik, after she had read the manuscript. Personally, I was against the idea of publishing it. This should have remained a private matter. But he wanted to see those pages in print, "to give support to other child survivors", and Verena encouraged him.'

In 1993, the year before Wilkomirski delivered his manuscript, he and Bernstein travelled to Majdanek, Auschwitz, Cracow, and Riga. One of Dr Bernstein's sons videotaped Wilkomirski during the tour (which is how Berman's documentary and other films came to include footage of him in those places). Bernstein said: 'Before we went to Majdanek, Bruno prepared detailed maps of the camp, from his memory. They were different from the maps in history books. When we got there, his maps turned out to be the correct ones, in all details and angles. In Riga, we came upon a house which he recognized as the house where the events he remembers took place. Later, we were told that this house had been a part of the Riga ghetto, just for two months. We also consulted with historians and other experts. One, in Riga, confirmed Bruno's memory of his escape on a ship. Another, in Cracow, looked at the maps he drew and told us that he must have been in Auschwitz, and in Majdanek, that there could be no mistake.'

By this stage, the association between Wilkomirski and Bernstein had become professional. They were working together in what Bernstein said was an 'interdisciplinary approach' as a historian and psychologist to help survivors (not just Wilkomirski) retrace their memories and find their identities. They wrote and presented a paper on the subject at several conferences. The paper mentions 'about fifty similar cases', but Wilkomirski's is the only one cited as an example. He is, in this way, both the researching 'historian' and the survivor/client. Later, when I enquired about the other fifty cases, I was told by Dr Bernstein, repeatedly, that, after what happened to Mr Wilkomirski, not one was willing to come forward.

10.

It is not entirely wrong of Wilkomirski to describe himself as a historian. He studied history at university after he dropped medicine, though he never completed his thesis on Jewish emigration between the two world wars, and history has remained his hobby and his interest. The 'Holocaust archive' in his farmhouse attests to years of private collecting that long pre-dated the publication of *Fragments*; after its publication he took on a much more public and authoritative role as a speaker and lecturer. In a Swiss documentary film on Wilkomirski (*Fremd Geboren—Born a Stranger*, 1997), he is seen lecturing students at Ostrava University in the Czech Republic. There, he speaks furiously about the fact that in all the Holocaust material he has studied, there is hardly anything about children. He makes this point often. He made it to me when we met. 'I was reading all those books about the Holocaust—and I kept wondering: where am I in all of this?' Then he corrected himself: 'I mean, where are the children?'

I took his question to some of the leading Holocaust historians: to Yehuda Bauer and Israel Gutman in Jerusalem, and to Raul Hilberg in Vermont. Bauer and Hilberg, especially, had come under fire from Wilkomirski for their negative response to his book. Yehuda Bauer, for instance, had been interviewed for a Swiss documentary and said that there were no children in Auschwitz.

When I met him at Yad Vashem, he smiled and declared: 'To begin with, I haven't read the book, so I have nothing to say about it.' He does, however, believe in the importance of witness accounts, not least those of children. 'Documents were often created to hide, rather than reveal, crucial data. They don't always tell the full story. Today, children's testimonies can add important information.'

He gave me the name of a woman who was in Majdanek as a child—though she was there for only a short while and after the period Wilkomirski's account would most likely place him there. How about children in Auschwitz? 'Perhaps, when the gassing was stopped in the second week of November 1944, there is a possibility that a handful survived.'

Israel Gutman has his office next door to Bauer's in the same building at Yad Vashem. He, too, began by saying that he wasn't prepared to judge the veracity of Wilkomirski's story, though, unlike Bauer, he had actually read it. 'But I think that in any case this is a very interesting and important phenomenon. And it proves that the power, the essence of what occurred in the Holocaust, to this day does not leave people alone.'

Was it likely to be true, given the historical record?

'Look...we know that during the Holocaust extraordinary things happened, which did not correspond to the general rules. This does not mean that I think that his story is true. It has to be checked very thoroughly, but—I don't think it's that important. Wilkomirski has written a story which he has experienced deeply, that's for sure. So that, even if he is not Jewish, the fact that he was so deeply affected by the Holocaust is of huge importance.'

Gutman himself survived the Warsaw Ghetto, Majdanek, Auschwitz and Mauthausen. He never talks about it. But I have to ask him—as he was in Majdanek himself—whether there were children's barracks there, as Wilkomirski describes.

'I was in Majdanek.' He paused. 'Not at that time. Majdanek went through different phases. So that I cannot answer you with one-hundred per cent certainty. And I also cannot say—and this is a big question—whether a child can remember. I don't know whether one should look at everything he said under a microscope, and start checking whether it could have happened the way it is written. He is not a fake. He is someone who lives this story very deeply in his soul. The pain is authentic.'

I said: 'Wilkomirski claims that established Holocaust historians like yourself do not take children's testimonies into account.'

'He is right, not necessarily about witness accounts in general, but about children. It's true, and it is a painful point that the children's fate has somehow gotten lost in the main and big body of work that was done in this area. Also because so very few children survived. How many children survived? A tiny percentage! Those that did were hurt by this response. Somewhere in this whole narrative the children's story got lost, to a large degree.'

His voice became even quieter. 'Look...I know what it was like to be a child in that huge suffering. There was always the question— how could it be? How could people be so inhuman? The world turned upside down, all the values and principles on which the world was based fell apart. The ones who were the least able to understand this were the children. Also because they were completely deprived of the childhood experience; instead they came into an environment where they were neglected, hungry, their life was very, very hard. If the Germans gave the Jews some leeway, it was because they needed them to work. The child did not have any of that.'

'How old were you at the time?'

'I wasn't a child. When the war broke out, I was sixteen. I was a young man, and in Poland at this age I had to act as a man. This is why I think I am sensitive to this topic, not only as a historian, but also personally.'

Was it possible that there were women and children in Majdanek?

'A short period before the liberation of Majdanek, at the end, yes.'

'Is there a chance that a small child would have been transferred to Auschwitz?'

There is a long, heavy pause. 'A child, from Majdanek to Auschwitz... I came from Majdanek to Auschwitz. I know what it means.' A long silence. 'I came from Majdanek to Auschwitz.'

I said: 'I cannot imagine it, and I cannot imagine how he could have survived, all alone.'

'It's a problem. You don't know what it was, a concentration camp. A concentration camp is a place where the number of people had to be precise, in the morning and in the evening, and everybody had to be counted at roll call. If the roll call wasn't exact, you could stand all night in the cold, until they found the person somewhere in a barrack, or someone fell. But it was also forbidden to have one extra. The problem is not just how he survived or managed day to day—the problem is: how did he breathe?'

Raul Hilberg, the author of the definitive Holocaust study, *The Destruction of the European Jews*, was rather less forgiving when I met him in Frankfurt. He met Wilkomirski at a conference at Notre Dame University, Indiana, in April 1998, and asked whether his book was fiction. Hilberg recalled: 'He pointed out indignantly that it said "memoir" on the jacket. When he gave his lecture at the conference, he basically recounted the contents of the book, adding details, such as his recent journey to Riga, where he found the house he lived in and talked to a local Jewish historian, Mr Vestermanis, who confirmed his memories.'

Raul Hilberg himself does not read novels; he is also 'against counterfactual material in fiction', and has a nose for what he describes as 'hearsay represented as observation'. He is sceptical about oral witness accounts. 'I found that a great percentage of the mistakes I discovered in my own work could be attributed to testimonies.'

Hilberg migrated from Vienna to the United States in 1938. In the American army, he was used to interrogate German prisoners. 'People can make up any stories about themselves, I've seen them do it.' For example: 'You don't know me; if I told you that I am not Jewish, but a German POW who stayed in Canada after the war, learned English and became interested in researching the Holocaust for some personal reason, wouldn't you have to believe me?'

[I would.]

When Hilberg was asked by the German weekly *Die Zeit* to evaluate the historical validity of *Fragments*, he read both the English translation and the German original, and came to the conclusion that there were many points which he considered impossible. 'I came across passages detailing incidents that seemed to me highly improbable or completely impossible. The description of partisan bands and German tanks in Poland was clearly an invention. The German woman who finds the boy in the farmhouse is wearing the kind of uniform which *Aufseherinnen* [female guards] wore only inside the camps; they never left the premises. In his book the woman says "Majdanek". Actually, the Germans always called the camp Lublin. If he played there right outside *Feld 5* (Sector 5) and an SS guard hurled him against a concrete wall, he must have been at the crematorium, again an altogether improbable situation. Presumably, he was then moved to Auschwitz, but there is no record known to me of Jewish children being transferred there from Majdanek. Finally, in Switzerland, he eats cheese rinds as though he came upon unexpected food in a concentration camp. By then, however, at least two years must have passed after his liberation.'

Then Hilberg added some questions of his own—not of the text but of how the text came to be published. 'As you can imagine, I was not the only one who wondered about the stories in the book. Not all sceptics are Holocaust specialists: one is interested in memory, another in the Eastern Front. The question then is: How did this book pass as a memoir in several publishing houses? How could it have brought Mr Wilkomirski invitations to the United States Holocaust

Memorial Museum as well as recognized universities? How come we have no decent quality control when it comes to evaluating Holocaust material for publication? If Wilkomirski's publishers had asked me beforehand, I would have saved them the embarrassment. If you get rid of all the inaccuracies, what remains?'

These are good questions. No publisher had the book scrutinized by a historian—Daniel Goldhagen read it but not (it would seem) to test its truth. Perhaps the publishers felt that the book was more likely to be appreciated for its literary and moral qualities, which certainly proved to be the case. Gary Mokotoff, a member of the board of the Jewish Book Council in the United States, told me that, though *Fragments* had won his council's prize for memoir, it would never have won in the Holocaust category. Why not? 'The facts did not add up. As a Jewish genealogist and student of the Holocaust, I knew that the book was historical fiction. It reminded me of Martin Gray's book [*For Those I Loved*], which was also a Holocaust memoir that was exposed as fiction. It worried me, because today you will find references to that book only on revisionist websites. These kinds of pseudo-memoirs may do real damage to survivors, by rendering each Holocaust memoir suspect.'

Gary Mokotoff wrote to the president of the Jewish Book Council detailing his concerns about *Fragments* three days after it won its award. His letter went completely unnoticed.

11.

But then, in the words of Wilkomirski's American publisher, Arthur Samuelson of Schocken Books (an imprint of Alfred Knopf/Random House), *Fragments* 'is a pretty cool book'. Samuelson has compared it to the work of Primo Levi. To me, he said: 'I admire it for its simplicity, humanity, lack of artifice. It made me look differently at my own child... I turn down Holocaust memoirs every day. This one is different.' When he had to explain *Fragments* quickly and effectively to book salesmen, he brought up the scene from *Schindler's List*, where a child is hiding alone in the toilet. 'They got it right away.'

What if it turned out not to be true?

'It's only a fraud if you call it non-fiction. I would then reissue it, in the fiction category. Maybe it's not true—then he's a better writer!'

Samuelson said he wanted to know the truth. 'So far, I have seen only allegations, but no proof. If you could show me a person who would say he'd played soccer with Bruno Dössekker/Binjamin Wilkomirski in a Swiss kindergarten, I would be convinced. On the whole, we relied on the German publisher's research.'

The book was translated from German into English by Carol Brown Janeway, a senior New York editor and the director of foreign rights at Knopf. Janeway had been shown the German manuscript of *Fragments* by Eva Koralnik and was immediately struck, she said, by its 'directness, its simplicity, the quietness of the voice, and the child's-eye view of the unbearable—how you see the world when this horror is all you know, and you have to find your way within it.' On behalf of Knopf she bought world English rights and took on the translation herself—something of an honour for the author because of Janeway's reputation (she also translated an even greater success, *The Reader* by Bernhard Schlink).

I asked if questions about the book's veracity troubled her. Janeway said it was 'ultimately impossible' for publishers to guarantee the truthfulness of their authors—that was why publishers' contracts contained a clause which, in some non-fiction work, required the author to warrant that the facts contained in a manuscript were true. Janeway went on: 'The relationship between publisher and author is one of trust—it isn't an adversarial relationship. But that, I think, is not the point here. If the charges made concerning Mr Wilkomirski turn out to be correct, then what's at issue are not empirical facts that can be checked, but spiritual facts that must be pondered. What would be required is soul-checking, and that's an impossibility.'

What did her last remark mean? I had no idea; it seemed to me that non-mystical facts were the essence of the matter here and that, if Wilkomirski had broken another contract—that between an author and the reader's trust—then his book should be reclassified as fiction or withdrawn. But then Janeway has a poetic touch with English. Her translation of Wilkomirski is, I would say, one of those instances which proves that a translated text can improve the original. The book reads much more fluently in English than in German; it flows, it acquires a kind of poetry. But there are some striking discrepancies between the German and English versions. I asked Janeway if Wilkomirski had approved them. Yes, she said: 'Mr Wilkomirski was involved in reviewing every page of the translation. He requested the change of a person's name, because she was still alive; I found the German chapter headings a little intrusive, and asked if we might omit them in the English version—he had no objection.'

Only later, after I turned to the English and German versions again, did I see quite how much freedom had sometimes been allowed. The most striking example comes when Binjamin, as a small boy in Switzerland, is caught begging for money during a school outing. The Swiss children tease him by chanting a nursery rhyme. In the German version: *'Der Bettelbub, der Bettelbub, er hat noch immer nicht genug'*; the beggar child, the beggar child, he still hasn't got enough. In Janeway's translation, this becomes: 'Beggar kid, beggar kid, there's never enough for the yid. Beggar kid, beggar kid.' The children's rhyme now rhymes 'kid' with 'yid', and in the process it has become anti-Semitic. The point here isn't to protect Swiss children of fifty years ago against charges of anti-Semitism; the point is that the translation contradicts Wilkomirski's account of perceptions of himself as a child in Switzerland; he has never claimed that he was known as a Jew at that time.

In other places, the English version helps to make the book more believable by simplifying Wilkomirski's language so that the thoughts it contains seem more childlike. For example, when Binjamin finds himself at a railway station—possibly among Poles—he is surprised by the prettiness of women's dresses and the general peacefulness of the scene. In English, he thinks: 'This isn't real peace. There's something wrong—it's only their peace!' In the original German, he thinks: *'Dies ist nicht ein echter Friede, ihm ist nicht zu trauen—es ist nur der Frieden der Sieger!'* or 'This isn't real peace, it cannot be trusted—it is only the peace of the conquerors!' A sophisticated thought for a boy who could have been no more than three at the time; and an incongruity smoothed out in English.

12.

I began to wonder about the support for Binjamin's story. Did anyone in the West, other than Lea Balint and his friend, Elitsur Bernstein, still believe Wilkomirski? In Eastern Europe he seemed to have greater credibility. People there, according to Bernstein, had vouched for the details of his account. I called Margers Vestermanis in Riga, the man Wilkomirski said had confirmed parts of his story. Vestermanis is a well-known local Jewish historian and a Holocaust survivor. He said he vaguely remembered having a conversation some years ago 'with an Israeli psychologist [Bernstein] and another very quiet man'. He said: 'I was very busy, there were many people waiting to talk to me. They asked me some strange questions about whether a three-year-old child could experience such things. I didn't have much patience for them.'

Vestermanis was certain that he could not have confirmed the authenticity of Wilkomirski's memory of escaping on a boat. 'It was impossible. The shore was a military zone, totally controlled. Even fishermen had difficulties accessing it.' I reported this conversation to Wilkomirski, who got very angry. 'But he even wrote it in his book! He wrote that sixty people were smuggled out of Riga by boat!' Back to Vestermanis: 'He is confusing things. I have written, in a small booklet about places of Jewish interest in Riga, about Janis Lipke, a Latvian man who did smuggle altogether fifty-six Jews out of Riga, of which fifty-one survived. But this took place over a long period of time, starting only in 1942—a year later than the period described by Wilkomirski.'

He confirmed a point made by Raul Hilberg: the child could not possibly have heard the cry 'Watch it: Latvian Militia!' because they were not called militia until the Soviets arrived. 'Latvian Jews all spoke Yiddish, and they would have referred to those forces in Yiddish as *bendeldike*—the men with the green armbands.' (He added: 'But it's a very powerful book. Wilkomirski captured perfectly how one never leaves the camps, even long after the war.')

Next to Majdanek. No historian I talked to could say for certain that there were barracks with Jewish children in Majdanek; yet, in a German documentary film (*Der Prozess*—The Trial) about the trial of SS guards from Majdanek (which took place in Düsseldorf from 1975 to 1981), there are references to two barracks with about 200 Jewish children in Majdanek in the sector described by Wilkomirski (*Feld 5*). These children were killed in a special operation during the spring and summer of 1943. Any that may still have been there by 3 November 1943 would have perished during Operation Harvest Festival, which began on that day. About 45,000 Jews were massacred within thirty-six hours in the entire Majdanek-Lublin complex, which comprised several camps. In Majdanek alone, about 17,000 Jews were shot within eleven hours.

There may have been barracks with non-Jewish children—mostly Polish and Belorussian—with perhaps a few Jews mixed in. This would certainly match Wilkomirski's memory of suddenly being with 'other children who spoke languages he did not understand'. He also told an Israeli researcher that during this time it was difficult for him to go to the toilet because he did not want the others to see that he was circumcised. (However, when I asked Wilkomirski whether he was circumcised, he refused to say; later he wrote me a long note implying that many Jews did not have their sons circumcised during the war, out of concern for their safety—an argument which does hold if he was born in Riga in 1938 or 1939.)

Majdanek was liberated on 23 July 1944. But Binjamin had to be somewhere between that time and his period at the Cracow orphanage after the war. He finds himself in another camp, which may be Auschwitz-Birkenau. His own position on this is not clear: before the doubts raised by Raul Hilberg and others, he said to many people that he was in Auschwitz. For example in an interview with Anne Karpf in the *Guardian* (11 February 1998) he told her that 'he now celebrates his birthday on January 22, for it was on this day that he emerged from Birkenau'. In a Swiss documentary, he is filmed with a woman of his own age who is an Auschwitz survivor. She says in the film: 'It's amazing to know that we were in the same place, he survived practically behind my back.' Wilkomirski nods gravely.

The same woman, who does not want to be named, was the only survivor who was willing to provide me with a statement of support for Binjamin Wilkomirski: 'I am sure Binjamin Wilkomirski is who he claims to be, and he was in Birkenau as a child. We both remember many of the same things, in the same way. Including a lot of things that only someone who was there at that time could know, and many things that would be remembered only by a small child.' Still, she did not remember him.

When Wilkomirski takes the story in his book to Cracow, he moves into a very well-documented period, despite the confusion in Poland immediately after the war. He provides checkable details of the orphanage and the children it contained. I managed to trace and talk to several people who had lived in the orphanage during the period described in the book. They live today in Israel, Germany, the United States, France and Brazil. Not one of them, during our phone conversations, could remember a boy who matched Binjamin's description. One of their carers, Pani Misia, mentioned by Wilkomirski in his book, is still alive. And yet, when Wilkomirski met her in 1994, she did not remember him either.

The orphanage was housed in a large 1930s building (which still stands) just off Augustianska Street in the Jewish quarter of Cracow, called Kazimierz. It was built before the war as a Jewish retirement home and turned into a brothel by the Germans. The orphanage moved to this building from Dluga Street, in another part of Cracow, in 1946. It catered for an influx of children who had spent the war in hiding, and it was very well run, registering each child's origins, dates and place of birth, and parental names. The children were fed, clothed and schooled and sometimes taken on excursions to the theatre. They spent their summer holidays in summer camp in the countryside. They remember the orphanage with affection and gratitude; after their wartime experience, it was a haven of comfort and security. Unlike Binjamin, none of the people I spoke to remembered any need to beg or desire to escape.

Prior to the filming of *Wanda's Lists* in Poland in 1994, Wilkomirski spent time with a group of people who had lived in the orphanage as children. Some of their meetings were filmed, though the footage was not included in the final edit. In the rushes, Wilkomirski can be seen with other people who are exchanging memories and information and looking at pictures of the orphanage. Elitsur Bernstein is there, too, translating for Wilkomirski.

At one point, Wilkomirski says in German that there was a garden next to the orphanage. Bernstein translates this into Hebrew as '*gina*', which means a garden. Julius Lowinger then exclaims, excitedly, 'yes, yes, there was', at which point Wilkomirski gestures to show something like a climbing frame. Bernstein says to his friend,

'Could this be me?' Wilkomirski wondered of the blond boy (front row, fourth left) in this picture of the Cracow orphanage c1946, and annotated the picture (see back cover) to this effect.

in German, 'He is confirming your memory.' It seems to have been deduced from this incident that Lowinger was agreeing with Wilkomirski about the presence of a playground with some sort of equipment; this was one of the proofs offered by Lea Balint in Jerusalem to Suhrkamp in Frankfurt. In chapter fifteen of *Fragments*, he wrote of how 'many years later' he recognized the 'house on Augustianska Street with the big staircase and the exercise bars in the playground'.

Perhaps the phrase 'many years later' refers to his trip to Cracow with Bernstein in 1993, or perhaps to an earlier trip alone. Whatever the case, the facts as remembered by all the other former orphanage children I talked to were different. Nobody could recall any equipment, exercise bars or swings. All of them—including Pani Misia, the carer—said the 'playground' was simply a large stretch of grass where the children played ball games. One person did recall some exercise bars being erected, but not until the 1950s.

There is more, unfortunately. In the same rushes, Wilkomirski is inspecting a photograph of the entrance to the orphanage and asks: *Was ist das?* He is told that it is the orphanage building in

Augustianska Street. But he does not recognize it, because (at that time) he had never seen it (he seems to have missed it during his trip to Cracow with Bernstein in 1993). Yet when I showed him the same picture four years later, he claimed to know the building well and, pointing out a modernist circular window near the door, said emotionally: 'That's the window I was so afraid of.'

Can nobody vouch for his presence there? In his book, Wilkomirski suggests that at least one person can.

We come, finally, to the case of the girl 'Mila' (or 'Karola' as she's called in the German edition). He devotes an entire chapter to her. She was older than him and gave him 'some sense of safety and peace'. They had met before—'[in] one of the many barracks probably, we weren't sure anymore'. She had survived through being thrown with her mother, by mistake, on to a heap of dead bodies. Now, in the orphanage, they befriend each other as lonely survivors of the death camps. Her mother has vanished.

Many years later, in Switzerland as adults, Wilkomirski and 'Mila' meet each other again:

> ...we met quite by chance. She was working as a translator, and I'd become a musician.
>
> Mila had managed to find her mother, and we went together to visit her—she was old by now—in a hospital. She died soon after that.
>
> Mila and I saw each other regularly now—we often had long talks. We discussed the present, but what we really meant was our past...
>
> We loved each other, and our love was fed by our sadness. But it was always accompanied by a fear of touching what actually bound us together.
>
> So, inevitably, we lost each other again.

'Mila' was, most probably, a girl who appears in different records as Martha Fligner or Karola Fliegner, born in Lemberg (Lvov) in 1931. The later parts of her life story are consistent with Wilkomirski's account. She now lives in Paris but spent some time in Switzerland, where her mother died.

Do I believe Wilkomirski knew her? Yes, certainly—in Zurich, when they were adults (Wilkomirski told me that they met in Zurich in the 1960s and then lost touch with each other until 1994). But when they were children in Cracow? That seems less likely. Establishing 'Mila's' identity has its own difficulties, but similar details in the records and the accounts of people who knew her in the orphanage suggest that Martha Fligner and Karola Fliegner are the same person. In the Red Cross files and in a list published by the Jewish Agency she is recorded as present in Cracow in 1945 under the name Karola Fliegner, born Lemberg, 1931, mother alive and father dead. Then, at some point in 1946, she moves to the Augustianska orphanage under the name Martha Fligner (perhaps she adopted the first name when she was hidden by Christians in the Ukraine during the war). 'Martha' is how everyone there remembers her, and also the name under which a short biography of her appears (with her photograph) in a fund-raising booklet about the orphanage, published by the orphan rescue and relief fund of the United Galician Jews of America in 1947. Martha Fligner, born Lemberg, 1931, mother present in Poland, whereabouts of father unrecorded.

In 1994, Wilkomirski seemed certain that Martha/Karola and the woman he knew in Switzerland twenty years later were one and the same. In a fax to his friend Elitsur Bernstein on 8 July that year, he circles her name in the Red Cross records and writes that, according to these records, she has spent the war in hiding and not (as his book records) in a camp. He also says that she later married in France, was by now called Carole, that she worked as a translator of technical texts from Russian and Polish, and that he knew her son, Claude. In the fax, he continues: 'Carole's mother...lived in Zurich near the Triemli. When she fell ill (cancer) I often visited her with a rabbi Weiss. She must have died at the end of the 60s or the beginning of the 70s.' (Rabbi Weiss has also died since.)

There are several problems with this. First, as Wilkomirski concedes in his private fax to Bernstein, Karola/Martha/Carole/Mila spent the war years in hiding and not in a camp. Second, she came to the orphanage only after the time Wilkomirski now implies he was there. Binjamin's departure from Cracow with 'Frau Grosz' is undated in the book, like every other event, but it is connected to a pogrom which seems to threaten his safety. There were several attacks on Jews in post-war Poland, but where and when was the pogrom that could have prompted young Binjamin's flight? At first, he suggested one in Kielce 'in the summer of 1947' (in fact, it occurred in July 1946) and his arrival in Switzerland the same year. Later, faced with documentary evidence that he started school in Zurich in April 1947, he did further research and 'discovered'—as he said to me— a small pogrom in Cracow in the summer of 1945, which could explain his earlier departure from that city. And indeed Cracow's Jewish quarter was attacked in August 1945. Nobody who was then at the orphanage, however, can remember this pogrom; the orphanage had still to relocate to Augustianska Street from its previous home in a non-Jewish part of the city and doesn't seem to have been threatened (there is no evidence for Wilkomirski's claim in an e-mail to me that the pogrom was 'directed primarily at Jewish orphanages'). And if Binjamin left in 1945, how could he have formed a friendship with a girl who arrived in 1946?

Only 'Mila' can properly answer these questions, but despite several approaches from me she declined to be interviewed. She is, however, the woman whom Lea Balint referred to as the witness who could 'really help Bruno if she could confirm his memories'. Sadly, according to Balint, she did not remember him at the Cracow orphanage.

So what role did 'Mila' play in the making of Wilkomirski's book? I think this: she was just another stage in his exercise of imaginative reconstruction. Perhaps it was from her, when they were both adults in Zurich, that he first heard the story of the orphanage on Augustianska Street.

Wilkomirski wrote in his afterword: 'Years of research, many journeys back to the places where I remember things happened, and countless conversations with specialists and historians have helped me to clarify many previously inexplicable shreds of memory...' Novelists sometimes take a similar route. They have an idea for a character and a story in a certain place and time; and then, just to make sure no topographical or historical solecisms crop up in the narrative, they might travel to a city to check its street-life and spend a few days in the local library. Wilkomirski wasn't dealing with a novel, he was dealing with his life; but I began to see how such a process (hugely amplified, a life's work) could have led to the writing of *Fragments*.

13.

Bruno Dössekker's obsession with the Holocaust began long before he met Elitsur Bernstein. In *Fragments*, he mentions two teachers who inspired him—a maths teacher, who was Jewish, and a history teacher, who was committed to describing the truth about Nazism. According to Lukas Sarasin, another student at the same school, Bruno then was 'a very happy adolescent, good-looking, popular with girls...his parents let him do whatever he wanted, he skied a lot, was interested in jazz and dancing'. But that seems to have been the public Bruno. His drawings and paintings from that time (he showed me examples) suggest a deeply troubled adolescence: a favourite is of a dark prison cell, which he pinned above his bed.

In Zurich, I met people who had known him in the 1960s and '70s. Two musicians, Daniel Bosshard and Gertrud Voegeli, said they used to meet him almost every day in the same café. According to Voegeli he was 'unusual, interesting, unhappily married with children' and always had stories to tell. 'He told us that he had been in the Warsaw Ghetto, and was saved from the Holocaust by a Swiss nanny, who brought him here. It was a very sad story, full of touching details. He also spoke about the famous Polish violinist, Wanda Wilkomirska, to whom he claimed he was related. Then he dropped that story. Sometimes he talked about being a Mossad agent. All these stories were still in the air in 1977 and 1978, when we lost touch as close friends.'

Bosshard, who is still close to Wilkomirski, remembered that he always said that he came from Poland, which he'd visited three or four times in the 1970s, looking for roots and connections. 'He used to say that his adoptive parents wanted him as a medical experiment. He also went to Biel in the 1970s, to find out about his papers. When he came back, he mentioned the name Grosjean, and said he thought she might have been the person who had brought him to Switzerland from Poland.'

According to Birgit Littman, an art historian who knew Verena and Bruno in the early 1980s, one chapter of *Fragments*, the episode in which Binjamin meets his mother in Majdanek, had an earlier life as a film script. In 1983, she was given the script to read. 'He wanted me to play the mother in the film.' But Littman 'did not find the story credible' and refused. Their friendship ended. The film was never made. A dozen years later, however, she received a copy of *Fragments* in the mail, with a hostile letter from Verena saying that the book's publication demonstrated the truth of Wilkomirski's story and that if she continued to 'spread lies' about the author, his lawyer would act. In other words, that Wilkomirski had at last 'proved' his identity in the eyes of the world by having his story accepted for publication—that he was his book. (Wilkomirski does not recognize Littman's account of the film project. 'The film was not my idea, it was the project of two young students, twin brothers, who wanted to film the story of a man who builds his own clarinets. My memories served only as background, and I wrote none of the screenplay myself.' However, one of those students, Rolando Colla, confirmed that the film was to have been called 'Binjamin' and included the scenes of the mother in the camp and hiding with his brothers in the farmhouse.)

The picture that emerges from these recollections (among others from people who knew him then) is of a man who thinks he may be Polish not Latvian, who may be related to a Polish violinist and not a Lithuanian town, but who has already, by 1980, made several trips to Eastern Europe. He has the rudiments of a story—his own story, episodic, a jumbled series of scenes from childhood—but he has yet to make it fully believable to others, and perhaps to himself. He needs to discover more detail, look further into the record, examine all possibilities.

Thinking of him as he must have been then, I thought of his memories of Majdanek camp. After *Fragments* was published, he recorded testimonies of his experience for the archives of Yad Vashem in Jerusalem and the Holocaust Memorial Museum in Washington. These accounts more or less repeat the story of the book (though the account he gave in Washington on 26 September 1997 contains serious discrepancies with other accounts, including his communications to me). It is the extra detail of them that is interesting. In his Washington testimony, he speaks of the Majdanek concentration camp with great precision and knowledge. He even knows the full names of some female camp guards—though they were normally known to inmates only by their nicknames. When I asked him about this, he said: 'We children knew the real names.'

I bear in mind Israel Gutman's wisdom: 'during the Holocaust extraordinary things happened, which did not correspond to the general rules'. But why would children rather than adult prisoners know a guard's real name? What seems more likely is that the adult Wilkomirski has studied everything about Majdanek he can lay his hands on: documents, books, films. In fact, I suspect (proof is impossible) that his knowledge of Majdanek is at least partly based on the German documentary, *Der Prozess*, which contains detailed descriptions of the camp, powerful witness accounts by both guards and inmates, and, unusually, a harrowing section on the children who were there. Wilkomirski often refers to his memories as being film-like. They are, I believe, more than that: they are, I believe, derived from films. In the Swiss documentary about him, *Fremd Geboren*, he is shown watching concentration-camp scenes on his television screen. His face has the same suffering expression as when he talks about being there himself. Perhaps, in some sense, he is.

And now I consider the main evidence against him. The birth certificate that says he was originally Bruno Grosjean, born Biel, Switzerland, 12 February 1941; the records which show Bruno Grosjean's adoption by the Dössekkers; the continual revision of his hypothesis; his acceptance of Yvonne Grosjean's legacy as her natural son in 1981; the reluctance of his 'afterword' to say as much as it could; his absence from the memory of anyone who might have known him in Cracow; his willingness to prove his blood-relationship to Maroco by DNA testing, no matter the damage to the credibility of his published account; and, crucially, an *unwillingness*—as disclosed by Ganzfried and repeated to me—to submit to DNA tests which might prove his relationship to Yvonne Grosjean's brother Max Grosjean. To take that one step might risk everything.

For all these reasons, I cannot believe that *Fragments* is anything other than fiction. And yet when I came back from his farmhouse that evening I was, as I said, convinced he was genuine. Anguish like his seemed impossible to fabricate. As Israel Gutman said in Jerusalem: 'Wilkomirski has written a story which he has experienced deeply, that's for sure.'

The question now, in Zurich again, is: What story and which anguish?

14.

According to the archivist in Adelboden, Bruno Grosjean arrived in that Swiss resort as a four-year-old boy on 20 March 1945. He came from Biel, where he was under the guardianship of one Walter Stauffer, who these days would be described as a care-worker. Stauffer and two assistants looked after the welfare of hundreds of children; in Bruno's case he seems to have acted with the authority *in loco parentis* from the boy's birth in 1941 until his legal adoption in 1957, when Stauffer signed the adoption papers (he retired in the following year and died soon after). At Adelboden, Bruno stayed in a children's home called Sonnhalde, which was turned into a pension in the 1950s. Sonnhalde was not an orphanage; it existed to give children a holiday in clean mountain air, and Bruno was probably sent to it for health reasons. (Two old ladies who live next door to the building remember that it had a playground, with swings.) Comments on Bruno's papers suggest that he was originally meant to stay for only two months. In fact, according to the papers, he was registered there until 13 October the same year, when he was placed with the Dössekkers (their discussions with his guardian about his adoption began in June 1945).

Did any member of his family visit him during those months? It seems that they did.

15.

In the late summer of 1998, after Wilkomirski discovered from Ganzfried that he had an 'uncle', he decided to go and see Max Grosjean in his home in Horgen, Kanton Zurich. Grosjean showed Wilkomirski and Verena pictures of his 'mother' and Bruno as a baby. No one present thought that they looked alike; Wilkomirski said that the photograph of Yvonne Grosjean did not in any way match his memory of his mother. Then Grosjean told Bruno/Binjamin a little of the family history. He had lost touch with his sister in the 1930s. Then, in 1940, she was involved in a car accident and he'd come to see her in hospital in Biel. While she was in hospital, it was discovered that she was pregnant. She was unmarried. She stayed in hospital until the birth, which had to be induced. She also received electric shock treatment to cure her partial paralysis. The uncle wanted to adopt Bruno, and sent his then fiancée—his present wife—to see him in Adelboden. She was shown Bruno in a group of other children, but was told that it was too late to adopt him. A 'doctor's family' had already applied and been accepted as foster parents. Neither Max Grosjean nor his fiancée/wife had ever seen Bruno again.

Wilkomirski talked to me about all this with remarkable ease. For him, Bruno Grosjean is a completely separate person. But when I expressed an interest in contacting the 'uncle' myself, Wilkomirski said that it would not be a good idea to disturb him. Therefore, I did.

On the telephone, Max Grosjean and his wife were quite happy to talk about what they remembered. They told me that Yvonne was very pretty, but not very 'reliable'; that she'd been hurt when a car had knocked her from her bicycle; that she didn't get along with her future sister-in-law, and therefore didn't want her brother to raise the child. After the birth and once she got better, she returned to her work in a watch factory in Biel.

The first four years of Bruno's life are not at all clear. Before he reached Adelboden, he was in the legal care of the Biel authorities, but where he was—in an institution, with foster parents?—Max Grosjean could not remember or would not say. Illegitimacy was a stigma; his mother was poor. But there are two photographs of mother and son together and the mother did, Mrs Grosjean said, visit him in the home in Adelboden at least once. Of course, once the adoption was agreed, she was not allowed to know where Bruno would go.

Then he used a word that I'd first heard from Wilkomirski. He said that he and his sister had been *Verdingkinder*. He said it sadly, and hinted at suffering and physical abuse. *Verdingkinder* (roughly 'earning children') were the children of the poor, sometimes orphans, sometimes illegitimate, sometimes with parents too impoverished to keep them. The traditional solution was a primitive welfare system; the creation of a caste of children who provided free labour for peasant families, in exchange for shelter and food. In the last century, *Verdingkinder* were sometimes sold at auction, like farm animals; beatings and sexual abuse were often part of their childhood. The system was finally abolished in the 1950s—neither a proud nor much-examined part of Swiss social history—but not before it had separated Bruno's mother and uncle when they were children; and, perhaps,

Yvonne Grosjean

made Bruno, as the illegitimate child of a *Verdingkind*, a natural candidate for separation from his mother, with or without her consent. I am not a psychologist; the temptations and dangers of literary or any other kind of psychology for the amateur are well known. Still, the similarities between *Fragments*, the early life of Benjamin Wilkomirski, and what we know of the early life of the real Bruno Grosjean are too striking to resist: obscure origins in a social class that polite Swiss society would rather not discuss; a childhood swamped with loss and change; institutions which might easily seem like child-prisons; distant memories of motherhood. In the book, the mother-substitute, Frau Grosz. In life, his mother, Frau Grosjean. 'I looked at her,' writes Wilkomirski of Frau Grosz as they travel on the train from Poland to Basle. 'She was staring at her hands and seemed to be a long way away. Something important, something that couldn't be changed, was going to happen.' Whether this is Grosz or Grosjean, Binjamin or Bruno, the destination is the same: adoption, the Dössekkers, a certain luxury but also coldness and formality in that villa up in the Zürichberg, overlooking a country where Binjamin/Bruno will begin to feel separate, and which he will come to dislike.

My second meeting with him in Switzerland wasn't really an interview. I just wanted to get a feeling for what he was like if we talked about subjects other than himself or the Holocaust. We met at his Zurich apartment and talked about opera and his favourite writers, Rilke and Goethe ('I love Faust'). He remembered rowing boats on the lake as a boy and, later, going as an adult back to his old home in Zürichberg to cook meals for the Dössekkers when they were old and frail. I may be wrong, but I sensed the agony of being Binjamin Wilkomirski had lifted for a while and that I was glimpsing Bruno Dössekker. I liked him. The Yiddish in his German had vanished.

To remove himself as far as possible from his native environment, he declared himself a Jew. If he sought a sense of community in Judaism, I doubt that he has found it—he practises a very solitary form. But to Bruno Dössekker, being a Jew was synonymous with the Holocaust. Swiss history has nothing remotely similar to offer, nothing so dramatic to survive, or to explain to a man where he came from, or how he is. □

65

Royal Festival Hall
Hayward Gallery
on the South Bank

CITIES ON THE MOVE

**Urban Chaos
and Global Change
East Asian Art, Architecture and Film Now**

13 May - 27 June 1999
At the Hayward Gallery

Please call **0171 921 0971** for a free leaflet with full
details of the exhibition and related talks and events.

www.hayward-gallery.org.uk

Literature on the South Bank

FICTION, POETRY AND TALKS

Wed 2 June, Purcell Room 7.30pm

Fiction International

Paul Auster with Kevin Jackson

Paul Auster, one of America's most
outstanding novelists and essay
writers, reads from his new novel
Timbuktu and talks about his writing
with **Kevin Jackson**.

Tickets £6.50 (concs £4)

Tue 15 June, Purcell Room 7.30pm

The *Sounding the Century* Lectures

Amos Oz with Sarah Dunant

How to Cure a Fanatic
Israel's foremost novelist on how
fanaticism begins at home. With
discussion chaired by **Sarah Dunant**.

Presented in collaboration with

Join our **free** mailing list for **advance information** about events and **priority booking**.
Call 0171 921 0971 or write to: Literature Events, Marketing Department, Royal Festival Hall,
Belvedere Road, London, SE1 8XX or email: ddezylva@rfh.org.uk

Royal Festival Hall
& Hayward Gallery **BOX OFFICE 0171 960 4242**

For your FREE Literature and Hayward Bulletins with full details
of all the above and more please call 0171 921 0971. Online: www.sbc.org.uk

GRANTA

BAD NATURE

Javier Marías

TRANSLATION BY ESTHER ALLEN

Elvis Presley in *Fun in Acapulco*

No one knows what it is to be hunted down without having lived it, and unless the hunt was constant and active, carried out with deliberation and determination and dedication and never a break, with perseverance and fanaticism, as if the pursuers had nothing else to do in life but catch you and before that look for you, keep after you, follow your trail, locate you and then, if you're lucky, wait for the best moment to settle the score. Being hunted, really hunted, isn't that someone has it in for you and stands at the ready to lay waste to you should you cross his path or give him the chance; it isn't that someone has sworn revenge against you and waits, waits, does no more than wait and therefore is still passive, or schemes in preparation for his blows, which as long as they're machinations cannot be blows, we think they'll fall but they may not, the enemy may have a heart attack before he sets to work in earnest, before he truly applies himself to harming us, destroying us. Or he may calm down, something may distract him and he may forget, and if we don't happen to cross his path again we may be able to get away; vengeance is extremely wearying and hatred tends to evaporate, it's a fragile, ephemeral feeling, impermanent and unable to last, so difficult to maintain that it quickly gives way to rancour or resentment, either of which is more bearable, easier to retrieve, much less virulent and somehow less pressing, while hatred is always in a tearing hurry, always urgent, I want him now, I want him dead, bring me the son of a bitch's head, I want to see him flayed and his body smeared with tar and feathers, a carcass, butchered and flayed, and then he will be no one and this hatred that is exhausting me will end.

No, it isn't that someone will harm you if given the chance, it isn't one of those civilized enmities in which someone takes a certain satisfaction in striking a name off the list of invitees to the embassy ball, or publishes nothing in his section of the newspaper about his rival's achievements, or fails to invite to a conference the man who once took a job away from him. It isn't the betrayed husband who does his utmost to requite the betrayal—or to do what he thinks will requite it—and see you betrayed in turn, it isn't even the man who trusted you with his savings and was had, buying in advance a house that was never built, or going up to his eyeballs in debt to finance a film when there was never even the slightest intention of shooting a single millimetre of footage, it's incredible how the movies lure and delude people. Nor is it the writer or painter who didn't win the prize that went to you and believes his life would have been different if only justice had been done back then, twenty years ago; it isn't even the peon thrashed a thousand times by the vicious and abusive capataz who is on close terms with the owner, the peon who yearns for a new Zapata in whose wake he'll slip a knife all the way down to his torturer's belly and, in passing, across the landowner's jugular, because the peon, too, lives in a state of waiting, or rather of the childish daydreaming we all fall into from time to time in order to make ourselves remember our desires, that is, in order not to forget them, and though repetition would appear to be in the service of memory, in reality it blurs and plays tricks on memory, and mutes it as well, relegating our needs to the sphere of that which is to come, so that nothing seems to depend on us right now, nothing depends on the peons, and the capataz knows there is a vague or imaginary threat, he suffers from his own dream, a dream of fear that only makes him the more brutal and vicious so as to repay in advance the knife thrust to the belly that he only receives in dreams, his own and those of others.

No, being hunted down is none of these things; it isn't knowing that you could be hunted down, it isn't knowing who would come to kill you if another civil war were to break out in these countries of ours, so prone to them and full of rage, it isn't knowing with absolute certainty that someone would stamp on your hand if it were clutching the edge of a cliff (a thing we don't usually risk, not in the presence of heartless people), it isn't fearing a bad encounter that could be avoided by walking down other streets or going to other bars or other houses, it isn't worrying that fate will make a mockery of us or the tables will turn against us one day, it isn't making possible or probable enemies or even certain but always future ones, committing transgressions whose atonement lies far ahead, almost everything is put off, almost nothing is immediate or exists, and we live in a state of postponement, life usually consists only of delay, signs and plans, projects and machinations, we trust in the indolence and infinite lethargy of the whole world, the indolence of knowing that things will come true and come to pass, and the indolence of carrying them out.

But sometimes there is neither indolence nor lethargy nor childish daydreaming, sometimes—though rarely—there is the urgency of hatred, the negation of reprieve and cunning and stratagems, which are present only if improvised by the intolerable resistance of the quarry, existing only as setbacks, without other value than to cause a slight adjustment to the planned trajectory of a bullet because the target has moved and evaded it. This time. But never again, or that's the hope, and if the bullet went astray there remains only to fire again, and again and again until the mark falls and can be finished off. When you're being hunted down like that you have the feeling that your pursuers do nothing but search for you, chase you twenty-four hours a day: you're convinced that they don't eat or sleep, they don't drink or even stop for one second, their venomous footsteps are incessant and tireless and there is no rest; they have neither wife nor child nor needs, they don't go to the bathroom or pause to chat, they don't get laid or go to soccer games, they don't have television sets or homes, at most they have cars to chase you with. It isn't that you know something bad could happen to you some day or if you go where you must not, it's that you see and know that the worst is happening to you right now, the most fearsome thing, and then the hunted one doesn't drink or eat or stop either; or sometimes he does, he stays still more out of panic than from any certainty of being safe and sheltered, more than a stillness, it's a paralysis, like an insect that doesn't fly away or a soldier in his trench. But even then he doesn't sleep except when exhaustion undermines what is happening right now and deprives it of reality, when all the years of his former life reassert themselves—it takes so long for habits to go away, the idea of an existence that isn't short-term—and he decides for an instant that the present is the lie, daydream or nightmare, and rejects it because it is so incongruent. Then he sleeps and eats and drinks and gets laid if he's lucky or pays, chats for a bit, forgetting that the venomous footsteps never stop and always go forward while his own perpetually innocent feet are detained or don't obey or might even be bare. And that's the worst thing, the greatest danger, because you must not forget that if you're fleeing you can never take off your shoes or watch television, or look into the eyes of someone who appears in front of you and might hold you back, my eyes only look

Javier Marías

back and those of my pursuers look ahead, at my dark back, and so
they are bound to catch up with me always.

It all happened because of Mr Presley, and that is not one of those
idiotic lines referring to the record that was playing the night we
met or the time we were careless or went too far, or to the idol of the
person who caused the problem by forcing us to go to a concert to
seduce her or just to make her happy. It all happened because of Elvis
Presley in person, or Mr Presley, as I used to call him until he told me
it made him feel like his father. Everyone called him Elvis, just Elvis,
with great familiarity, and that's what adoring fans and detractors
alike are still calling him even after his death, people who never saw
him in the flesh or exchanged a single word with him, or, back then,
people who were meeting him for the first time, as if his fame had
made him the involuntary friend or unwitting servant of one and all,
and this may be normal and even justifiable, however much I disliked
it, for the whole world did already know him even then, didn't they?
And they still do. Even so, I preferred to call him Mr Presley and then
Presley alone, by his surname, when he told me to drop the element
that made him feel so elderly, though I'm not sure he didn't later
regret the request a little, I have the feeling he liked to hear himself
called that at least once in his life, Mr Presley or señor Presley,
depending on the language, at the age of twenty-seven or twenty-
eight. And that—the language or its fringes, its most ornamental
aspects—was what brought me to him, when I was hired to be part
of his troop of collaborators, assistants and advisers for what was
supposed to be six weeks, that was how long it was supposed to take
to shoot *Fun in Acapulco*, which I think came out in Spain under a
different title, as usual, not *Diversión en Acapulco* or *Marcha en
Acapulco* but *El ídolo en Acapulco*. I never saw it in Spain.

But here not long ago I did buy the record that went with it,
the original soundtrack, which happened to catch my eye as I was
looking for something by Previn. I got it because it made me laugh
and brought back memories that for a long time I had decided I
would rather forget, just as everyone else in the crew had
undoubtedly decided to forget them, and had tried hard to forget
them, and succeeded: the liner notes to the record once again trot

72

out the old lie that has now been consecrated, the false history. The notes say Presley never set foot in Acapulco during the making of the film, that all his scenes were shot at the Paramount Studios in Los Angeles to spare him the trouble and the trip, while a second crew went to Mexico to shoot landscape stills and footage of locals in the streets to be used as backgrounds, Presley outlined against the sea and the beach, against the streets as he rides a bicycle with a boy perched in front, against the cliffs of La Perla, against the hotel where his character worked or wanted to work; he played a traumatized former trapeze artist named Mike Windgren, I always remember names, more than faces. The official version has prevailed, as happens with almost everything, but it is a highly doctored version, as official versions generally are, no matter who provides them, an individual or a government, the police or a movie studio. It's true that all the footage that actually appears in the film—as it was first shown and in the video version that exists today—was shot in Hollywood whenever Presley is on camera, and you hardly lose sight of him in the whole movie. They were very careful not to keep or use a single shot with him in it that hadn't come out of the studios, not a single one that could have contradicted the official version given by the producer and by señor Presley's entourage. But that doesn't mean there wasn't other footage that was cut, painstakingly and deliberately cut, in this case, and possibly fed to the flames or into the maw of a shredder, reduced to a celluloid pulp, not a trace must remain, not a millimetre, not a single frame, or that's what I imagine. Because the truth is that Presley did go to Mexico on location, not for three weeks but for ten days, at the end of which he not only abandoned the country without saying goodbye to anyone, but decided he had never been or set foot there, not for ten days or for five or even for one, Mr Presley hadn't budged from California or Tennessee or Missouri or wherever it was, he hadn't set foot in Acapulco or in Mexico itself and the person who'd been interviewed and seen by tourists and Acapulqueños—or whatever they're called— during those days in February was only one of his many doubles, as or more necessary than ever for this production because Presley's character, in order to get over the nasty shock of having dropped his brother from a trapeze, with the consequent shattering of his morale and his flying brother's body (smashed to bits), had to throw himself into the Pacific from the heights of the brutal cliffs of La Perla in the final or rather penultimate scene of *Fun in Acapulco*, a title on which no one had wasted any great mental energy. That was the official version of Presley's sojourn in Mexico, or rather his lack of a sojourn; it's still around, I see, which to some extent is understandable. Or perhaps it's simpler than that, perhaps it's just that there is never a way of erasing what's been said, be it true or false, once it's been said: accusations and inventions, slanders and stories and fabrications, disavowal is not enough, it doesn't erase but adds, once an event has been told there will be a thousand contradictory and impossible versions long, long before the event is annihilated: denials and discrepancies coexist with what they refute or deny, they accumulate, add up, they never cancel it out but ultimately sanction it for as long as people go on talking, the only thing that can erase is to say nothing, to say nothing for a very long time.

Thirty-three years have gone by since then and eighteen since señor Presley died, and he is dead, though the whole world still knows and listens to and misses him. And the truth is that I knew him in the flesh and we were in Acapulco, absolutely, he was there and I was there, and in Mexico City, where we flew more often than we should have in his private airplane, trips that took hours, at ungodly times of the night, he was there and I was there, though I was there longer, far too long, or so it seemed to me, the time of a chase lasts like no other because every second counts, one, two and three and four, they haven't caught me yet, they haven't butchered me yet, here I am and I'm breathing, one, two and three and four.

Yes: we were there, we were all there, the film's entire crew and señor Presley's entire entourage, which was far more extensive, he travelled—but that may be an exaggeration: he moved—with a legion at his back, a battalion of more or less indispensable parasites, each with his own function or without any very precise function, lawyers, managers, make-up artists, musicians, hairstylists, vocal accompanists—the invariable Jordanaires—secretaries, trainers, sparring partners—his nostalgia for boxing—agents, image consultants, costume designers and a seamstress, sound technicians, drivers, electricians, pilots, financial expediters, publicists, promo people, press people, official and unofficial spokesmen, the president of his national fan club on an authorized inspection or to deliver a report, and of course bodyguards, choreographers, a professor of diction, mixing engineers, a teacher of facial and gestural expression (who wasn't able to do much), occasional doctors and nurses and an around-the-clock personal pharmacist with an implausible arsenal of remedies, I never saw such a medicine chest. Each claimed to be answerable to certain others in an organized hierarchy, but it was not at all easy to know who answered to whom nor how many divisions and subdivisions there were, how many departments and teams, you would have needed to draw up a family tree or that other thing, I mean a flow chart. There were individuals whom no one was supervising at all closely—everyone thought they were taking orders from someone else—people who came and went and prowled and milled around without anyone ever knowing exactly what mission they were on, though it was taken for granted that they had a mission, back then no one was very suspicious, Kennedy hadn't been assassinated yet. All of them had the initials 'EP' embroidered on their jackets, shirts, T-shirts, overalls or blouses, in blue, red or white, depending on the colour of the garment, and any over-eager bystander who asked his mother to do a little embroidering for him could have passed himself off as a member of the crew without further difficulty. No one asked questions then, there were too many of us for everyone to know everyone else, and I think the only person who tried to keep an eye on things a little and supervise the whole group was Colonel Tom Parker, who was Presley's discoverer, or tutor or godfather or something like that, they told me (no one was very well informed about anything), and whose name appeared in the credits of all Presley's films as 'Technical Adviser', a vague title if ever there was one. His appearance was quite distinguished and severe and even somewhat mysterious in that motley setting; he was always well dressed and wearing a tie, his jaw tight as if he never relaxed, his teeth clenched as if he ground them in his sleep, he spoke very softly but very sternly right in the face of the person he was addressing, making sure his listener was the only one who heard him even if he were speaking in a room full of people, who were often whiling the time away in unbridled gossip. I'm not sure where the Colonel part came from, whether he really had been in the army or it was only some kind of whim and he called himself Colonel in nominal fulfilment of some truncated aspiration. But if so, then what was to prevent him from calling himself General? His lean figure and carefully combed grey hair inspired respect and even apprehension in most people, so much so that when his presence made itself felt on the set or in an office or a room the place began to empty out, imperceptibly but rapidly, as if he were a man of ill omen, as if no one wanted to be exposed for long to his Nordic eye, a translucent eye, difficult to meet head-on. Though he wore civilian clothing and his demeanour was more senatorial than military, everyone, including Mr Presley, always called him Colonel.

My own role was certainly not indispensable but resulted from one of Presley's caprices; I was hired only for that single occasion. And there we all were, the regulars of his formulaic movies, all copied from each other—*Fun* was the thirteenth—and the newcomers, all of us there for the indolent shooting of a ridiculous film, without rhyme or reason, at least in my opinion, I'm still amazed that the screenwriter actually received any money—a guy named Weiss who was incapable of making the slightest effort, he hung around the set paying no attention to anything but the music, I mean the music Presley sang at the drop of a hat with his inseparable Jordanaires or another group of vocal accompanists who went by the offensive name of The Four Amigos. I don't really know what the plot of the film was supposed to be, but not because it was too complicated, on the contrary, it's hard to follow a plot when there is no plot and no style to substitute for one or to distract you; even after having seen the film later—before the premiere there was a private screening—I can't tell you what its excuse for a plot was. All I know is that Elvis Presley, the tortured former trapeze artist, as I said—but he's only tortured sometimes, he also spends a lot of time going swimming, perfectly at ease, and romancing women uninhibitedly—wanders around Acapulco, I don't remember why, let's say he's trying to shake off his dark past or he's on the run from the FBI, maybe they thought the fratricide was deliberate (I'm not at all clear on that, I could be mixing up my movies, thirty-three years have gone by). As is logical and necessary, Elvis sings and dances, performing in various places: a cantina, a hotel, on a terrace facing the daunting cliff. From time to time he stares, with envy and some kind of complex, at the swimmers—or divers—who plunge into the pool with tremendous smugness from a diving board of only average height. There's a lady bullfighter, a local, who has a thing for Elvis, and another woman, the hotel's publicist or something like that, who competes with the matadora for him, Mr Presley was always very successful with women, in fiction as in life. There's also a Mexican rival named Moreno who jumps off the diving board far too often, frenetically, pausing only to taunt Windgren and call him a coward. Presley competes with him for the publicist, who was none other than the Swiss actress Ursula Andress, in a bikini or with her shirt capriciously knotted across her midriff and ribbons winding through her wet hair, she had just made herself universally desirable and famous— particularly among teenage boys—by appearing in a white bikini in the first James Bond adventure, *Agente 007 contra el doctor No*, or whatever it was called in Spain; her Acapulcan bikinis weren't cut very high and didn't live up to expectations, they were far more chaste than the one she wore in Jamaica, Colonel Tom Parker may have insisted, he seemed to be a gentleman of some decorum or maybe he was unwilling to tolerate any unfair competition with his protégé. Running around somewhere in all that was also a pseudo-Mexican boy, greatly over-endowed with the gift of the gab, whom Windgren befriended—the two amigos—without knowing why or for what purpose: that boy was an epidemic of talk and deserved to be avoided and ignored even in the elevators, which in fact was what we all did every time he came chattering towards us thinking that the fiction carried over into life, since in the movie he was a boon companion to the former trapeze artist embittered by the fraternal fatality and by Moreno the mean diving champ. That was the whole story, if you can call that a story.

And somewhere in there, very depressed, were also two veterans of the cinema whose attitude, between humiliated and sceptical, contrasted with the festive atmosphere of that thirteenth production. (We should have thought more about the number.) One was the director Richard Thorpe; the other, the actor Paul Lukas, a native of

Hungary whose real name was Lukács. Thorpe was around seventy years old and Lukas around eighty, and both found themselves at the end of their careers playing the fool in Acapulco. Thorpe was a good-hearted and patient man, or, rather, a heartsick and defeated man, and he directed with little enthusiasm, as if only a pistol shoved into the back of his neck by Parker could convince him to shout 'Action' before each shot. 'Cut', though, he would say more energetically, and with relief. He had made terrific, very worthwhile adventure films like *Ivanhoe* and *Knights of the Round Table*, *All the Brothers Were Valiant* and *House of the Seven Hawks* and *Quentin Durward*, he had even worked with Presley on his third film, back in less formulaic days, directing *Jailhouse Rock*, *El rock de la cárcel*, 'that was something else altogether, in black and white', he rationalized to Lukas during a break in the shooting; but discreetly, he wasn't a man to offend anyone, not even the provincial magnate McGraw or the producer Hal Wallis, who was also well along in years. As for Lukas or Lukács himself, he had almost always played supporting roles but he had an Oscar to his credit and had taken orders from Cukor and Hitchcock, Minnelli and Huston, Tourneur and Walsh, Whale and Mamoulian and Wyler, and those names were permanently on his lips as if he wanted them and their noble memory to conjure away the ignominy of what he was afraid would be his final role: in *Fun in Acapulco* he played the vaguely European father of Ursula Andress, a diplomat or government minister or perhaps an aristocrat come down so far in the world that he now worked as a chef at the hotel. During the entire shoot he never had one chance to take off the lofty white hat—far too tall, it had to be starched stiff to stay up—that is the cliché of that profession, I mean while he was on the set mouthing trite phrases that embarrassed him, because as soon as Thorpe mumbled 'Cut' with a yawn, and even if another take was being shot immediately, Paul Lukas tore off the loathsome headgear in a rage, looked at it with a disdain that may have been Hungarian—in any case, an emotion never seen in America—and muttered audibly, 'Not a single shot, dear God, at my age, not one shot of my glistening pate.' I was glad to learn two years later that this was only his penultimate film; he was able to bid his profession adieu with a great role and an excellent performance, that of the good

Mr Stein in *Lord Jim*, along with true peers such as Eli Wallach and James Mason. He was always polite to me and it would have pained him to say his farewell at Mr Presley's side.

It must not be inferred from this that I looked or look down on Mr Presley. On the contrary. There can't have been many people who admired him and still admire him more than I do (though without fanaticism), and I know I have enormous competition in that. There's never been another voice like his, another singer with so much talent and such a range, and in addition to that he was a pleasant, good-natured man, far less conceited than he had every right to be. But movies...no. He started out taking them seriously, and his earliest films weren't bad, *King Creole* for example (he admired James Dean so much that he knew all his parts by heart). But Mr Presley's problem, which is the problem of many people who are uncommonly successful, was the boundless extravagance it forced him to: the more success someone has and the more money he makes, the more work and the less freedom he has. Maybe it's because of all the other people who are also making money off him, and who exploit him, force him to produce, compose, write, paint or sing, squeeze him and blackmail him emotionally with their friendship, their influence, with pleas, since threats aren't very effective against someone who's at the top. Then again, there can always be threats; that's a given. So Elvis Presley had made twelve films in six years, in addition to multiplying himself in a thousand other varied activities; at the end of the day, the movies were only a secondary industry in his conglomerate. Behind this kind of person there are always businessmen and promoters who have trouble accepting that from time to time the manufacturer of what they sell stops making it. The fact is I've never seen anyone who was as exploited as Mr Presley, anyone who put out so much, and if he wanted to avoid it he wasn't helped by his character, which wasn't bad or surly or even arrogant—a little belligerent at times, yes—but obliging; it was hard for him to say no or put up an opposition. So his films got worse and worse, and Presley had to make himself more and more laughable in them, which was not very gratifying for someone who admired him as much as I did to see.

He wasn't aware of it, or so it seemed; if he was, he accepted the ridiculousness without making any faces about it and even with a touch of pride, it was all part of the job. And since he was a hard and serious and even enthusiastic worker, he couldn't see how his roles looked from the outside or make fun of them. I imagine it was in the same disciplined and pliant frame of mind that he allowed himself to grow drooping sideburns in the Seventies and agreed to appear on stage tricked out like a circus sideshow, wearing suits bedecked with copious sequins and fringes, bell bottoms slit up the side, wide belts like a novice whore, high-heeled goblin boots, and a short cape—a cape—that made him look more like Superrat than whatever he was probably trying for, Superman, I would imagine. Fortunately I didn't have any dealings with him during that period, not even for ten days, and in the Sixties when I knew him he didn't have to stoop so low, but neither was he free of the extravagant notions that happened to occur to other people, and I'm afraid it was in *Fun in Acapulco* that he got stuck with the worst of those bright ideas.

Every time I watched them shooting a scene I thought, 'Oh no, my God, not that, señor Presley,' and the amazing thing was that none of it seemed to bother Mr Presley, he even enjoyed the horror, with his undoubted capacity for kidding around. I don't think he was pleased or proud; it was just that he didn't have the heart to raise objections or make negative comments that would disappoint whoever it was that had come up with today's delirious concept, whether it was Colonel Tom Parker or the choreographer, O'Curran, or the producer Hal Wallis himself, or even that quartet with the objectionable name, The Four Amigos, whose flashes of inspiration came in pairs. Or maybe he had so much confidence in his own talent that he thought he could emerge unscathed from any fiasco; certainly in the course of his career he sang about everything and in all languages—for which he had no gift whatsoever—without any resultant collapse of his reputation. But we didn't know that yet. 'Oh no, dear God, spare him that,' I thought when I found out that Presley was going to play the tambourine and dance wearing a Mexican sombrero and surrounded by folkloric mariachis—one group was the Mariachi Aguila, the other the Mariachi Los Vaqueros, I couldn't tell them apart—while he sang 'Vino, dinero y amor', everyone joining in on the chorus, in a cantina. 'Oh Lord, don't let it happen,' I thought when they announced that Mr Presley would have to wear a short, tight jacket with a frilled shirt and scarlet cummerbund to sing the solemn 'El Toro' while stamping like a flamenco dancer. 'Oh no, please, what will his father think,' I thought as he perpetrated 'And the Bullfighter Was a Lady' wearing some approximation of a Mexican rancher's garb and swirling a bullfighter's cape over his carefully coiffed head or throwing it around his shoulders with the yellow side up as if it were a cloak. 'Oh no, that's going too far, that's regicide,' I thought when I read in the screenplay that in the final scene Presley was to sing 'Guadalajara', in Spanish, at the edge of the cliff, cheered on insincerely by all the mariachis together. But that's another story, and the linguistic disaster was no fault of mine.

That was what they hired me for. Not just to avoid linguistic disaster, much more than that: everything was to be pedantically perfect. I had been in Hollywood for a couple of months, doing whatever came my way, I had arrived with some letters of recommendation from Edgar Neville, whom I knew a little bit in Madrid. The letters weren't very useful—almost all his friends were dead or retired—but at least they allowed me to make a few contacts and stave off starvation for the time being. I was offered little jobs lasting a week or two, on location or at a studio, as an extra or an errand boy, whatever came up, I was twenty-two years old. So I couldn't believe it when Hal Pereira called me to his office and said, 'Hey Roy, you're Spanish, from Spain, right?'

My last name, Ruibérriz, isn't easy for English speakers, so I quickly became Roy Berry, and people called me Roy, that was my Christian name over there, or first name, as they say, and I appear as Roy Berry, in tiny letters, in the credits of certain films made in '62 and '63, I'd prefer not to say which ones.

'Yes sir, Mr Pereira, I'm from Madrid, Spain,' I answered.

'Terrific. Listen. I've got something fantastic for you and you'll be getting us out of a last-minute jam. Six weeks in Acapulco; well, three there and three here. Movie with Elvis Presley. Holiday in Acapulco'—that was the initial title, no one was ever prepared to put his brain to any stress over that film—'He's a lifeguard, trapeze artist,

I'm not sure, I'm joining up tomorrow. Elvis has to talk and sing a little in Spanish, right? Then suddenly he drops this bomb on us, claiming he doesn't want to have a Mexican accent; he wants it to be pure Spanish as if he learned it in Seville, says he found out they pronounce the letter 'c' differently in Spain and that's how he wants to pronounce it, OK, you're the one who knows about that. So the ten million Mexicans we've got swarming around here are no use at all, he wants a Spaniard from Spain to stay with him through the entire shoot and be in charge of his classy accent. We don't have many of those around here, Spaniards from Spain; what do we need them for? it's ridiculous. But Elvis is Elvis. We won't take no for an answer. You'll be hired by his team, and you'll take your orders from him, not us. But Paramount will pay you; Elvis is Elvis. So don't expect to make any more than what you're making this week. What do you say. We're leaving tomorrow.'

There was nothing to say, or rather I was speechless. Six weeks of easy, safe work, at the side of an idol, and to top it all off, in Acapulco. I think that for the first and last time I blessed the place of my birth, which doesn't usually bring me any advantages, and there I went, off to Mexico, to do hardly anything, since Mr Presley had to pronounce very few Spanish phrases in the course of the film, things like *'muchas muchachas bonitas'*, *'amigo'* and *'gracias'*. The hardest part was 'Guadalajara', he had to sing the whole song in the original lyrics, but that was scheduled for the third week of the shoot and there would be plenty of time to practise.

Mr Presley won me over right away, he was a funny, friendly man and after all he was only five or six years older than I was, though at that age even five or six years is enough to make the younger one be in awe of the more experienced, and even more so if the older one is already legendary. The concern with his accent was no more than a passing whim, and as it turned out he was completely incapable of pronouncing the Madrid 'c', so we settled for the Seville 'c'; I promised him that this was indeed the famous Spanish 'c', though he found it suspiciously similar to the Mexican 'c', which, as a matter of principle, he wanted to avoid. I ended up being employed more as an interpreter than as a professor of Spanish diction.

He was restless and needed to be doing something all the time, he had to get out of Acapulco as soon as the day's filming was over, so we would take his private plane and a few of us would go to Mexico City—five of us could fit, including the pilot, it was a small plane, the five amigos—or we would all go in several cars to Petatlán or Copala, Presley couldn't stand to spend the day and the night in the same place, though he also got tired of the new place right away and we always went back a few hours later, and sometimes a few minutes later if he didn't like what he saw, maybe it was only the trip that appealed to him. But he also had to work the next morning, and what with all the to and fro we would sleep from two or three a.m. to seven; after three or four days of that the rest of the excursionists were worn out, but not Presley, his endurance was incomparable, a man in a perpetual state of explosion, and used to giving concerts. He spent the whole day singing or crooning, even when he was under no professional obligation to do so, you could see he had a passion for it, he was like a singing machine, endlessly rehearsing with The Jordanaires or the mariachis or even The Four Amigos, and in the plane or the car, if conversation hadn't set in, it wouldn't be long before he started humming and the rest of us would join him, it was an honour to sing with Presley, though I hit a lot of false notes and he would laugh and gleefully encourage me, 'Go on, Roy, go on, just you by yourself, you've got a great career ahead of you.' (We switched back and forth between slow and fast numbers, and I've sung along with him above the clouds of Mexico on one of my favourites, 'Don't', and on 'Teddy Bear'—PA-palala, PA-palala—. You don't forget a thing like that.) His mania for singing made everyone involved in the shoot a little frenetic, or at least excited, Wallis's people and Presley's people, no one can take a life of non-stop music in their stride, I mean without being a musician. Even the good Paul Lukas, at his advanced age and with his great burden of annoyance, hummed at times without realizing it, I heard him humming 'Bossa Nova Baby' between his teeth, though in his defence that song really sticks in your mind, I'm sure he didn't realize what he was doing. Presley sang it with a bunch of guys wearing glittering green jackets and holding tambourines.

But most unbearable of all were the kind of people who not only let themselves be carried along on the tide of song and incessant humming but went looking for it and egged Mr Presley on in order to feel they were on his level or ingratiate themselves, trying to out-Elvis Elvis. There were a number of them among that vast company, but the most grotesque of all was McGraw, the small-town magnate, a man of about fifty-five—my age now, awful thought—who, during the days he spent on location with us, behaved not like a young man of twenty-seven (Presley's age) or twenty-two (mine) but like a fourteen-year-old in the full frenzy of burgeoning pubescence. George McGraw was one of the many inappropriate individuals Presley swept along in his wake for reasons that were not at all clear, maybe they were big investors in his conglomerate, or people from his home town whom he tolerated for that reason or owed old favours to, like Colonel Tom Parker, possibly. I found out that George McGraw had several businesses in Mississippi and maybe in Alabama and Tennessee, in any case in Tupelo, where Presley was born. He was one of those overbearing types who are incapable of rectifying their despotic manners even when they're very far outside the five-hundred-square-mile area in which their remote and doubtless crooked business dealings have influence. He was the owner of a newspaper in Tuscaloosa or Chattanooga or even in Tupelo itself, I don't remember, all of those places were often on his lips. It seemed he had tried to make the town in question change its name to Georgeville, and, having failed in that ambition, he refused to give his newspaper the city's name and christened it instead with his own first name: *The George Herald*, no less, in daily typographic retaliation. That was what some people called him in derision, George Herald, reducing him to a messenger (I've known other men like him since then: editors, producers, cultural businessmen who quickly lose the adjective and are left with the noun). I remember joking with Mr Presley about those towns in his native region, he thought it was hilarious when I told him what Tupelo means in Spanish ('your hair' he repeated, laughing uproariously), especially since it sounds so much like toupee. 'They seem completely made up, those names,' I told him, 'Tuscaloosa sounds like a kind of liquor and Chattanooga like a dance, let's go have a couple of tuscaloosas and dance the chattanooga,' with Mr Presley everything went fine if you joked around a lot, he was a cheerful man with a quick, easy laugh, maybe too quick and too easy, one of those people who are so undemanding that they take to everyone, even airheads and imbeciles. This can be a little irritating, but you can't really get angry with that kind of simple soul. Anyway, I was on the payroll.

George Herald, I mean McGraw, was no doubt very boastful of his friendship with Presley and would imitate him in the most pathetic way: he wore a sorry excuse for a toupee, an overly compact mass that looked like Davy Crockett's coonskin cap from the front, and from the side, since there was no beaver's tail, like a bellboy's hat, though without the chinstrap. He admired or envied Presley so much that he wanted to be more than Presley, he didn't want to lag behind him in any respect, but to be a kind of paternalistic partner, as if the two of them were singers at the same level of success and he were the more experienced and dominant. Except McGraw couldn't sing at all (except in the airborne choruses of that ill-fated journey which for me was the last), and his unhealthy rivalry with Elvis was no less imaginary. He would shamelessly appropriate Elvis's phrases, so that if Elvis said to the pilot and me one afternoon, 'Come on, Roy, Hank, let's go to FD,' referring to Mexico City, Federal District in his language, and then added: 'FD sounds like a tribute to Fats Domino, let's go to Fats Domino' (whom he admired tremendously), McGraw repeated the quip a hundred times until he had entirely stripped it of any conceivable charm, 'We're off to see Fats Domino, to Fats Domino we go.' You start to hate the joke. In the throes of this half-adulatory, half-competitive zeal, he spent the two days of his visit exaggeratedly tripping the light fantastic wherever he happened to be (on the beach, in the hotel, in a restaurant, in an elevator, in what was supposed to be a business meeting) as soon as he heard a few notes nearby or even in the distance, and there was always music playing somewhere. He danced in the most unseemly fashion, like someone who's pretending to be crazy, aided and abetted by a towel which he rubbed at top speed against his shoulders or along the backs of his thighs as if he were a stripper, it was truly a vile spectacle since he was husky verging on fat but moved like a hysterical teenager, shaking that broad head from which not one of his Davy Crockett hairs ever came unglued, and spinning his tiny feet like tornadoes. And he did not stop. In the plane, on the trip out (for me there was no return trip), we had to ask Presley not to sing anything that was too fast, because the owner of the *George Herald* would immediately go into his dance fever—those wee vicious eyes of his—and endanger our airborne equilibrium. McGraw didn't like slow tunes, only 'Hound Dog', 'All Shook Up', 'Blue Suede Shoes' and so on, songs that let him go nuts and do his number with the towel or whatever scarf or handkerchief happened to be at hand, his indecent bump and grind. It may be that he was what today we would call in Spanish *un criptogay*, a homosexual who hides it even from himself, but he boasted about never letting a tasty chick—his expression—get away from him without putting his hands on her or making some lewd remark.

That night, in addition to Presley, whom he always watched pathologically, he had his eye on an actress, very young, very blonde, who played a bit part in the film and who was part of our expedition to the FD, I always went along to act as interpreter, Hank could get out of it when we went by car. But that night we were flying. The girl was named Terry, or Sherry, the name has gotten away from me, it's strange, or not so strange, and McGraw had the gall to compete in that arena, too, with Presley, I mean he was putting the moves on her without waiting to see if the King had any plans in that respect, which was a serious lapse in manners in addition to being a delusion, since it was clear to one and all that the young lady had ideas of her own which in no way included the moronic magnate.

It wasn't Presley's fault, or mine, except secondarily, it was primarily McGraw's fault, and for that reason alone have I spoken, very much against my will, of that fake frontiersman. When the five of us walked into a dance hall or discotheque or cantina—five if we had flown to Mexico City; ten or fifteen if we were in Acapulco, Petatlán or Copala—a riot would usually break out the moment those present realized that Presley was there, and women would be fainting all over the place. As soon as the owners or managers realized he was there they would put an end to the commotion the more bold-hearted girls were making and throw out the swooners so that Elvis wouldn't get annoyed by them and leave right away—I've seen nightclub bouncers scaring off harmless teenage girls with their fists, we didn't like it but there was nothing else to do if we wanted to have a quiet tuscaloosa or watch a chattanooga—and once order had been re-established, what generally happened was that all eyes without exception were on us, to the great detriment of whatever show was being performed on stage, and everything was limited to that and a few furtive autographs. Once we had a kind of forewarning of what happened that night, a few young fellows got jealous; they started trying to provoke us and made some seriously inappropriate remarks. I decided it was best not to translate any of it for Mr Presley and convinced him to get out of there, and nothing happened. Those guys had knives, and sometimes you see the capataz embodied in anyone with a bulging wallet.

We happened to wander into an inhospitable and not very well-policed joint, or else the thugs inside were there to protect the owners rather than any patron, even if he happened to be a famous gringo. We would stop in wherever we felt like it, going by how the dive looked from the outside and what its posters promised, pictures of singers or dancers, almost always Mexican, a few unconvincingly Brazilian women. There were quite a lot of people inside, in an atmosphere that had a listless, thuggish savour to it, but it was the third stop of the evening and we hadn't been stinting on tequila, so we went over to the bar and stood there all in a row, making room for ourselves in a way that wasn't exactly the height of good manners, anything else would have been out of place.

Across the dance floor was an eye-catching table of seven or eight people, looking rich but not at all high-class, five men with three women who may have been rented for the night or hired on a daily basis, and both men and women were staring at us fixedly despite the fact that we had our backs to the dance floor and to their table. Maybe they were just guys who liked to watch other people dancing from up close; the women danced, but among the men only one did, the youngest, a limber individual with high cheekbones and the look of a bodyguard, a look he shared with two others who stayed in their places and didn't leave their bosses alone for a second. They didn't look as if they had any connection to the place, but they turned out to, and one of their bosses did too; he was a common enough type in Mexico, around thirty-five with a moustache and curly hair, but in Hollywood they would immediately have put him under contract as a new Ricardo Montalbán or Gilbert Roland or César Romero, he was tall and handsome and wore his shirtsleeves neatly rolled up very high in order to display his biceps which he was constantly testing out. His partner, or whatever he was, was fat with a very fair complexion, more European blood there, his hair combed straight back in a dandified way, and too long at the nape of the neck, but he didn't dye it to take out the grey. Nowadays we'd call them *mafiosos lavados*, 'whitewashed gangsters', but that expression wasn't in use then: they were intimidating but for the time being irreproachable, owners of restaurants or stores or bars or even ranches, businessmen with employees who accompanied them wherever they went and protected them when necessary from their peons and even from some capataz gone wrong. In his hand the fat man had a vast green handkerchief that he used, by turns, to mop his brow or to fan the atmosphere as if he were shooing flies away or performing magic tricks, sending it floating out over the dance floor for a second.

Our arrival hadn't created much of a stir because we had our backs to the room and because Hank, who was enormous, stood, looking very dissuasive, between Mr Presley and the three or four women who first came up to us. After a few minutes, Presley spun around on his bar stool and looked out at the dance floor; there was a murmur, he drank as if nothing were going on and the buzz diminished. He had a certain glassy look that could sometimes appease a crowd, it was as if he didn't see them and cancelled them out, or he would shift his expression slightly in a way that seemed to promise something good for later on. He himself was calm just then, drinking from his glass and watching the *hermanos Mexicanos* dancing, sometimes a kind of a melancholy came over him. It didn't last.

But there was no stopping the exasperating George McGraw who of course was relentless when it came to making demonstrations of his own prowess; if he saw Presley in a moment of calm, far from adapting to the mood or following his lead, he seized on it to try to outshine and eclipse him, fat chance. He wanted Sherry to dance with him, practically threatened her, but she didn't go with him to the dance floor and made a crude gesture, plugging her nose as if to say

that something stank, and I saw that this did not pass unnoticed by
the fat guy with the oiled-back locks, who wrinkled his brow, or by
the new César Montalbán or Ricardo Roland who flexed his right
biceps even higher than usual.

So McGraw got out on the floor, swaying his hips all by himself
and taking very short little steps, his button eyes ablaze with the
trumpeting rumba that was playing, and he couldn't manage to keep
from displaying his repertory of dreadful movements or from emitting
sharp, ill-timed cries that were like a mockery of the way Mexicans
yip to urge someone on. Hank and Presley were watching him in
amusement; they burst out laughing and young Sherry started
laughing too, out of contagion and flirtation. The owner of the
George Herald was dancing so obscenely that his crazed thrusts of
the hip were getting in the way of some of the women on the dance
floor, and the bodyguard with high cheekbones who moved as if he
were made of rubber shot him dead with a glance from his Indian
eyes, but nothing stopped him. The other dancers did stop and stood
aside, whether out of disgust or in order to get a better view of
McGraw I don't know: he was giving his trapper's or bellhop's cap
such a vigorous shaking that I was afraid it would go sailing off and
come to a bad end, forgetting that he wore it securely glued to his
scalp. The problem was that he didn't travel with his towel, and he
must have considered it an indispensable element in his dance
routine; consequently, as the pale-skinned fat man, in a moment of
carelessness, flung his handkerchief up to aerate the atmosphere,
McGraw filched it from him without so much as a glance and
immediately flung it over his shoulders, holding it by the two ends,
and rubbing it against himself, up and down, with the customary
celerity that by then we had seen all too often. The fat man kept his
limp hand extended during the moment following the loss, he didn't
pull it back right away as if he hadn't given up on recovering his
beloved green handkerchief—some kind of a fetish maybe. In fact,
he tried to reach it from his seat when McGraw came his way in his
increasingly indecorous dance. What finally made the fat man lose
patience was a moment in McGraw's sashayings when he withheld
the handkerchief and started voluptuously towelling it across his
buttocks. The fat man stood up for a second—he was a very tall fat

man, I saw—and grabbed the handkerchief away from the dancing fool in irritation. But the dancer gave an agile spin and, before the fat man had resumed his seat, took it back again with an imperious gesture, he was used to having his way and having his orders followed back in Tupelo or Tuscaloosa. It was a comical moment, but I wasn't happy to see that Gilbert Romero and his crowd were not at all amused, because it really was funny, the fat man and the semi-fat man quarrelling over the green silk handkerchief next to the dance floor. I was even less happy to see what happened next: the impatient expression on the stiff-haired fat man's face changed to brutal cold rage, and he seized the handkerchief back from McGraw with a swipe of his big hand at the same time as the elastic bodyguard delivered a blow to the magnate's kidneys that made him fall to his knees, his dance stopped dead. As if he were well-rehearsed at this sort of gesture—but how could he be?—the fat man's next swift move was to twist the handkerchief around the kneeling McGraw's neck and start pulling on the ends to strangle him right then and there. The cloth lost all its glide in a second and stretched thin and unbelievably taut, like a slender cord, and its green colour disappeared, a cord that was tightening. The fat man pulled hard on the two ends, his complexion red as a steak and his expression heartless, like a man tying up a clumsy package hurriedly and mechanically. I thought he was killing McGraw on the spot, like a flash of lightning and without saying a word, in front of a hundred witnesses on the dance floor, which in an instant emptied out completely. I admit I didn't know how to react, or maybe I felt that at last we would be free of the small-town magnate, I did no more than think (or else the thought came later but I attribute it to that moment): 'He's killing him, killing him, he is killing him, no one could have seen it coming, death can be as stupid and unexpected as they say, you walk into some honky-tonk without ever imagining that everything can end there in the most ridiculous way and in a second, one, two and three and four, and every second that passes without anyone intervening makes this irreversible death more certain, the death that is happening, as we watch, a rich man from Chattanooga being killed by a fat man with a bad character in Mexico City right before our eyes.'

Then I saw myself shouting something in Spanish out on the dance floor, all of us were there, Presley grabbing the lapels of the rubber man who managed to twist away from a hard blow, Hank with the handkerchief in his hand, he had given the fat man a shove that sent him flying back to his seat and sent all the glasses on Roland's table crashing. This crew weren't carrying knives, or not just knives, they were full-grown men, not peons but capatazes and landowners, and they carried pistols, I could see it in the way the other two thugs moved, one at the chest and the other on the hip, though Montalbán restrained them, opening out a horizontal hand as if to say 'five'. Hank was the most excited, he always carried a pistol, too, though fortunately he hadn't put his hand on it, a man with a gun gets more excited when he sees he may be using it. He wadded the handkerchief into a ball and threw it at the hotheaded fat man saying in English, 'Are you crazy or what? You could have killed him.' The silk floated in its journey.

'¿Qué ha dicho ese?' Romero asked me immediately, he had already realized I was the only member of the group who spoke the language.

'Que si está loco, ha podido matarlo,' I answered automatically. 'No es para tanto,' I added on my own account. What *was* the big deal?

It was all coming to nothing, every second that went by now, every panting breath we all drew made the tension diminish, an altercation of no importance whatsoever, the music, the heat, the tequila, a foreigner who behaved like a spoiled brat, he was standing up with Sherry's help, coughing violently, he looked scared, unable to comprehend that anyone could possibly have harmed him. He was all right, either there hadn't been time for much damage to be done or the fat man wasn't as strong as he looked.

'La nena vieja se puso pesada con el amigo Julio y Julio se cansa pronto,' said Romero Ricardo. 'Será mejor que se la lleven rápido. Váyanse todos, las copas están pagadas.'

'What did he say?' Presley asked me immediately. He had his own urgent need to understand, to know what was happening and what was being said, I saw him slipping into belligerence, the ghost of James Dean descended upon him and sent a shiver down my spine.

His own movies were too bland to satisfy that ghost. Hank jerked his head towards the door.

'That we should get out of here fast. The drinks are on them.'

'And what else? He said something else.'

'He insulted Mr McGraw, that's all.'

Elvis Presley was a good friend to his friends, at least to his old friends, he had a sense of loyalty and a lot of pride and it had been many years since he had taken orders from anyone. It's only a step from melancholy to brawling. And there was his nostalgia for boxing.

'Insulted him. That guy insulted him. First they try to kill him, then they insult him. What did he say? Come on, what did he say? And who is he to tell us to get out of here anyway?'

'*¿Qué ha dicho?*' now it was Roland César's turn to ask me. Their inability to understand each other was enraging them, a thing like that can really grate on your nerves in an argument.

'*Que quién es usted para decir que nos vayamos.*'

'*Han oido, Julio, muchachos, me pregunta el gachupín que quién soy yo para ponerlos en la calle,*' Montalbán answered without looking at me. I thought it was odd (if there was time for such a thought) that he said I was the one asking who he was: it was Presley who was asking and I was only translating, it was a warning I didn't pay attention to, or that I picked up on too late, when you relive what happened, or reconstruct it. '*Soy aquí el propietario. Aquí soy el dueño, por muy famoso que sea su patrón,*' he repeated with a slight tremor of one of his mobile biceps. If he was the owner, as he claimed, he was very unfriendly, my boss didn't impress him, they hadn't come over to say hello when we came in and now they were throwing us out. '*Y les digo que se larguen y se lleven a la bailona. La quiero ya fuera de mi vista, no espero.*'

'What did he say?' It was Presley's turn.

I was getting tired of the double onslaught of this crossfire. I looked at McGraw, *la bailona*, as Romero had called him, he was breathing more easily now but was still terrified—the tiny psychotic eyes were glazed—he was pulling at Hank's jacket to get us to leave, Hank was still making gestures with his head tilted towards Presley, Sherry was already heading for the door, McGraw leaning on her, maybe taking advantage, he was one of those guys who never learn.

Fat Julio was in his seat, he had recovered his composure after his exertions, his whiteness had returned like a mask, he was following the conversational match with his hands crossed (rings glinting), like someone who hasn't given up on the idea of re-entering the fray.

Before answering Presley I thought it was a good idea for me to say something to Ricardo: '*El no es quien usted cree. Es su doble, sabe, su sosias, para hacer las escenas de peligro en el cine, estamos rodando una película allí en Acapulco. Se llama Mike.*'

'*El parecido es tan logrado,*' Julio interrupted sarcastically, '*que le habrán hecho la cirugía estética a Mike, como a las presumidas.*' He wiped the by now utterly revolting handkerchief across his forehead.

'What did they say?' Presley insisted. 'What did they say?'

I turned towards him.

'They're the owners. We'd better go.'

'And what else? What were you saying about Mike? Who's Mike?'

'Mike is you, I told them that was your name, that you're your double, not yourself, but I don't think they believe me.'

'And what did they say about George? You said they insulted him. Tell me what those guys said about George, they can't get away with just saying whatever they want.'

This last comment was a genuine piece of North American naivety. And that was where my share of the blame came in, though Presley and I were to blame only in the second place, and the guilty party was primarily McGraw, maybe I was only to blame in the third place. How could I explain to Mr Presley, at that moment, that the tough guys were using nouns in the feminine gender to refer to McGraw, *la nena vieja, pesada, bailona,* English nouns have no gender and I wasn't about to give him a Spanish lesson right there on that dance floor. I glanced over at *la nena vieja, la bailona*—I'm the same age now that he was then—he was smiling weakly, walking away, the coward, he was starting to feel as if he were out of danger, he was tugging at Hank, Hank was tugging a little at Presley ('Let's go, Elvis, it doesn't matter'), no one was tugging at me. I gestured my head towards César Gilbert.

'OK. He called Mr McGraw a fat faggot,' I said. I couldn't avoid

Javier Marías

putting it like that and I couldn't help saying it, I wanted the owner of the *Herald* to hear it and not be able to make any display of his despotism or punish anyone or do anything except swallow the insult. And I wanted the others to hear it, pure childishness.

But I hadn't been thinking about what a stickler Presley was and for an instant I'd forgotten the ghost. We'd all been drinking tequila. Mr Presley raised one finger, pointed it at me dramatically and said, 'You're going to repeat this word for word, Roy, to the guy with the moustache, don't you leave out one syllable. Tell him this: you are a goon and a pig, and the only fat faggot here is your little girlfriend there with the handkerchief.' That was what he said, with that way of twisting his mouth he sometimes had that inspired distrust in the mothers of his youngest fans. His insults were a little on the schoolboy side, nothing about bastards or sons of bitches, those words had more weight in the Sixties. He paused for a second, then, with his finger still pointing, added, 'Say that to him.'

And I did say that to Ricardo César, I said it in Spanish (stammering a little): '*Usted es un matón y un cerdo, y la única maricona gorda es su amiguita del pañuelo.*' As soon as I said '*maricona gorda*' I realized it was the first time those exact words had been spoken there, really, though they weren't much more offensive than '*bailona*' or '*nena vieja*'.

Presley went on: 'Tell him this, too: We're leaving now because we want to and because this place stinks, and I hope someone sets fire to it soon, with all of you inside. Say that, Roy.'

And I repeated in Spanish (but in a less wounding tone and a softer voice): '*Ahora nos vamos porque queremos y porque este lugar apesta, y espero que se lo quemen pronto con todos ustedes dentro.*'

I saw how Gilbert Ricardo's biceps were quivering like jelly and a corner of his moustache twitched, I saw fat Julio open his mouth like a fish in feigned horror and run his fingers across his rings as if they were weapons, I saw that one of the two thugs at the table openly pulled back the front of his jacket to exhibit the butt of a pistol in its holster, like an old print of one of Pancho Villa's men. But Ricardo Romero stretched out his hand to the horizon again, as if he were indicating 'five', which was not at all comforting because there were five of us. Then, with the same hand, he briefly signalled towards me with the index finger pointing upwards, as if he were holding a pistol and his thumb were the raised safety. Sherry was at the door by then, along with McGraw whose hand was clutching his damaged loin, Hank was pulling at Presley with one hand and kept the other in his pocket, as if he were gripping something. I already said no one was pulling at me.

Presley turned around when he saw I had translated everything, and in two shakes he was there with the others at the door, the meaning of the way Hank had his hand in his jacket was clearly unmistakable, to the Mexicans, too. I followed them, the door was already open, I was the straggler, all of them were walking outside, quickening their step, they were already out, I was about to go after them, but the rubber man shoved in between Presley and me, his back in front of my face, he was taller and made me lose sight of the others for a second, then the rubber man went out with the others, and the bouncer who'd been standing at the door keeping an eye on the street came in and closed the door before I could get through it. He stood in my way and kept me from passing.

'Tú, gachupín, te quedas.'

I had never believed it was really true that we Spaniards are known as gachupines in Mexico, just as I never believed the other thing they told us when we were kids, that if you were ever in Mexico and ordered 'una copita de ojén'—an anisette—to the rhythm of seven thumps on the bar of a cantina—or even if you thumped rhythmically seven times and didn't say a thing—they'd open fire on you without further ado because it was an insult. It didn't occur to me to try and verify this just then, I didn't much feel like having anisette, or anything else.

This time it wasn't Gilbert Montalbán who called me gachupín but Julio, and he was looking more irate and uncontrolled to me, I'd watched him knotting up.

'Pero mis amigos ya se marchan,' I said, turning around, 'I have to go with them. No hablan español, you saw.'

'Don't worry about that. Pacheco will go with them back to the hotel, they'll arrive safe and sound. But they'll never be back here, eso es seguro.'

'They'll come back for me if you don't let me leave,' I answered, trying to glance furtively back at the door, which did not open.

'No, they won't be back, they won't know the way,' it was César Roland speaking now. 'You wouldn't know how to come back here either, if you left. I'm sure you weren't paying attention to the street we're on, you guys wandered away from the centre a little bit without realizing it, it happens to a lot of people. But you're not leaving; you have to spend a little more time with us tonight, it's early still, you can tell us about the *Madre Patria* and maybe even insult us some more, so we can listen to your accent.'

Now I really wasn't happy.

'Look,' I said, 'I didn't insult you. It was Mike, he told me what to say to you and all I did was translate.'

'Ah, you didn't do anything but translate,' the fat one interrupted. 'Too bad we don't know if that's true, we don't speak English. Whatever Elvis said we didn't understand, but you we understood, you speak very clearly, in a little bit of a rush like everyone else back there in Spain, but we hear you loud and clear, and you can rest assured that we're listening. Him, no, your boss we couldn't, he was speaking English, right? We never learned to speak it, we didn't get much of an education. Did you understand what the gringo said, Ricardo?' he asked Gilbert or César, who was, in fact, named Ricardo.

'No, I didn't understand either, Julito. But the *gachupín* yes; we all understood him very well, isn't that right *muchachos*?'

Neither *muchachos* nor *muchachas* ever answered when he said things like this, they appeared to know that on such occasions their involvement was merely rhetorical.

I turned my head towards the door, the big bouncer was still there, almost as big as Hank; with a jerk of the chin he let me know he wanted me further back inside the dive. 'Oh Elvis, this time you really have robbed me of my youth,' I thought. They must have tried to come back inside when they saw I wasn't coming out but Pacheco wouldn't let them, maybe he even pulled his gun on them. But Hank had a gun, too, and in the street it was three against one, not counting Sherry, so why didn't they come back for me? I still hadn't lost all hope but I lost it a second later when I saw that the Villista with the butt of his pistol on display had left the table and was coming towards me, but only to go by and continue on out to the street, the bouncer let him pass, then closed the door again. He put a hand on my shoulder as he was opening it, a hand the weight of a steak, immobilizing me. Maybe the thug was going to help the rubberized Pacheco, maybe they weren't going to escort my group back to any hotel—there was no hotel, just the plane—but settle the score with the others just as they were going to with me, only outside the joint that belonged to them, *dar el paseo* that's called: going for a ride.

I didn't know which was better: if the others were being prevented from rescuing me or if they had left me in the lurch. Rescuing me. The only one who might have felt any obligation to do that was Mr Presley, and even then: we'd only spent a few days together, I was an employee or peon, no more, and after all I spoke the local language and would know how to take care of myself; Hank didn't seem like a bad guy or a man to abandon anyone, but he was a capataz and his primary duty was to look out for Mr Presley and bring him back safe and sound from that bad encounter, anything else was secondary, they would look for me later, when the King was far away and out of danger, what a disaster if anything should happen to him, for so many people. But I wouldn't be disastrous for anyone. As for McGraw and the girl, no one could criticize McGraw for leaving me there until hell froze over if he wanted to, I hadn't lifted a finger for him when he was being strangled on a dance floor to the sound of a rumba. The music started up again, it had been interrupted by the altercation, but not by death which seemed to have arrived among us. I felt a shove on my back—that steak, so raw— and walked to Ricardo's table, he urged me to sit down, motioning with his hand towards the seat left empty by the Villista thug. It was a friendly gesture, he was wearing a deep red handkerchief around his neck, very clean and neatly tied, I only had to try to get them to forgive me for words that were not mine but that had been on my lips, or had become real only through my lips, I was the one who had divulged them or deciphered them, and that was incredible, how could they hold me accountable for something that didn't proceed from my head or my will or my spirit. But it had come from my tongue, my tongue had made it possible, from my tongue they had grasped what was happening and if I hadn't translated those men would have had no more than Presley's tone of voice to go on, and tones of voice have no meaning, even if they are represented or imitated or suggested. No one kills over a tone of voice. I had been the messenger, the intermediary, the true deliverer of the news, the interpreter, I was the one they had understood, and maybe they didn't want to have serious problems with someone as important and famous as Mr Presley, the FBI itself would have crossed the border to hunt them down if they had so much as scratched him, petty gangsters know above all who they can tangle with and who they can't, who they can teach a lesson to and who they can bleed, just as capatazes and businessmen know, but not peons.

I spent that whole eternal night with them, the entire group, women and men, we went to a string of bars, we would all sit down around a table and watch some dances or a song or a striptease and then move on to the next place. I don't know where I was, every time we went somewhere new we travelled in several cars, I barely knew the city, I watched the street signs go by, a few names stayed with me and I haven't ever gone back to Mexico City, I will never go back, I know, though Ricardo must be nearing seventy by now and fat Julio has been dead for centuries. (The thugs won't have lasted, that type has a brief, sporadic life.) Doctor Lucio, Plaza Morelia, Doctor Lavista, those few names stuck in my head. They assigned me—or maybe it was his choice—to the company of the fat man for the duration of the evening's festivities, he was the one who most often chatted with me and asked me where I was from and about Madrid, when I told him, what my name was and what I was doing in America, about my life and my brief history which perhaps began then, maybe he needed to know who he was going to be killing later that night.

I remember he asked me, 'Why the name Roy? That was what your boss called you, right? That's not one of our Spanish names.'

'It's just a nickname they use, my name is Rogelio,' I lied. I wasn't about to tell him my real name.

'Rogelio *qué más*.'

'Rogelio Torres.' But you almost never lie entirely, my full surname is Ruibérriz de Torres.

'I was in Madrid once, years ago, I stayed at the Hotel Castellana Hilton, it was pretty. At night it's fun, lots of people, lots of bullfighters. In the daytime I didn't like it, everything dirty and too many policemen in the streets, as if they were afraid of the citizens.'

'It's the citizens that are afraid of them,' I said. 'That's why I left.'

'*Ah muchachos, es un rebelde.*'

I tried to be sparing in my information yet courteous in my conduct, he wasn't giving me much of a chance to show how nice I could be. I told an anecdote to see if they would think it was charming or funny, but they weren't inclined to share in my humour. When someone has it in for you, there's nothing to do about it, they'll never acknowledge any merit in you and would rather bite their cheeks and lips until they bleed than laugh at what you're saying (unless it's a woman, they laugh no matter what). And from time to time one or another of them would remember the reason for my presence there, remember it out loud to keep everyone simmering:

'Ay, why doesn't the *muchacho* like us,' Ricardo said suddenly, fixing his eyes on me. 'I hope his wishes haven't come true during our absence and we don't find El Tato reduced to ashes when we go back. That would be most distressing.'

Or Julio would say, 'It's just that you had to go and choose such an ugly word, Rogelito *revoltoso*, why did you have to call me a *maricona*, you could have said I was a fairy. That would have hurt me less, now, you see how things are. Feelings are a great mystery.'

I tried to argue each time they came at me with this: it wasn't me, I was only transmitting; and they were right, McGraw had asked for it and Mike hadn't been fair at all. But it was no use, they clung to the extravagant idea that I was the only one they had heard and understood, and what did they know about what the singer had said in English.

The women sometimes spoke to me, too, but they only wanted to know about Elvis. I stayed firm on that point and never wavered, that was his double and I'd hardly seen the real Elvis during the shoot, he was very inaccessible. In the third place we dropped in on Pacheco appeared, and seeing him really shook me up. He went over to Ricardo and whispered in his ear, his Indian eyes on me. Fat Julio pulled his seat over and lifted a hand to his ear in order to hear the

Javier Marías

report. Then Pacheco went off to dance, the man loved a dance floor. Ricardo and Julio said nothing, though I was looking at them with a questioning and undoubtedly worried expression, or maybe that's why they didn't say anything, to worry me. Finally I worked up the nerve to ask: '*Perdone, señor,* do you know if my friends got back all right? The other gentleman was accompanying them, no?'

Ricardo blew cigarette smoke in my face and picked a shred of tobacco off his tongue. He took advantage of the occasion to smooth his moustache and answered, flexing his biceps (it was almost a tic), 'We have no way of knowing that. It looks like there's a storm brewing tonight, so God willing they'll crash.'

He looked away deliberately and I didn't think it was advisable to insist; I'd understood him well enough. He could only be referring to the flight, so Pacheco must have taken them back to the airport on the outskirts of the city where we had landed, and now he had told Ricardo about it: no hotel, a small plane, otherwise there was no way Ricardo could have known, no one ever mentioned the airplane in El Tato and I hadn't mentioned it since then. Now I really did feel lost, if Presley and the others had taken off for Acapulco I could say my last farewell. I had a feeling of being cut off, of abyss and abandonment and enormous distance or dropped curtain, my friends were no longer in the same territory. And what never occurred to me, neither then nor over the course of the five days that followed, was that the abyss would become or had already become much larger right away, and the territory more remote, that they decamped immediately in light of what had happened, alarmed by McGraw and Sherry and Hank and convinced of the manifest unsafety of that country for Presley; nor that in Acapulco I would find, when I arrived bruised and battered at the end of those five days—five—only the second unit that even today the liner notes speak of, left there partly to shoot more stills and partly as a detachment in case I appeared; nor that after that night Presley would never again set foot in Mexico but give his entire performance as the trapeze artist Mike Windgren in a movie studio, my idea about the double was put to use; nor that I would not manage to be present for the climactic scene in which 'Guadalajara' was sung, and which would, for that reason, become the most ludicrous display of the

Spanish language ever heard on a record or seen on a screen, Presley sings the entire song in the original lyrics and you can't understand a thing he says, an inarticulate language: when they finished filming the scene everyone crowded around and slapped his back with insincere congratulations ('*Mucho*, Elvis'), they told me later; he thought his unintelligible pronunciation was perfect and no one ever informed him that he was mistaken, who would dare, Elvis was Elvis. I never investigated the question very thoroughly but apparently it did happen the way I thought it had: they forced Mr Presley to leave me stranded, first Pacheco with his threats or his pistol, then McGraw and Colonel Tom Parker and Wallis with their terrible panic. You don't like to think that your idol has let you down.

I was feeling hopelessly lost, I had to find some way to get out of there, I asked for permission to go to the men's room and they let me but the other bodyguard came along, the one with the pistol in his armpit, a slow-moving, heavyset guy who was always at my side, in the bars and also in the cars during the trips from one bar to the next. They had dragged me with them that whole night like a package they were guarding, without paying much attention to me and as part of the entourage, amusing themselves from time to time by scaring me, though they hadn't even made me their primary source of entertainment, they were a somewhat sluggish and not very imaginative group, the same ones must have been getting together almost every night and they were sick of it. I was a novelty, but the routine did not fail to swallow me up, as it must have swallowed up everything.

And in the fourth place, or was it the fifth (I started having trouble keeping track), they finally got tired of the whole thing and gave up on the evening.

We were a few kilometres outside the city, I didn't know if it was south or north, east or west. It was a place along a highway, a place of last resort, surrounded by open country, you recognize these places in any part of the world, people go only to drag the night out a little longer, half-heartedly and in seclusion. There were very few people there and even fewer a couple of minutes later, in fact we were on our own, two very tired girls, Pacheco, the heavyset bodyguard, Ricardo and Julio, the manager of the place and a waiter who was serving us, all the waiters seemed to be friends or even employees, maybe Ricardo was the owner of this place, too, or maybe his fat partner was. Ricardo had drunk a lot—who hadn't—and was dozing off a little, lolling on to the low-cut blouse of one of the women. They were criminals of little standing, whitewashed gangsters, their crimes were not organized.

'Why don't you get it over with now and we'll all go to sleep, eh Julito?' Ricardo said with a yawn.

Get what over with, I thought, nothing had started. Maybe the fat one was going to give me some sort of punishment, or maybe they were going to leave me there. But they hadn't dragged me along with them the whole night for nothing. Or maybe the fat one was going to put me to death, the pessimistic thought always coexists with the optimistic, the daring idea with the fearful, and vice-versa, nothing comes alone and unmixed.

Fat Julio's white jacket was stained with sweat, he was sweating so profusely that it had soaked through his shirt and even his jacket, the combed-back hair looked greyer and had rebelled over the course of that eternal night, the long ends at the back of his neck had started to curl and were almost in little ringlets. His white skin was pale now, there was intense tedium in his eyes and there was bad nature, too. All at once he stood up in all his great height and said, '*Está bien*, as you wish.' He put a hand on my shoulder (his was more like a fish, wet and stinking, it almost squelched when it made contact) and added, looking at me, '*Anda, muchacho,* come with me a while.' And he pointed to a back door with a small window through which vegetation or foliage was visible, it seemed to open on to a little garden or an orchard.

'Where? Where do you want us to go?' I exclaimed in alarm, and my fear was obvious, I couldn't help it, I was suffering from nervous exhaustion, that was what they called that condition then, *un agotamiento nervioso.*

The fat man grabbed my arm and jerked me violently to my feet. He twisted it around and immobilized it behind my back. He was strong, but it cost him some effort to manage that, you can always tell.

'Out in back there, to have a little chat, you and I, about

mariconas and other things before we all go to bed. You need to sleep, too; it has been a very long day but life, on the other hand, is short.'

The start of that day was lost in remote time. We had shot some scenes in Acapulco that morning, with Paul Lukas and Ursula Andress, it seemed impossible. He had no idea how far away that was.

The others didn't move, not even to watch, it was the fat man's private business and there are no witnesses to these things. With his left hand he pushed me towards the back door, with the right he kept up the pressure on my arm, a swinging door that kept swinging, we came out into the open air, there was indeed a storm forecast for that night and a hot wind had already sprung up and was shaking the bushes and, further back, the trees in a grove or thicket, or so it seemed to me as I stepped out on to grass and instantly felt it against my face, dry grass, without missing a beat the fat man had put me on the ground with a fist to the side, he wasn't going to waste any time fooling around. Then I felt his enormous weight straddling my back and then something around my neck, the belt or the handkerchief, it had to be the green handkerchief that had been forced to interrupt its work a few hours before and now he was knotting it around my throat again, the package all tied up at last. It wasn't only his hand, his whole fat body stank of fish and the sweat was pouring off him, and now there was nothing, no music or rumba or trumpet, only the sound of the wind rising or maybe fleeing from the storm, and the squeaking hinge of the door we had come through, out on to the stage of my unforeseen death in a back yard on the outskirts of the City of Mexico, how could it be true, you wander into some dive and you don't imagine that here begins the end and that everything finishes obscurely and ridiculously under the pressure of a crumpled, greasy, filthy handkerchief that's been used a thousand times to mop the forehead, neck and temples of the person who is killing you, killing me, he is killing me, no one could have foreseen it this morning and everything ends in a second, one, two and three and four, no one intervenes and no one is even watching to see how I die of this certain death that is befalling me, a fat man is killing me and I don't know who he is, only that his name is Julio and that he's Mexican and without knowing it he has been waiting twenty-two years for me, my life is short and is ending against the dry grass of a back yard on the outskirts of the City of Mexico, how can it be true, it can't be, and it isn't because all at once I saw myself with the handkerchief in my hand—the silk floating—and I ripped it in rage, and I had thrown off the fat man with the strength of my dark back and my desperate elbows that dug into his thighs as hard as they could, maybe the fat man took too long tying up my throat and his strength deserted him, just as he took too long tying up McGraw in order to send him to hell, you need more than the first impulse to strangle someone, it has to be kept up for many more seconds, five and six and seven and eight and even more, still more because each of those seconds is counted and counts and here I am still and I'm breathing, one, two and three and four, and now I'm the one who grabs a pick and runs with it raised over my head to dig it into the chest of the fat man who has fallen and can't get up quickly enough, as if he were a beetle, the dark sweat stains tell me where to strike with the pick, there is flesh there and life there and I must finish both of them off. And I dig the pick in, one and two and three times, it makes a kind of squelching, kill him, I kill him, I am killing him, how can it be true, it is happening and it is irreversible and I see him, this fat man got up this morning and didn't even know who I was, he got up this morning and never imagined that he would never do it again because a pick is killing him that had been waiting, thrown down in a back yard for a thousand years, a pick to split open the grassy soil and also to dig an unexpected grave, a pick that may never have tasted blood before, the blood that still smells more like fish and is still wet and welling out and staining the wind that is rushing away from the storm.

The exhaustion ends then, as well, there's no longer fatigue or haze and perhaps not even consciousness, or there is but without mastery or control or order, and as you spring into flight and begin to count and look back you think: 'I have killed a man, I have killed a man and it's irreversible and I don't know who he was.' That is unquestionably the verb tense you think of it in, you don't say to yourself 'who he is' but inexplicably and already 'who he was' and you don't wonder whether it was right or wrong or justified or if there was some other solution, you only think of the fact: I have killed a man and I don't know who he was, only that he was named Julio and they called him Julito and he was Mexican, and he was once in my native city staying in the Castellana Hilton and he had a green handkerchief, that's all. And he knew nothing about me that morning, and he never learned my real name and I will never know anything more about him. I won't know about his childhood or what he was like then or if he ever went to high school as part of his scanty education which did not include the study of English, I'll never know who his mother is or whether she's alive and they'll give her the news of the unexpected death of her fat Julio. And you think about this even though you don't want to because you have to escape and run now, no one knows what it is to be hunted down without having lived it and unless the hunt was constant and active, carried out with deliberation and determination and dedication and never a break, with perseverance and fanaticism, as if the pursuers had nothing else to do in life but catch up with you and settle the score. No one knows what it is to be hunted down like that for five nights and five days, without having lived it. I was twenty-two years old and I will never go back to Mexico, though Ricardo must be nearing seventy now and the fat man has been dead for centuries, I saw him. Even today I stretch my hand out horizontally and look at it, and say to myself, 'five'.

Yes, it was best not to think and to run, run without stopping for as long as I could hold out now that I no longer felt hazy or fatigued, all my senses wide awake as if I had just risen from a long sleep, and as I went deeper into the thicket and was lost from sight and the first rumblings of thunder began, I could distinctly make out, through the wind, the sound of the venomous footsteps setting off with all the urgency of hatred to destroy me, and Ricardo's voice shouting through the wind, 'I want him now, I want him dead and I will not wait, bring me the son of a bitch's head, I want to see him flayed and his body smeared with tar and feathers, I want his carcass, butchered and flayed, and then he will be no one and this hatred that is exhausting me will end.' □

GRANTA

THE TRUTH
COMMISSION

PHOTOGRAPHS AND TEXT BY
JILLIAN EDELSTEIN

In April 1996 an extraordinary process began in South Africa. The Truth and Reconciliation Commission, under its chairman Archbishop Desmond Tutu, held its first public hearings to investigate over thirty years of human-rights violations under apartheid. The Commission had been founded in the belief that truth was the only means by which the people of South Africa could come to a common understanding of their past, and that this understanding was necessary if the country was to forge a new national identity in the future. Encouraged by the possibility of amnesty more than 7,000 perpetrators came forward to confess their crimes, and, hoping for justice and reparation, around 20,000 victims made statements to the commissioners over the two years that followed. The hearings took place in township halls, churches and civic centres all over South Africa, and in many cases, victims and perpetrators sat in the same room to give or listen to evidence.

When I went back to South Africa to visit my family in 1996, I watched footage of the early hearings on television. There were dramatic and emotionally wrenching scenes—wheelchair-bound Joseph Malgas, a veteran of the ANC, described his torture by the security police and broke down. Archbishop Tutu wept. The wailing of Nomonde Calata, one of the widows of the four murdered activists known as the 'Cradock Four', halted the proceedings as she described her husband's disappearance and torture. I came back to London, wrote up a proposal, and put it to various magazines in order to get financial help with a story I knew would take several years to complete.

Perhaps the concepts of good and evil, the problems of ethics and morality are complicated and tedious. The media wallowed in Nelson Mandela's release from prison, the Mandela divorce, and the betrothal of Nelson to Graca Machel, but the intricacies of a new nation redressing its past didn't seem to hold much interest for them. Early in 1997, however, with partial backing from the *New York Times Magazine*, I began to take photographs. I set up studios in rooms adjacent to the hearings, visited victims in bleak and sprawling townships all over the country, photographed ex-Cabinet ministers in their suburban mansions and witnessed painful scenes beside mass graves. One of my least expected pictures came during the hearing of Mrs Winnie Madikizela-Mandela in Johannesburg at the end of 1997. Behind the main hall were a series of rooms—one for Winnie's counsel and the Mandela family; one for the members of the Mandela United Football Club and their prison wardens, and another for my makeshift studio. I had asked permission to photograph Jerry Richardson, the man

Mrs Winnie Madikizela-Mandela consulting with her lawyers at the hearing into the death of Stompie Seipei in Johannesburg. Previous page: witness seat at a hearing in Cape Town.

jailed for killing the young black activist, Stompie Seipei. I had also put in a request to photograph Mrs Seipei, Stompie's mother. By accident, they ended up in my room at the same moment. Richardson boldly announced that he would like to be photographed with Stompie's mother. Mrs Seipei nodded her head in gentle acquiescence. A victim and perpetrator in the same frame. I felt a strange combination of emotions as I retreated under my black hood to check the inverted image on the glass.

The Commission's work is not complete. The Amnesty Committee, whose proceedings are due to end this July, is deliberating on its verdicts. After that, legal proceedings will begin for those for whom amnesty has been refused. The process of the Truth Commission has been a controversial one, but so far it is hard to think it has been anything but invaluable. Joyce Mtimkulu, who discovered that her son Simpiwo had been poisoned by the security police, then detained, arrested and killed, seemed to speak for many when she told me, after listening to the testimonies of those responsible, 'at least now we know what happened'.

The Mandela United Football Club

In November 1997, Mrs Winnie Madikizela-Mandela appeared at a human-rights violation hearing in Johannesburg. Many black parents had testified about the disappearance of their children after they had come into contact with the Mandela household, particularly the group of men known as the 'Mandela United Football Club' who referred to Winnie as 'Mommy'. In 1988 they kidnapped Stompie Seipei, a fourteen-year-old activist, with three other teenagers, claiming he was a police informer. His body was found on 6 January 1989. At the summation of the hearing, Archbishop Tutu had to beg Mrs Mandela to ask forgiveness for her misdeeds, and to apologize to Stompie's mother. Mrs Mandela denied the allegations of torture, murder and abductions linked to her name.

The testimony of Mananki Seipei, Stompie Seipei's mother

'In 1989 on 30 January, two ministers from Johannesburg Methodist Church arrived… They said it was on 29 December in 1988 when Stompie was taken from the Methodist Church together with his friends. They were taken to Mrs Winnie Mandela's house. They said to me they…are still searching for Stompie, they don't know whether is he alive or is he dead… On 14 February 1989 they took me and we went to Brixton. We went to Diepkloof Mortuary. That's where I identified Stompie. His body was decomposed, but your son is your son… After having been killed he was thrown into the river between New Canada and Soweto… I had a deep look at him. I saw the first sign. I said, "I know my son. He doesn't have hair at the back." His eyes were gouged, and I said, "This is Stompie." He had a scar on his eye. I looked at his nose, and he had a birthmark. I looked at his chest and I could see a scar, because he fought with another boy in Tumahole… They brought his clothes… His white hat was there. I looked at his shoes, a new pair of running shoes. I said, "Yes, they are Stompie's." I said, "He used to wear size four." …They said to me, "Do you think we should believe you that it is Stompie?" I said to them, "Yes, you have to." They came back and they gave me hands. They said, "He is your son. We could identify him through his fingerprints."'

Mrs Mananki Seipei, the mother of Stompie Seipei, with Jerry Richardson, a member of the Mandela United Football Club, who was imprisoned for Stompie's death; Johannesburg, December 1997. He carried a football at the hearing believing it had 'muti'—magical properties.

Jerry Richardson was known as the 'coach' of the Mandela Football Club. He was arrested in 1989 for his part in the murders of Stompie Seipei, Lolo Sono and Anthony Tshabala, and in 1990 was sentenced to death, later commuted to life imprisonment. In 1997 he was called by the Truth Commission to testify at Mrs Mandela's hearing and he told the court that his orders came from Mrs Mandela and that he reported to her after the murders had been executed.

'The first thing that I did to Stompie was to hold him on both sides...throw him up in the air and let him fall freely on to the ground. And Mommy was sitting and watching us. He was tortured so severely that at one stage I could see that he would ultimately die. We kicked him like a ball.'

Dr Abu-Baker Asvat, a friend of Winnie Mandela, refused to treat Stompie after he had been beaten. He said he should be admitted to hospital. Dr Asvat was murdered in his surgery in January 1989.

Jerry Richardson (holding football), with Zakhele Cyril Mbatha (second from left) and Thulani Dlamini (fourth from left), two members of the Mandela United Football Club imprisoned for the murder of Dr Abu-Baker Asvat; also Charles Slovo Zwame (third from left), and three prison guards, Niapo (far left), Roberts (far right) and Ntengo (seated).

Above: Two young men from New Brighton township listening to the Biko amnesty hearings at Centenary Hall, Port Elizabeth, in December 1997. Translations usually went on throughout the hearings in English, Afrikaans, Xhosa, Zulu and other languages and dialects.

Opposite: Belgium Biko, younger brother of Steve Biko, at the Biko family home, Ginsberg location, King William's Town, February 1997.

Steve Biko

Steve Biko, the leader of the Black Consciousness movement, died in Pretoria on 12 September 1977. He was beaten into a coma during interrogation by security officers in the Eastern Cape city of Port Elizabeth and then driven, manacled and naked in the back of a police Land-Rover, over 700 miles to Pretoria. The inquest found that he had died of head injuries inflicted over a period of several days during scuffles with members of the security police. In January 1997 five security policemen came forward to confess to Biko's killing. One of the five, Gideon Nieuwoudt, was among the most feared security policemen in the Eastern Cape. His application for amnesty was successfully opposed by the Biko family—his widow, Ntsiki, his two sons, Samora and Nkosinathi, and his sister Nbandile Mvovo.

Opposite: Gideon Johannes Nieuwoudt (left) and Mike Barnardo, a member of the witness protection team, in Cape Town, 31 March 1998.

The Pebco Three

On 8 May 1985, Qwaqwahuli Godolozi, Sipho Hashe and Champion Galela, leaders of the Port Elizabeth Black Civic Organization (Pebco), went to meet a British diplomat at the airport. They were never seen again. Although it was suspected that the police had been involved in their disappearance, for fifteen years their widows, Monica Godolozi, Elizabeth Hashe and Nomali Galela, did not know what had happened to them. In 1996, Joe Mamasela, a security policeman at Vlakplaas, the training ground for the counter-insurgency movement outside Pretoria, told the Truth Commission that the three men had been led into an 'animal shed' at Post Chalmers where they had been interrogated. He said: 'It was brutal. They were tortured severely. They were brutalized. I strangled them. They were beaten with iron pipes on their heads, kicked and punched. They were killed, they died one by one. I have never seen anything like it in my life. It was blazing hell on earth.'

Opposite: Post Chalmers, an isolated police station off the national road some twenty miles from Cradock in the Eastern Cape where brutal tortures and murders took place, among them the killing of the Pebco Three.

Above: The son of Champion Galela, New Brighton Township, December 1997.

Opposite: Monica Godolozi with her daughter, Papama, who was five years old when her father disappeared; New Brighton Township, February 1997.

Father Michael Lapsley, ANC activist and chaplain, Cape Town 1997
Father Lapsley, a New Zealander, was a pacifist when he arrived at the University of Natal in 1973. But, he explained to the Truth Commission, 'I realized that if you were white and did nothing to change the situation you were actually a functionary of the apartheid government.' He was deported by the South African government in 1976 and went to Lesotho, where he joined the ANC and trained Anglican priests. In 1983 he moved to Zimbabwe, where he was denounced as 'the ANC's chief external ecclesiastical propagandist'. In April 1990, after the release of Nelson Mandela, he received a letter bomb believed to have been sent by a government death squad. He lost an eye and both his hands. 'Hands transmit love...tenderness ...I endured an endless and intensely overwhelming sorrow over the loss of my hands...when they brought me the prosthetic hands, I started crying...because they were so ugly... Now I have these and it is actually amazing what they can do.'

Father Lapsley's testimony: 'It was a normal warm autumn day...April...when I became the focal point of all that is evil. I returned from a series of lectures in Canada. A pile of mail had accumulated on my desk, among others something with an ANC letterhead. The envelope stated that it contained theological magazines. While I was busy on the phone...I started opening the manila envelope on the coffee table to my side. The first magazine was Afrikaans...that I put aside, I can't read Afrikaans. The second was in English. I tore off the plastic and opened the magazine...and that was the mechanism that detonated the bomb... I felt how I was being blown into the air...throughout it all I never lost my consciousness...

'Someone had to type my name on the manila envelope; somebody made the bomb. I often ask the question: "What did these people tell their children they did that day?" However, the fact that such a sophisticated bomb found its way through the post to me... I lay sole responsibility for that with F. W. de Klerk. De Klerk knew of the hit squads...but De Klerk chose to do nothing about it.'

Annemarie McGregor, Paarl, Western Cape, March 1997
Mrs McGregor's son was a member of the South African Defence Force.
He was killed at Oshakati, on the Namibian–Angolan border, during cross-
border operations into Angola and Mozambique. She was presented with
his body in a bag and instructed not to open it but to obey the military code
of secrecy. She was told that his body was intact. She testified before the
Truth Commission in an attempt to discover what had happened to her son.
How had he died? Was it his body that she had buried?

Opposite: General Magnus Malan, in retirement, Pretoria, June 1997
General Malan, Minister of Defence between 1980 and 1991, was
responsible for authorizing cross-border raids into Mozambique and Angola.
He also authorized the setting up of the Civil Cooperation Bureau, an
undercover unit of the South African Defence Force dedicated to protecting
South Africa's borders from the alleged 'communist invasion'. In 1997
Malan was one of three former military generals who announced they were
willing to take responsibility for all military incursions across the border,
although the SADF frustrated the investigations of the Truth Commission
by refusing to open their files.

Letlapa Mphahlele, Cape Town, February 1997
Mphahlele was a member of the Azanian People's Liberation Army
(APLA), the military wing of the Pan African Congress. In July 1993,
he was part of an APLA group which launched a machine-gun attack
on the congregation at St James's Anglican Church in Kenilworth,
Cape Town. Eleven people were killed and fifty-eight injured. It
became known as the St James Church Massacre.

Opposite: Marilynn Javens, St James's Church, Kenilworth, May 1997
Mrs Javens's husband, Guy, was killed in the St James Church
Massacre. As her way of dealing with this tragedy, she goes back to
the same church every day to pray. She said, 'If it were not for the
Lord I would not have survived.'

The Cradock Four

In June 1985, Sparrow Mkhonto and Fort Calata, two leading anti-apartheid activists whose activities were being monitored by the security police, disappeared with two others on the way to a meeting in Cradock in the Eastern Cape. Their mutilated bodies were found the following week. They were later known as the 'Cradock Four'. Shortly after their funerals, the first State of Emergency was declared in South Africa.

Sindiswa Mkhonto and Nomonde Calata still live in Cradock. In April 1996, Calata described the moment she realized that her husband was dead, the day after he did not return home: 'Usually the *Herald* was delivered to my home... I looked at the headlines, and one of my children said: "Mother, look here in the paper...the car belonging to my father has been burnt." At that moment I was trembling, because I was afraid of what might have happened to my husband—because if his car is burnt down like this, I was wondering what happened to him.'

Opposite: Sindiswa Mkhonto (left) and Nomonde Calata, Cradock township, February 1997.

Brigadier Willem Schoon, Pretoria, September 1998, after having applied for amnesty for the attempted murder of Marius Schoon in Botswana in 1981.

Roger 'Gerry' Raven, explosives expert, responsible for the letter bombs which killed Ruth First in 1982 and Jeanette and Katryn Schoon in 1984, and for the bomb blast at the ANC headquarters in London in 1982.

The Schoon letter bomb

In 1984, Jeanette Schoon, the wife of Marius Schoon, and their six-year-old daughter Katryn, were killed in Lubango, Angola, where they were living in exile from Botswana. According to Craig Williamson, the spy who masterminded the attack, the Schoons were ANC and SACP (South African Communist Party) operatives. Williamson, who had infiltrated the ANC network, had been on good terms with the Schoons and had stayed with them in Botswana. 'When I heard what the result of this attack had been,' he told the Truth Commission in September 1998, 'it was like being hit with a bucket of cold water.'

Gerry Raven and Craig Williamson applied for amnesty for the death of the Schoons, and for the death of Ruth First, the wife of Joe Slovo, head of the military wing of the ANC, who was killed by a letter bomb in Maputo, Mozambique in 1982. Raven tried to persuade the Commission that it was possible for him to have made the Schoon bomb and fitted it into the envelope without noticing who the letter was addressed to and without leaving any fingerprints. In his amnesty statement, he said: 'Williamson said that the letter [that killed the Schoons] had been intended for Marius Schoon, but that it served them right.' In September 1998 Brigadier Willem Schoon, a member of the South African security forces, applied for amnesty for the attempted murder of Marius Schoon in Botswana in 1981.

Opposite: Craig Williamson (far right), the spy responsible for organizing the letter bomb which killed Jeanette Schoon and her six-year-old daughter, Katryn; Pretoria, September 1998.

Above: Marius Schoon at home in Johannesburg, 18 January 1998. He attended the Truth Commission hearings into the death of his wife and daughter in Pretoria in September 1998. He died in February 1999.

Robin Slovo, the daughter of Joe
Slovo and Ruth First, at the
hearings in Pretoria, September
1998. She was accompanied by her
sisters, Shawn and Gillian.

Inkatha–ANC violence

On 5 March 1993, Nkanyiso Wilfred Ndlovu and Mabhungu Absalom Dladla, members of the Inkatha Freedom Party, opened fire on a minibus at Enkanyezini in Natal killing sixteen people. In their amnesty application they claimed that they were avenging the deaths of six schoolchildren who had been ambushed and murdered in the area a few days earlier by ANC members. Ndlovu and Dladla had already been sentenced to over sixty years in prison but were called to testify to the Truth Commission. Ndlovu said the crime was motivated by the fact that he wanted to intimidate the ANC so they would stop attacking IFP members. (It was discovered that some of the murdered people were not even ANC supporters.) Dladla said he felt 'justified to go and retaliate and pay revenge. The ANC had killed young and innocent children. All these children were the children of the IFP members. Some of the children, three of them, belonged to my cousins.'

Nkanyiso Wilfred Ndlovu applying for amnesty to the Truth Commission in Durban, Natal, 26 March 1998.

Applicant

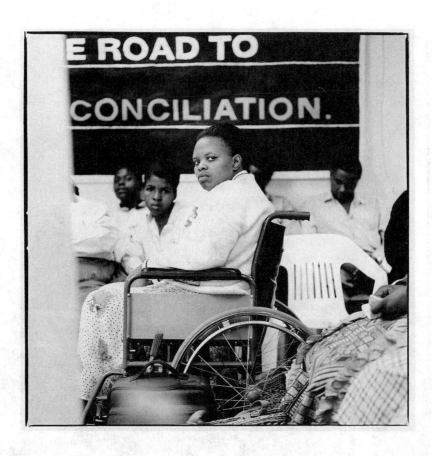

Above: Ziningi Mkhize, at the amnesty hearings in Durban, Natal, March 1998.
She was travelling in the minibus when it was attacked at Enkanyezini. She was left paralysed by
her injuries. She attended the hearings to witness the amnesty applications made by Ndlovu and
Dladla.

Opposite: Mrs Shezi (left) and Mrs S'thembile Jiyane at the hearings in Durban, March 1998.
Mrs Jiyane, Mrs Shezi and Ziningi Mkhize are cousins. Mrs Jiyane's twenty-three-year-old sister,
Bonisile Ngcobo, died in the minibus attack.

Five perpetrators

These five former policemen confessed to committing forty-one murders between them during the 1980s. In 1987, three of them strangled, suffocated and then shot a suspected ANC member, Richard Mutase, and his wife, Irene, leaving the murdered couple's six-year-old son alone with the bodies. Also present was Joe Mamasela, a former ANC activist who became a security policeman and in 1994 turned state's evidence and swore affidavits which resulted in other members of the security police coming forward to confess their crimes.

Captain Jacques Hechter's testimony

'When the woman opened the door, Mamasela pushed her with a gun to a back room... We switched off the lights, but left the television on so that it seemed that someone was there. We then hid behind the couch. Then a vehicle arrived: his Mazda. He came to the door and found it locked. He was struggling with the lock when we jerked him inside... He fought like a tiger and he shouted wildly. To bring him under control I started to strangle him, and Van Vuuren smothered him with a pillow over his face. He then fired four shots with his AK-47. The pillow was the silencer. Then we called Mamasela: "Come on! We're finished." Just as we were walking out we heard a shot from inside the house... When Mamasela joined us we asked what the shooting was about. He told us that he killed the woman because she saw his face. It was also only afterwards that we learned that there was a child in the house.'

From left: Warrant Officer Paul van Vuuren, Brigadier Jack Cronje, Colonel Roelf Venter, Captain Wouter Mentz and Captain Jacques Hechter, Pretoria, 1997.

Exhumations at Boshoek, Northern Transvaal, March 1998
As a result of evidence given at the Truth Commission hearings,
exhumations of unmarked graves began all over the country. On 17
March 1998, the bodies of three young ANC guerrillas were
exhumed at a farm in Boshoek in the Northern Transvaal. These
men had been killed by security police in November 1985 and taken
to Abraham Grobelaar's farm to be buried. Thirteen years later, the
crowds of relatives and onlookers waited patiently in the hot sun
amid the stink and uncertainty as, instead of three bodies, the diggers
unearthed a mass grave of twelve. Apart from the three young men,
the bodies could not be identified and their coffins were marked A1,
A2, A3 up to A9.

A Critique of Postcolonial Reason

Toward a History of the Vanishing Present

GAYATRI CHAKRAVORTY SPIVAK

Are the "culture wars" over? When did they begin? What is their relationship to gender struggle and the dynamics of class? In her first full treatment of postcolonial studies, a field that she helped define, Gayatri Chakravorty Spivak, one of the world's foremost literary theorists, poses these questions from within the postcolonial enclave. Her book is an attempt to understand and describe a more responsible role for the postcolonial critic. It tracks the figure of the "native informant" through various cultural practices—philosophy, history, literature—to suggest that it emerges as the metropolitan hybrid. It ranges from Kant's analytic of the sublime to child labor in Bangladesh. Throughout, the notion of a Third World interloper as the pure victim of a colonialist oppressor emerges as sharply suspect.

$49.95 / £30.95 cloth • $24.95 / £15.50 paper • author photo: Julio Etchart

Walter Benjamin

Selected Writings, Volume 2: 1927–1934

MICHAEL W. JENNINGS, GENERAL EDITOR

In the frenzied final years of the Weimar Republic, amid economic collapse and mounting political catastrophe, Walter Benjamin emerged as the most original practicing literary critic and public intellectual in the German-speaking world. Volume 2 of *Selected Writings*, covering the years 1927 to 1934, displays the full spectrum of Benjamin's achievements at this pivotal stage in his career.

Previously concerned chiefly with literary theory, Benjamin during these years does pioneering work in new areas, from the study of popular culture (a discipline he virtually created) to theories of the media and the visual arts. His writings on the theory of modernity—most of them new to readers of English—develop ideas as important to an understanding of the twentieth century as any contained in his widely anthologized essay "The Work of Art in the Age of Technological Reproducibility." This volume brings together previously untranslated writings on major figures such as Brecht, Valéry, and Gide, and on subjects ranging from film, radio, and the novel to memory, kitsch, and the theory of language.

Belknap Press • 14 halftones • 704 pages • $37.50 / £23.50 cloth
photo: Walter Benjamin, 1929. photo by Charlotte Joël. Courtesy Theodor W. Adorno Archiv, Frankfurt

HARVARD UNIVERSITY PRESS
US: 800 448 2242 • UK: 0171 306 0603 • www.hup.harvard.edu

GRANTA

GOAL 666

Stacey Richter

W̲e must love nature, and we must rape nature for Satan! What would daylight be without the night? What would a clearing be without the woods? All your fairy dust, all your little white Christmas lights that twinkle, your Stardust Woman on the lite rock radio station—it would all be nothing without the dark and heavy elements of Doom/Black Metal music. When I'm on stage I feel aggression, power, rage—the everlasting lust for domination! The other side is the feminine side, the soft and pink parts that must also be cherished, as the moon is cherished, but we must remember this: We are not of the light. We are the harbingers. We are Lords of Sludge, the most revered Doom/Classical Goth Metal band in Washington state!

The Vikings did nothing but invade! Those fur-covered Goths were crazy and ultimate, the baddest of ass. When a Viking died he went to Valhalla, an indoor heaven where dead warriors engaged in perpetual battle! The northern tradition continues still, with hellish great Scandinavian metal bands like Dissection, Dark Tranquillity, Exhumation and Wizards of Ooze playing some of the most malevolent tunes to which Lord Satan ever lifted a pointed ear! I have the deepest reverence for the Norderland tradition, which was why I was honoured to join Lords of Sludge, a Swedish heavy-metal band that lost their lead singer when he ran off to become a hermit. He's practising asceticism in the deepest forest! Their loss, my gain—since I'd been perfecting my top-secret method of Satanic throat singing and was finally ready to be a part of a great Doom/Black Metal band like Lords of Sludge. I'd been known as a tenor in church choir, but by wedging a ping-pong ball behind my teeth I perfected a means of producing a low rumble in the back of my throat that was evil in the extreme. Black Metal is spirit and power!

The three Swedish lads came from the cold-land town of Uppsala, and were covered with tattoos of screaming skulls and flaming crosses—pussying great! That was my first impression. Like their Viking ancestors they were ultra-pale with fierce hanks of hair falling in dirty curtains around their faces. I thought, 'These are manly men!' and after the audition we all slapped each other on the back and had a hearty laugh over the throbbing music—punctuated by light, lilting passages of classical acoustic guitar—that we would produce for the Dark Lord, who was a diehard metal fan as every diehard metal fan knows. Those crazy Swedes! That first night they introduced me to the tradition of the sauna, which they'd built of stone and wood in the back of the house they'd both rented and painted entirely black, inside and out. After we were sufficiently heated, Anders, the lead guitarist, a strapping Swedish man with mega-antisocial facial tattoos and a wide, hairless chest, led us naked and sweating into the lush, snowy woods beyond the house. We rolled our bare, hot bodies in the fresh winter snow—ah nature, we must love nature and rape it for Satan—we leaped around like satyrs scouring the woods for wayward virgins. Men! We were naked men, three Swedish and one American man.

After that night we had a masculine bond, so I was slow to notice details I might have caught earlier. Though Anders had mega-fierce tattoos and Stefan, the small but muscular drummer, had huge, furry sideburns creeping across his cheeks, and Max had the extremely Satanic name of Max—there was something not right about these men. There was an air of innocence to them. Despite the fiery badness of The Lords, and their lusty embrace of songs I had written, these guys were scrupulous about washing their hands after using the bathroom. They returned all their phone calls promptly and refrained from resting their forearms on the dinner table. Going for a meal with these guys was like going to a Victorian tea-party: napkin on the lap, chewing with the mouth closed, salad fork, dessert spoon, and so on.

The contagion was severe. Before I knew it I was uttering phrases like, 'Would you mind turning up the treble in my monitor just a smidgen?' Our leader, Anders, would bound into practice, right on time, his strong Nordic features aglow, so filled with vitality that the little spiral tattoo on his cheek seemed to twirl. Ten minutes later, the two of us were deep in a conversation (about literacy, Sweden has an amazing ninety-nine per cent rate). The other two maniacs were listening attentively, nodding and occasionally throwing in a pertinent fact (free daycare). No one was even smoking and I had totally forgotten about Goal 666 (for our Mexican *hermanos, Meta Número Seis, Seis, Seis*): Corrupt the World/Spread the Metal!!!

Maniacs, brothers, Vikings: lend me your hellishly buzzing ears. We must labour with guitar and anvil to spread the fire of pure heavy metal! They say entropy is inevitable but we must still toil to ensure the decay progresses! In my own life, only constant vigilance has been able to halt the creep of flowering vines up the balcony of my meagre studio apartment. Only a daily regimen of Satanic throat-singing and a pentagram drawn with chicken blood on my doorstep has kept kittens from being born in the back seat of my Camaro, butterflies from deciding my workplace was a bitchin' stop on their migration route and my neighbour Maria from constantly bringing me hot dishes covered with cloth napkins. My sister always tells me I am a sweetheart, but with effort I find I am not a sweetheart. If I didn't take care, my voice would slip back up to a clear, tenor register and I might find myself humming, on a warm spring day, snatches of Rodgers and Hammerstein show tunes. Yet, I've been able to avert the light so that diehard blacking metal still burns on in the many hatred-thrashing parts of my soul! We must not allow beauty to exist without corruption. Listen all maniacs! We must not give up the fight!

Because here's what happened. One afternoon I strolled into practice (still wearing my smock from Speedy Pro, where I'm a reproduction technician) and there, beneath the flaming, day-glo painting of the Fallen Angel himself, stood a girl. She had short, bleached hair and a lot of bitchin' ink sticking out of her leather vest, which she wore without a shirt. Pussy is advantageous but should be ornamental in the extreme! This chick was not ornamental, was not our first groupie, because right away I noticed she was perched over a musical instrument. Hold on to your lunch. It was a synthesizer.

Of all the limp-dick instruments in the universe, the synthesizer is the most flaccid. Guys who wear lipstick play synthesizer music for horny little fairies to dance to—I don't need to tell you this. It's well known among bitchin' sons of Lucifer the foul fiend and those Swedish men were well aware of this. Well aware. Anders entered the cement bunker where we practised our art, his stringy hair swinging about his broad shoulders, and introduced me to the girl. Her name, he said, was Liv. She was from Amsterdam, where she had been a member of an experimental music collective dedicated to bringing microtonal compositions to shut-ins, the institutionalized, and old people. Liv grinned and came out from behind the synthesizer to shake my hand. She wore a short leather skirt and that tiny vest as I mentioned. Her body was tremendous, a fierce combination of soft and athletic, so stunningly proportioned that it could have popped out of a lingerie catalogue, but I found her face scrunched and ugly, like a pug's. The overall effect was confusing and for a moment I found I couldn't say anything as Liv sprang behind the synthesizer and began to bang on the keys.

I don't know a lot about synthesizers, but the sounds Liv managed to hack out startled me. Instead of the floaty tones I expected, she produced muscular, ugly noises that reminded me of hooks piercing sheet metal in hell. Then, she flipped some switches and made some other sounds that were like live cats being skewered by white-hot knives. Nonetheless I was repulsed, as the synthesizer itself is a sissy instrument and should never be included in a rain of dark riffs. Particularly if played by a female, whose place it is to be soft and pink and stay in her scented room, praying to the moon.

While Liv played she had a big grin plastered on her face; beside her Anders laughed and tapped his foot. They seemed to be having a wonderful time. Then, abruptly, she stopped. 'Anders,' she called, her odd little face bright with delight, 'fetch me my valise!'

Anders obeyed, hustling across the room to grab a small satchel and dropping it at her feet.

'I have brought a gift for you,' she announced. She pulled out a record and presented it to me. It was a copy of 'Head Abortion', a rare single from Flayed Open, one of my favourite Swedish bands.

'Anders said you needed this. I located it in Europe!' Liv tossed back her head and giggled, and her face softened and spread into a more human countenance. Then she and Anders began to laugh like children, or adults on drugs. I watched them and smirked, fully aware that they were trying to break down my resistance, but the dark power and spirit had made me formidable! Through a careful regimen of self-control I'd become fully immune to joy and could not be seduced by the playful laughter of my bandmates! Liv stumbled and collapsed on top of Anders. Despite the dirt, ash and dried residue of various liquids on the floor, they began rolling around down there. I think they were having a tickle fight. Her miniskirt edged up and I glimpsed a flash of panty. The next thing I knew, Liv grabbed my leg and pulled me down.

I was beginning to think Liv might make an acceptable groupie, but she could never, ever play in our band.

At a meeting at Pepe Lou's, Anders, our trusted leader, solemnly declared Liv the newest member of Lords of Sludge. Max took the news calmly, grunting slightly and never pausing in his consumption of tater tots with ketchup. Max's English skills were rather poor and he rarely said anything anyway. I thought I detected a slight scowl on the face of Stefan, beneath the facial hair that had been spreading and spreading since the day we first met until it covered his entire face, from just below the eyes to the top of his collar. I found this facial hair very werewolf-like and antisocial and approved of it vigorously. As for myself, I sat silently, chewing iceberg lettuce with Russian dressing, rehearsing in my head all the reasons why Liv could not join the band and plotting a scathing delivery for my objections. But before I had a chance to actually offer them, Liv jumped up from the table and began dancing a heavy-metal victory dance, stomping her boots and flashing the double-eared sign of Satan with both hands. 'Lords of Sludge,' she hooted, 'Lords of Sludge!' Her scrunched face turned red with enthusiasm. At the next table, an old lady began to blow a rape whistle.

Liv had a nest of hair in her armpits and I could see it well as she slid into the booth and draped her arm around the cringing crone. 'What's wrong, little mother? Have I given you a fright?'

The lady shrank back with the whistle dangling from her mouth. It seemed she regarded Liv with deep suspicion. Max was laughing gleefully at this, as were Stefan and Anders, and I knew my chances of ousting Liv were fading.

'I want not to harm you,' she said to the senior, 'but to please you. May I kiss your cheek?'

'Don't you dare,' the old lady hissed, edging away from the armpit.

'I won't kiss you then, mother. I'm from across the sea and my customs must seem strange.'

'Get away,' the elderly woman said, but something in her had calmed and she said it without conviction. She'd let the whistle fall back into her purse and started to nibble on her eggs. Liv removed her arm from around the woman and began to chat with her politely, hands clasped in front of her on the table. Like the Swedes, she had lovely manners, and in a few moments Liv had charmed her foe utterly. The two sat chatting softly about whatever it is women talk about; then they were exchanging phone numbers.

After a while Liv bounded back to our table, sprightly-go-lucky, bragging that she had subdued the old one. The Swedish men applauded with delight and piled their extra tater tots on to Liv's plate. They began an animated discussion about walking clubs for the elderly in different European countries while I slumped in the corner, one lone man, fuming.

The forest is our mother, and we must destroy the forest! When I see pocked mountain slopes, cleared of trees, I feel virile, hulking, masterful. When I see the machines of my fellow men chewing through groves in which I played as a child, consuming glens in which I picnicked with my mother and sister when I was a boy, I feel enlarged. We are men, in charge, ploughing our masculinity into the earth, and in my heart I'm gladdened those places are destroyed because then I'll never be tempted to return to the dimpled, the pink, the fluffy. A true metal head knows innocence is irretrievable.

And so, to me, it was obvious Liv's femininity would corrupt us, soften us, wash us out to shades of pastel, but I figured if I complained the guys would kick me out of the band. Then where would I be? I'd be a clerk in a copy shop without a band. I'd be another minimum-wage worker in a leather jacket popping in to the convenience store on the way home to buy a twelve-pack of beer with wadded bills and a handful of change. I didn't want to leave the rock-and-roll life. It was just beginning to happen for us. We'd finally managed to schedule a gig, and I was looking forward to playing in front of an audience. Then there was the fact that I loved it. For me there was nothing more satisfying than our give-and-take of energy, the unselfish sharing of talent, skills and inspiration. When everything was working right, when all of us were in harmony, it was beyond bitchin'.

I was also genuinely fond of the Swedish men and their messy hair and the sauna where we often spent the evenings. Liv began to join us in the sauna as well, and I admit I appreciated the chance to spend time next to a live naked girl. Now and then she rubbed against me and laughed. She tugged at the towel around my waist and requested to see 'the nature of my unit'. Later, she and Anders traipsed off to the bedroom together while the rest of us watched television and snacked on pickled herring.

Many nights, after warming in the sauna, we'd go running naked through the woods behind the house. I knew that over the hill was a shopping mall, and next to that a ploughed lot where they were putting in a parking tower, but from our vantage point it almost seemed like we were in a primeval forest. When we got tired of running we'd leap backwards into the drifts and thrash about, making angels in the snow. Of course, my angel and the angels of the Swedish men were dark and brooding, fallen soldiers of Satan. Twigs, piss, and pine branches helped the effect. But Liv's angels were luminous. No matter how hard she tried to thrash out something sinister, her angels were always feathery. They seemed to float on the snow, and cupped the moonlight like a silver goblet.

'Liv,' said I, 'you must be a Stardust Woman. You are not of the darkness like us.'

Liv laughed and made the double-eared sign of Satan in the air. 'You are mistaken, Gabe (for Gabe is my name), I am quite badly bitchin'!' Her silver laughter filled the air. 'Dark power,' she sang, prancing in the snow. 'Dark power to all the children!'

'No,' I replied. 'Look at your angels. They look real. You are full of light, Liv. You are a good witch.'

'She is full of hatred!' Anders insisted, smashing a fist into his palm.

Liv looked at the two of us, then threw her head back and laughed, her short, bleached hair catching the moonlight like a piece of dandelion fluff.

'I do not think,' I said, very quietly, shivering in the drifts, 'that she is full of hatred.'

It was a frosty night, and soon the other men fled back to the sauna. Liv, though, seemed immune to temperature. She bounced around, licking snow off tree branches. I was freezing and my toes were turning blue but I couldn't stop watching her. I admit I sort of liked being alone with her, naked. She had a chance to take a look at the nature of my unit if she wanted, but she seemed more intent on eating snow. The unit was pretty shrunk up from the cold anyway.

Liv bounded between the pines. 'I'm pollinating,' she said. 'I take the snow from tree to tree. I am a pollinator.'

'Liv,' said I, 'you are a freak!'

She bounced over and poked me in the stomach. 'You small turd,' she whispered. 'You are a turd, and I'm a turd too!'

'I beg your pardon?'

'Ha! You try to act mean, but I see what a dumpling you are!'

What an odd, odd, odd feeling Liv gave me—for a second, when she pronounced the word 'dumpling', I was overwhelmed by an urge to grab her hand and skip off into one of those red, dripping sunsets they have on Seventies greeting cards. It was an electric, honeymoon feeling, full of fun and frolic and utterly devoid of evil, loathing or resentment. It was what I feared most—that deep down, in my core of being, I harboured a little flame of light.

I've always wanted desperately to be bad. I've always wanted to be extremely evil, full of hatred. I've always wanted people to exclaim, when I walk into a room: *Look at that fellow! He is truly bad!* Instead of saying what they usually say, which is nothing, or at most: *Look at that fellow, he has one of those pointy devil beards like our friend Skizz.* Skizz is not bad; Skizz is a nice guy. I've tried to be self-centred and an asshole; I've tried to follow the path of Satan; I've tried to absorb all the meagre boredom and antipathy that's been thrown my way by coaches, teachers and popular girls and radiate it back, larger, grander and more corrosive than ever, but I have a set of reflexes I can't control. I have an overwhelming desire to help those in trouble, or to talk to a person at a party if they seem to feel out of place, or to take stray animals home and love them. But I still feel a heavy sense of rejection and ugliness around my person. No one ever talks to me at a party if I feel out of place. No one ever wants to take me home and love me.

Heathens, take heart! Remember, the Vikings sailed the seas to find fresh, new places to invade! We must push ourselves daily to be worthy of the Dark Lord! As I trudged home that dark night from the house of the Swedish men, my boots crunching through the virgin snow, I rededicated myself to the task of corruption. I made a resolution to be as bad as possible. I would take the sparkly things of this world—including Liv, especially Liv—and muddy them. I would be smelly and dirty, of the dark, like a bat.

My resolve only grew stronger as the day approached when we were scheduled to play at Hole in One, a great Doom/Metal bar that had once been a great Golf/Sports bar. We had a show on a Friday night and were stoked to play hellish great songs dedicated to Satan! In the weeks before the gig, our practices intensified. It became more important than ever that we work together. Hey, I'm no party pooper. I stashed my hatred, I nurtured it like a coal in a bucket of peat, saving it for later, when it would be most effective. This was the time to practise our Doom/Black Metal music, including songs I'd written myself, like 'The Bad Watcher Watches' and 'Eater of my Soul'. I observed Liv's luminous blonde head bob and sway during practice; I listened to her synthesizer rumble and croak, and I waited. She would get hers, I thought. I'd really give it to her.

'More melody,' Liv said, perched over her keyboard like a pretty songbird. 'We must make our music fiery with melody!'

The Swedish men were in complete agreement. I, too, knew that the mighty power of Scandinavian metal music came from its ability to reconcile euphony with discord. Together, under Liv's guidance, we strengthened our songs, making them more tuneful. Liv designed vigorous, bold melodies on her keyboard; they were like the beams and rough-hewn buttresses on which our songs rested. Liv and I had to work especially closely, since lyric and melody go hand in hand. The Swedish musicians devised flourishes that enriched the whole. We started practice at five p.m. and played most nights until eleven. We improved steadily. We ordered pizza. After a while, even on days when we weren't practising, our songs stuck in my head. It was happening. The Lords were mutating from a great band into an awesome one.

I would guess the Vikings had some sort of ritual they performed before going into battle. Perhaps they danced around a block of ice, or killed a she-goat. As modern-day warriors we had our own ritual of bodily adornment and preparation that we referred to as 'getting ready for the gig'. This took me quite some time, and it seemed to require a similar amount of effort for the Swedish men, because when I arrived at the club, there they all sat, on time as usual, with their hair teased and lacquered into various startling arrangements. Anders' tattoos were especially dark. His hair was shiny but stringier than ever and I thought I detected a touch of mascara. Stefan had combed his facial hair downwards and looked more bestial than any human I'd ever seen; Max was clad entirely in black (OK, we all were) and had polished the silver pentagram around his neck. But of us all, Liv had been the most transformed by her preparations. She wore a boned, black bra that really showed off her figure. On her feet were pink go-go boots, and she'd painted a spider web across her cheek that completely camouflaged her canine quality. The truth is she looked quite beautiful.

I was almost swayed. It occurred to me that Liv was a nice girl with a good disposition and that I might this one time show some mercy—but in my heart I knew I must be fierce! Besides, I'd already decided how to strike. From my little sister I'd learned a foolproof way of wounding girls, and so mustering all the darkness within me, all the hostility and thrashing evil, I turned to Liv, who was sitting by her synthesizer, polishing the keys, and said, 'Wow. That outfit makes you look really fat.'

For a moment Liv seemed taken aback. The spider web across her face curved downward while she took in my blacking evil countenance, the hatred spewing from within me. She looked at me with her muddy brown eyes, directly into my smoking core.

'Oh Gabe! You had me going for a minute! Such a kidder! You're such a lamb.' The spider web expanded when she giggled.

Then I was on stage, standing in a pool of hot light. I held a microphone in my fist and something was feeding back through the PA. Anders fiddled with some knobs and the room grew silent except for the creaking of my leather trousers. I felt fuzzy and confused. I shaded my eyes and looked into the audience: not a bad turnout. Maybe a hundred metal heads slumped around in front of the stage; a few skinny girls, but mostly guys with bored faces and long, clean hair and freshly laundered, ripped T-shirts. They seemed to be in various stages of drunkenness. Behind me, Stefan crouched over his drum kit like a feral animal. To my right, Anders stood with his guitar hanging in front of his hips while Max waited expectantly behind his bass. At my side stood Liv, perched over her synthesizer with an elfin sparkle in her eye.

It was silent. I was waiting for something to happen, but nothing happened. I waited to feel malicious and potent but felt light and perky instead. Then, on Liv's count we sprang to life. Max plucked out the throbbing bass line to 'The Bad Watcher Watches', an extremely Satanic song—this song makes 'Parricide 2' seem like a trip to the petting zoo. Anders joined in with his growling but nonetheless buoyant guitar line. Entwined between was Liv's lilting, sinister melody, which sounded a little like a calliope in a movie about a clown who eats children.

We sounded awesome. It was like we'd been practising together our entire lives. Every part slid into place and blended with the others, without a thought. The crowd started to churn and wind around itself. I could feel the floorboards vibrating as we played louder, harder; my Satanic throat-singing featured strongly in this song and I felt the cells peeling off my larynx as I struggled to sing in a deeper, more frightening register: *He watches us/The bad watcher watches us/Ooooo/He watches us/Toil from the mountain top...*

The crowd had begun to gyrate and shake. By the second chorus, they were going totally berserk. So many heads of hair were banging in front of me that the skirt of the stage looked like a field of wheat in a wind storm. I stepped out of the lights to give the other guys a chance to take their solos. Anders began wailing on his instrument. He leaned forward and banged his head—his hair was actually getting caught in the strings of his guitar, but he didn't slow down—he was lost in the crunch of the music and the heat of the lights and the smell of the fans sweating below us. He was playing flourishes I'd never heard anywhere before, much less from Anders; wild, scrubbing riffs that were nevertheless melodic and tinged with sadness. That his guitar was merely an electrified construction of wire and wood and a couple of old pick-ups seemed unimaginable—it was more like a fallen angel spewing out the wickedest rock and roll from the lower intestine of hell! I closed my eyes. When I opened them, Anders' fingers were bleeding all over the pick guard.

Then Stefan took a drum solo. He was like a mutant woodland creature with advanced hand-eye coordination; his sticks flew over the kit so quickly they blurred. The kids in the audience stared at him with their mouths hanging open. Then he stopped, hands raised, perspiration gushing down his ribs. All was silent. No one in the crowd so much as hooted. Slowly he brought both hands down at once; bam. Then up and down again. Bam. He was beating a slow rhythm with all his might on the snare, only the snare. Bam, bam, bam—it was trance-inducing. It was like caveman music. The crowd loved it. We all loved it.

It was time for Liv to begin her synthesizer solo. Notes as soft as petals hung in the air beside the serrated snarls of a ruthless predator dismembering her prey. Liv's head drooped as her fingers leaped across the keys, urging forth a driving, overwhelming rock-and-roll moment. How could I have ever called the synthesizer a pansy instrument? The crowd roiled and churned. An odd tingling consumed me as I watched them, a kind of warm numbness. As Liv pushed the tune farther into the realm of the melodious, I began to feel almost ill with a kind of unpleasant pleasure, like being tickled. Something was happening—something was grasping at me; I had a sense it was grasping all of us. I was being swept up by a breezy, harmonious wave of major chords struck with pep. Then, after a weird, underwater period where I thought I might faint, my head cleared, and I understood what was happening.

A melody issued from Liv's organ, a melody effusive and irrepressible. It was contagious. It was sweet. It was Rodgers and Hammerstein's 'Happy Talk', from the musical *South Pacific*, and I was belting it out. A rich, dulcet tenor sprang from my throat as helplessly I found myself constructing the musical question: *You've got to have a dream! If you don't have a dream! How you gonna have a dream come true?* My mind filled with all the Carpenters songs I had loved and I thought of how I always tried, as a boy singing in the shower, to get my vowels to sound as velvety and overstuffed as Karen Carpenter's did. I couldn't help it then; a tide of pent-up joy washed over me. It was uncontrollable, it was uncool and wrong, and I was *so* happy. I was so happy I felt sick. It was as though all the loathing and resentment I'd been nursing at least since I was a sophomore in high school had burst like a soap bubble, had been popped and defused and dried out, and all that was left inside me was a lather of pure euphoria. I was so happy I thought I might melt.

We were of the light, bedazzling all. Liv arched over her synthesizer, singing, while the Swedes strummed joyfully along. Anders was banging out sweet, chiming chords on his guitar, an expression of blank rapture on his face. Max was laughing and bobbing from his knees. We were making something lovely. Together we thrilled to the power of creation. Below, our fans stared, openmouthed with horror. Liv lifted her fingers from the keyboard and began to do the happy talkie dance with both hands. ☐

GRANTA

ADULTS
Claire Messud

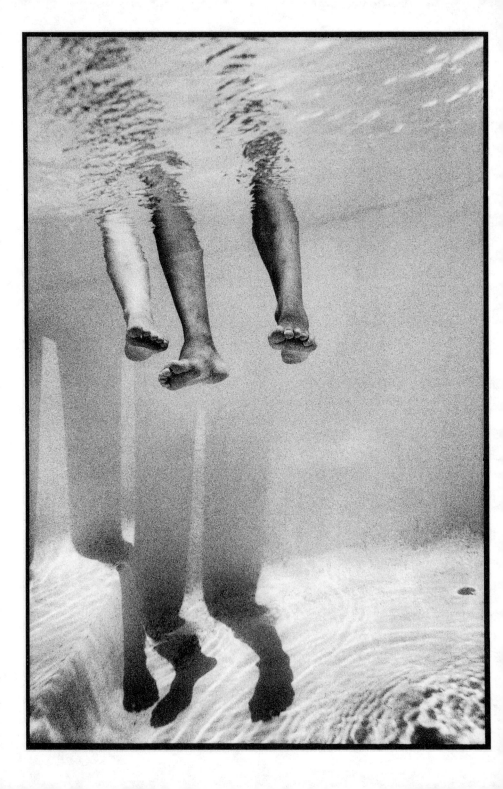

Those summer evenings were all alike. As Marie-José used to say, we had to make the time pass. Of its own accord, it didn't, or wouldn't: the days lingered like overripe fruit, soft and heavily scented, melting into the glaucous dusk. We gathered by the hotel pool, on the cliff top, after supper, watching the sky falter into Prussian blue, to blue-black, and the moon rising over the Mediterranean, the sea spread out before us, whispering and wrinkled. Every night the white, illuminated bulk of the island ferry ploughed its furrow across the water and receded to the horizon, the only marker of another day's passage.

Almost still children, we scorned the games of tag and cops and robbers that the younger kids delighted in, spiralling their pursuits outwards from the round benches by the parking lot to the furthest foliated corners of the grounds. We idled instead, and smoked, and talked, and were so bored we made a virtue of being bored. And we flirted—although most of us had known each other for years, and had spent each summer swimming and playing together, for so long that we knew each other's skin and laughter and illusions like our own, we flirted. It made the time pass.

I can't recall now whose idea it was, first, to swim at night. We spent our days in the water, in the murky, boat-bobbed brine of the bay, or in the electric indigo of the swimming pool, its surface skimmed with oily iridescence. We lived in our bathing suits, tiny triangles of colour, and worked (it was the closest that we came to work) on bronzing our skin evenly, deeply, until it held its tinge even through the winter months. We filed from beach to pool to beach again, up and down the tortuous paths, past the aloes in which, in earlier years, we had carved our initials, careful scars in the prickled, rubbery flesh. Why we felt the need to swim again, I do not know: perhaps because our water games were still those we had always played, a sphere into which self-consciousness had not yet intruded. We tussled in pairs on the pool's rim, struggling to push each other in, jumped from the overhanging balustrade into the shallows (although this manoeuvre had been strictly forbidden since a guest had cracked his skull attempting it), flaunting our elegant leaps from the diving board and, squealing, we chased each other the length of the pool, the prize a firm shove on the top of the head and a spluttering sinkage.

Claire Messud

Our games were loud: they echoed in the trees. The higher our pitch the more we felt we enjoyed ourselves. In the daytime, the adult guests lounged in disgust by the water's edge, cursing our explosions and the rain of chlorinated droplets that they scattered; or else they forged, stoic and frowning, a measured breaststroke through our midst, their wake immediately swallowed by our flapping arms and legs. But at night, the pool, lit from below, wavered, empty, avoided by the grown-ups who wandered through the distant hotel bar or dawdled, debating, over endless suppers, their voices rising and falling above the cicada chorus. The nearest thing to swimmers were the swooping bats that shot along the waterline in search of insects, attracted by the light. And so, around ten o'clock one evening in July, or possibly even later, one among us—Thierry, the son of the accountant, a boy who never seemed to grow and whose voice obstinately refused to change, who compensated for his size with awkward arrogance and tedious pranks—suggested that we chase away the bats and reclaim the shimmering depths for ourselves. Familiar in the sunlight, the pool in the dark was an adventure, all its shadows altered. We had no towels and, beneath our clothes, no suits, so we stripped naked, our curves and crevices hidden by the night, and plunged.

We were eight or nine, the children for whom the hotel was home and those for whom it was each summer the equivalent. Our gropings and sinkings and splashings were more exciting for our nakedness, our screams correspondingly more shrill. We didn't think of the adults: why would we? We didn't even think of time. The night swim was a delicious discovery, even though our heads and arms, when protruding to the air, were cold, and our bodies riddled with goose-bumps. Ten minutes, maybe twenty. We weren't long in the water, and it is still difficult to believe we were so very loud, when my grandfather emerged on to his balcony, a dark form against the living room lights, with the bulge of the plane tree like a palaeolithic monster yapping at his feet.

He declaimed, his voice hoarse and furious. People were trying to think, to sleep. This was a place of rest, and the hour unconscionable... We had no right, in short, to swim. We dangled, treading water, cowed into silence for a moment until someone—

Thierry, no doubt—began to hiss across to me, half-laughing, inaudible to my grandfather, about how the old prick should be silenced.

'Tell him you're here,' he whispered. 'Just tell him you're here and that'll shut him up. Go on. Or else he'll blabber on all night. Go on!'

Others—Marie-José and Thibaud and Cécile and the rest—took up his exhortation: 'Go on, Sagesse, go on.' Their voices lapped like waves that my grandfather, slightly deaf and still ranting, could not distinguish.

'Grand-père,' I shouted, finally, my voice high as a bell. 'It's us. It's me. We're sorry. We didn't mean to disturb you.'

'Get out right now,' he yelled back. 'Get out, get dressed and go home. It's the middle of the night.' Everyone sniggered at this: we were of an age and station to believe that people who went to bed, who got up in the morning and went out to work, were some kind of a joke—'Does your father know you're here?'

'Yes, Grand-père, he knows.'

My grandfather snorted, disgusted, a theatrical snort. 'Go home, all of you,' he said, and turned, fading back into the light, regaining his features and the high, greyed dome of his forehead.

We scrambled from the pool, a dripping huddle, muttering.

'Your grandfather, man,' said Thierry, jumping up and down with his hands clasped over the shadow of his genitals. 'He is something else.'

'It's not Sagesse's fault,' said Marie-José, putting a damp arm around me. 'But he is, you know, a jerk.'

'He's a bastard to work for, my father says,' said a skinny girl called Francine, her teeth chattering. Her father was the head groundsman.

'My father says the same,' I said. Everyone laughed, and just then a bat nosedived and almost clipped the tops of our heads. We screamed, in unison, and tittered guiltily at our screaming.

'Be careful,' said Thibaud, one of the summer residents, the son of nouveaux riches from Paris and the boy I had my eye on. 'Or he'll come back out.' He growled. 'Rottweiler.'

We dissolved again.

Claire Messud

That was the first night. When Marie-José dropped me at home, my clothes stuck clammily to my skin and my long hair was both damp and viciously tangled by the wind made by her moped. Marie-José had waved and blown a kiss from within her bubbled helmet, and as she putted back along the white gravel drive to the road, my mother opened the door.

Our house, the home in which I had lived most of my life, had the same marble stillness as the hotel, the same capacity for echoes and light. You could feel people in it or, more often, their absence, even standing in the foyer before the naked statue of Venus on her pedestal, with the brushed aluminium elevator door like another artwork beside her. The front hall stretched up two storeys, and the air high above seemed to hover, waiting to be disturbed.

My mother could slip through the house without moving that air, when she chose to. Her face, too, could remain still—even when she spoke, even when she was nervous—like a terrified mask, with its sharp planes and dark, hooded eyes.

'Not in bed?' I asked, as casual as I could be, plucking at my tats with my fingers as I pushed past her into the living room.

She fidgeted with the buttons of her blouse, and spoke to me in English, her language and that of my earliest childhood, used between us now only as the language of confidences and reprimand. 'Your grandfather called.'

'He did?' I sank into the middle section of the huge, death-white sofa, aware that my jeans would leave two wet bulbs beneath my buttocks. I spoke in French. 'And how was he?' I put my feet up on the coffee table, careful even as I indulged this act of war not to go too far: I placed them on a large, perfectly positioned book, and did not touch, let alone smear, the polished glass.

'Livid.'

I waited, still busy with my hair, tangling and untangling it like Penelope at her loom.

'He's furious with you and your friends. All that noise! In the middle of the night, Sagesse! The hotel is full of guests, for God's sake.'

'It wasn't very late. All we did was go swimming. It's one of the rules, that we be allowed to. He didn't have to yell at us.'

'Your grandfather is under a great deal of strain.'

'He's a jerk is what he is, who yells at people just because he can. Some of them—Renaud, or Thibaud, or Cécile and Laure—they're guests at the hotel. What right does he have to do that?'

'Your grandfather—' my mother's eyes were pleading, but then she made a sudden click of exasperation. 'I don't want to talk about your grandfather and what's wrong with him. That's not the point.'

'Oh no?'

'The point is an abuse of privilege.'

Small and neat, my mother had done her best to impersonate a Frenchwoman: her dark hair was pulled back in a tidy chignon, her blouses and skirts were cut in the latest fashion, and she favoured trim navy cardigans that pointed up the slimness of her shoulders. But something in her face, in the shape of her head or the way that she held it, gave away her foreignness, the way a transvestite is betrayed by her wrists or the line of her back. Perhaps it was just her anxiety; because my mother was constantly anxious. But the result was an inability to take command. Her scoldings were always half-hearted, as if she didn't really believe in them, as if she were criticizing herself and found the duty excruciating.

Then again, there was the awkwardness of my mother trying to take on the voice of her father-in-law: for too long, for ever, I had heard and overhead the railing, the whining, the fury—the range of melodramatic expostulations that characterized my mother's emotional expression, much of it directed against her husband's family, against the very man whom she was now forced to represent; and if not, then against the whole of France, in a sweeping, metonymical gesture that fooled no one. The criticism never fell where we all, silently, sinkingly, knew that it must, on the key to her imprisonment: my brother Etienne.

I could, you see, have begun with my brother; or even with my parents, and their meeting, in a café in Aix-en-Provence one April afternoon, when the sun was sinking and the parade of eccentrics, in imitation of the metropolis, marched the boulevard like puppets in a theatre for the sole benefit of this eager young American, on a year's release from her sedate women's college where the turbulence of the decade had failed to stretch its tentacles, and of the handsome (so he was, she tells me), gallant young Frenchman who leaned forward to watch the delight in my mother's eyes.

Or, indeed, I could have begun with the squalling of my own birth, which occurred at the time of the fall of Saigon, a matter of record for each of my parents in their different ways. For my father, because his colonial blood led him to grieve at the ultimate loss of another, former, outpost of French glory, when the final anguished battles of his own vanished Algeria were little more than ten years old. Whereas my mother, who hailed from the rolling comfort of Massachusetts, whose interest in and grasp of the political were always vague at best, saw the moment in a rush of nostalgia for America, that vast and only intermittently familiar territory, in pain and internally divided as she, in exile, was herself. And yet, somehow, I, slippery and screaming, could grow up believing that none of it— neither war, nor America—had anything to do with me. All stories are made up, after all, as much of what is left out.

As for my brother, why was he the more significant when I already crawled in my playpen, my parents' grave error made flesh? Because some things are truer than others, more inescapable, less dependent on the mad or imagined confluences of the mind. And what happened at my brother's birth was one of these inescapable things. Those precious minutes between the first wrenching push that propels the infant's head out of the womb, downwards, and its arrival into the brutal fluorescence that marks the beginning of its life—in the case of my brother, those precious minutes bled and fed into another, longer, more terrifying gap, in which the doctor and the midwife panicked, and presumably my gasping brother also, trying as they could, all of them, my mother too, desperate but unknowing, to drag him into the world. Perhaps he himself hesitated, sensing the agonies before him, feeling that he would not, could not, go ahead with life. He cannot tell us. Deprived too long of oxygen, his tiny limbs, blued, curled in upon his torso, his waving baby's neck slackened, and his mind...who knows where his mind went, or where it is, or whether it rages still behind his grinning eyes? He relinquished in those precious moments all possibility of language: nobody will ever know what Etienne may think, as he hunches, strapped at the waist and again at the chest, convulsing cheerfully in his wheelchair, with a thin, glistening trail of spit always reaching, like a wet spider's web, towards the ground. He was, the doctors pronounced almost immediately, incapable of motor coordination and severely mentally retarded: little more than a vegetable, by the reckoning of the world. For my parents, this was the clanging of their prison. But for me, two years old when they came home with him, my path was already chosen. We were the same, I decided, cooing over the silent bassinet, and I, at least, would not abandon him. If he could not learn to speak, we would share what words I possessed. I would move for him, and bring home to him the odours of the park, the beach, the schoolyard. We would be fine. And from that moment, too, I despised him as much as I loved him: he was—he is—my limitation.

My parents rose to their fate with Catholic dignity, against the advice of many—including, I was eventually to learn, their priest. We kept him and loved him, or tried to; and having chosen his name beforehand—now so inappropriate as to be laughable—they stuck with it, which is how my brother came to be called Etienne Parfait. To myself, and when I spoke to him, he was *plus-que-parfait*, more than perfect, pluperfect, an irretrievable tense in the language he would never speak.

To interrupt my mother's lecture, I asked her, knowing full well the answer, where he was.

'Your brother is asleep,' she said. 'Of course.'

'And *Papa*?'

'Your father had to go out.'

I nodded. I was tired, and so was she.

'Listen, Sagesse,' she ventured, in conciliatory French, her hand reaching to smooth my crumpled hair. 'Don't do it again. Tell the others not to. I assure you, your grandfather...it's not the best time. He's not... Your father says things at the hotel are worse. Not business-wise, just... Your grandfather is under a lot of strain. He's being difficult. For everyone?'

'I understand.'

I didn't really understand. How could I? I went up and kissed Etienne as he slept, the rasping suction of his breath a distraction from the irritation I felt, more and more, with my parents. I cocooned his narrow, tousled head in the draped net of my hair and breathed in time with him, his smell of glycerine soap and faintly, too, of urine, mingling with the chlorine and sweat of myself. I put my mother's warning away in the padlocked box in my head where I stored such information. That is to say, I forgot about it.

I had good cause to forget. I, my mother and father, the Bellevue crowd, the entire town—we were all distracted in the days that followed by a local event of sudden national importance. Our town, long waning in significance, ugly duckling of the glamorous Mediterranean coast, did not often merit mention in the faraway Parisian newspapers. Accustomed to provinciality, we went about our business as if we were invisible, occasionally puffed with resentment at the metropolitans, but blithely unaware that our own scrabbling tensions might have resonance beyond themselves. In this instance— in this summer bombing, or, more accurately, in this failure to bomb, we brought down upon ourselves a scrutiny neither anticipated nor welcome.

The morning after our unpopular swim, I trailed downstairs near nine to find my father still at home, eating his breakfast in a fan of sunbeams, the *Figaro*, zebra-striped by the light, held close in front of his shiny, new-shaven face.

Slit-eyed with sleep, dressing-gowned, illicitly barefoot (shoes were a rule in our house, if only espadrilles), I muttered a greeting and drifted past him to the kitchen, where the tiles were cool on my soles. There, arms akimbo, my mother stood eyeing the toaster, in which her preferred—her American—*pain de mie* was audibly crisping.

'Why's he still here?' I asked, filling a pot with water. 'You want more coffee?'

'He got in very late. I was asleep myself. Paperwork, something.'

I raised an eyebrow.

'And then this tragedy...'

'What tragedy? Not another heart attack?' The previous year, a Bellevue guest had succumbed, in his bathroom, in an inelegant posture, to fatal angina.

'The bombing. There's been a bombing.'

'Where?'

'Here. In town. It's incredible. Right here.'

'Gosh.' I tightened the belt of my dressing gown.

'Just like Algiers, when he was a boy—it's the first thing he said.'

'What happened?'

'It's in the papers. They're not entirely sure, but they think they know...'

What they thought they knew from the start, what they eventually decided was fact, amounted to this: two young men and a young woman, locals, dirt ordinary, none of them over twenty, and the girl only precariously past eighteen, had built a pipe bomb in the basement of one of the boys' homes. This bomb had been intended, it appeared, for a nightclub in the old quarter near the port that was much frequented by Arabs. There was no doubt—given the young men's activities in the preceding months, including their disruptive attendance at a National Front rally and, more troubling still, their arrest for the random beating of a young Frenchman of Moroccan descent—what they were after. The girl, it was thought, was merely a girlfriend: her commitment to the nationalist cause was undocumented.

In any event, the trio had paid for their malice with their lives. Whether the timer had been ineptly set, or whether the bomb had been too sensitively wired, tripped by a pothole or a sudden braking, they had exploded only themselves and their black Fiat Uno, with a tremendous bang and a shattering of glass, just outside the downtown shopping centre at 1.12 a.m. exactly, as indicated by a frozen watchface that belonged to one of the young men. The agitators were in little pieces, as was their vehicle, and the road that had been beneath it was cratered like a small quarry.

When I jested, bringing my bowl of coffee to rest with both my hands, that there was slight cause for mourning—'The bad guys did themselves in, right? So, big deal.'—my father looked at me over his newspaper with an unreadable expression, his eyes wide and sombre, his flesh scrubbedly gleaming, and he rasped, 'Don't talk about things you know nothing about.'

'Ex-cuse me.' I rolled my eyes at my mother, who busied herself with the crumbs around her plate and did not speak.

'If you had seen what I've seen,' my father said—and even I knew, at my tender age—why, even Etienne most probably knew, had he but been able to say so—that my father almost never referred to his youth, and specifically not to those dark years at its end, before he left Algeria for France; or certainly not in front of his children; and I thought, even hoped, that he might now say more. But he lapsed back into silence, his conditional clause hovering in the air, then withdrew momentarily behind his newspaper, only to snap its pages into ragged folds and pull back from the table, sloshing the milk in its jug and causing a precariously balanced jam spoon to clatter stickily from its jar.

'I'm late,' he said. 'I'll probably be late again tonight. Tomorrow's the Joxe dinner. And remember, the day after we're at *Maman*'s.'

'How could I forget?' asked my mother, who had licked the jammy spoon and stowed it on her plate.

He kissed us, dry, perfunctory kisses. His face at rest bore—was it a tint, an angle, a shadow?—an indefinable mask of sorrow.

On Friday, I bowed out of my customary routines to accompany my mother to the market. I washed my hair for the outing, and braided it wet, knowing that at bedtime, unfastened, it would ripple down my back in rare wavelets, and be still damp.

I loved our trips to the outdoor market downtown. Usually my mother made hastier forays to its smaller sibling near the beach. It was handier when she had Etienne in the car: she could park and leave him, and see him even as she filled her baskets. To go into town, she had to leave Etienne with Magda, his nurse. It was an expedition, a treat, and she preferred to go with me.

The town market stretched the length of a narrow street in the old quarter, running downhill from a small fountain near the shopping centre to the plaza opposite the edge of the quay. The stands lined the asphalt on either side, and behind the stands, forgotten, lay the stores which remained even when there was no market, dusty, odd caverns selling Chinese herbal remedies, or curtain rods and broomsticks, or plate glass and mirrors cut to size.

We liked to start at the top of the street and walk down, slowly, sniffing and pressing and sampling and chatting in the gentle current of fellow housewives, the odd runty husband or wizened grandfather as notable as the yapping dogs among us.

We had not reckoned, that morning, on the bombers' funerals. We hadn't thought twice about it. Not that the funerals were to take place downtown, or anywhere near the market; but the nightclub, the avowed target, was only a few blocks from the stalls. There was, in the town, much sentiment and much of it divided on the matter of the bombing. In addition to the regular gamut of French citizenry, there were many, like our family, white refugees from Algeria, some of whom sympathized passionately with the bombers; and many *harkis*, the Algerians who had sided with the French during the war, who feared the rekindling of old tensions; and many more recent North African immigrants, suddenly terrorized and enraged. As if to set fire to this dry tinder, the National Front (how like my mother, I note in retrospect, not even to have been aware of it!) had dispatched representatives to the funerals to march in solidarity with the grieving parents. They weren't quite calling the dead youths heroes, but the phrase '*Morts pour la France*' had been bandied about and was already, had we but wandered the alleys behind the market, spray-painted, along with swastikas, on the brickwork and stucco throughout the predominantly Muslim neighbourhood.

We had not thought of it, and did not think of it, but as we ambled into the fray at the top of the market street, we could sense something askew. The shoppers leaned in to one another in their discrete groupings, with a corresponding edging away—so very slight—from those who were different. Some stallholders held hissed conversations; some pointedly ignored their neighbours. Even the market's children seemed knowingly subdued.

My mother, in her careful attire, her Vuitton bag on her arm, her chignon tight, did not resemble many of the other market-goers. It was not, on that day, that her un-Frenchness showed; it was a matter, rather, of too successful an emulation of a certain type of Frenchwoman. We detected, in our slow and cheery perusal of the tables, a certain frost from their attendants; but attributed it to the fact that we looked too long and bought too little.

It was the olive woman halfway down on the right who surprised us: the olive woman next to the stall selling only Spanish melons. We lingered in front of her display for a time, eyeing and sniffing the briny, garlicky, slick smell of the olives. She had fat green ones speckled with red chillis, and tight oval kalamatas, and little withered oil-cured black ones like over-sized raisins. My mother wanted to ask to taste one type of olive she did not know—spherical, large and almost red—but the olive woman's evil glare dissuaded her.

The olive woman was vast, her shelf of bosom quivering beneath a fading black T-shirt, her moon-pale, dimpled arms crossed over her belly. Her black hair was hacked around her puffed cheeks, and her chin, a great bony jut in her flesh, resisted gravity's pull into the billowing cushion of her neck. Above her lip quivered a dark caterpillar of moustache, which rendered her more, rather than less, frightening. Her eyes, shiny as her blackest olives, glittered hostility.

Having decided not to request a sample, my mother asked merely how long the reddish olives might keep in the refrigerator.

To which the woman, summoning her bulk, replied, 'You're not from here, are you?'

My mother—for whom revelation of her Americanness was an agonized obsession—shook slightly as she insisted, 'Yes, I am. I shop at the other one, the little market, by the beach.'

The olive woman snorted, as if this were a likely story. 'If you live here, where do you live?'

'Up the Corniche. On the hill.'

'Oh yeah? What street? Name it. I bet you can't. Name it.'

My mother, who had been in retreat from the outset, stopped. 'I don't think that's any of your business.'

'Maybe not. All right. It's how you're dressed.' The olive woman's mouth was set in a grim little gape. She did not possess all her teeth. 'I thought you were with *Them*. Flown in to make trouble.'

'With "Them"?' repeated my mother.

'With the National Front. The way you're dressed. Here for that funeral. Are you sure you're not with the National Front?'

My mother shook her head in sharp, insistent little shakes as she backed away from the olive woman and her wares. It seemed to me that the people around us were cocking their ears, listening without wishing to appear that they were, guarding their opinions but preparing, if need be, for a fight. As my mother retreated, and I with her, sinking into a hole made for us by the crowd, the olive woman glared, and raised phlegm, with a harsh ratcheting, in her throat. She spat vigorously on to the mucky pavement. 'That's what I think of the National Front,' she called after us accusingly, her moustache glistening and aquiver.

My mother trembled, almost teary, in the wake of this incident.

'Don't let it bother you,' I assured her, tucking my arm in the crook of hers as we resumed our downhill course. 'She was a crazy lady. As if you were in the National Front!'

'It's the intensity of her unpleasantness that surprises me,' my mother said. 'She was so *angry*, and why?'

'Because you're dressed nicely, that's all. Let it go, mom. What are you going to do, buy your clothes in the market just to please her?'

My mother brightened at the notion. 'A red sequin miniskirt and go-go boots—what do you think?'

'I think I'd stick to buying fish.'

That evening, we went for supper to my grandparents' apartment. It was always a production to take Etienne there, because the Bellevue, and in particular its staff block, had not been designed with wheelchairs in mind. No matter which path one took—whether around the main drive, past the hotel and the pool, in a wide loop, or straight up from the gate to the back parking lot and the staff building beyond—there were steps to be negotiated. My mother and I panted and struggled while Etienne, drooling on to his fine white shirt, bucked and crowed and tried to reach for our hair or our arms or our shiny necklaces, and we all arrived at my grandparents' door flushed and dishevelled.

'Come in, *chéris*,' urged my grandmother, from within her cloud of Guerlain (a particular perfume concocted, appropriately enough, for the Empress Eugénie). Even though we were the only supper guests, an evening *en famille*, she had powdered and rouged, had draped her neck with jewels, and her body in flowered silks. 'The men are just sorting out the drinks.' I hadn't seen my grandfather since before the swimming pool incident, although my grandmother had roundly chastised me on his behalf the following day. I wasn't certain whether or not to apologize directly, to clear the air but possibly to elicit an indignant tirade, or whether to pretend nothing had happened and hope for the best. I would gauge the lay of the land, I told myself, and react accordingly.

We assembled in our specific places around the coffee table, my father and grandfather in facing armchairs, my mother and me on the sofa—which was particularly high, or deep, so that we both had to choose between dangling our feet above the ground and perching at the front of the slippery cushions: I always chose the former and she the latter—and my grandmother, with Etienne parked at her side, closed the circle, in a tapestry chair with carved legs and futile little armrests: a lady's chair.

Before sitting, I kissed my grandfather hello. He seemed preoccupied, and registered no displeasure. Indeed, he seemed barely to register who I was. But then, when drinks had been poured and I was quietly crunching potato chips from a blue bowl, I caught him frowning at me, his eyebrows, ever exuberant (their hairs were very long), working, as if the sight of me in the middle distance had provoked an aggravating memory.

My grandmother was telling a story about an ageing Italian opera singer who had visited the hotel every year for a decade—a woman we all knew, who wore grand, flowing tunics and who annually pinched my cheeks between her curiously strong fingers—when my grandfather interrupted her.

'Our country, in this time, has a problem of manners,' he began. 'It is not a *uniquely* French problem—indeed it stems in part, I, like many, would contend, from the influence of your country,'—he nodded at my mother—'although not, naturally, from your own gracious influence. What preoccupies me, however, as a nationalist—and I'm not afraid to say it, implying thereby only a love and a reverence for my nation, culture and history *above all other* nations, cultures and histories, which is perfectly natural and in no way implies disrespect for those others—anyway, as a nationalist and a Frenchman, I am concerned with the manners and mores of *this* country, and of our people. And it seems to me—' here his roving, appropriative gaze, which had been sliding like oil around the assembly, and beyond, to the Provençal plates on the wall and the darkening corner of sea he could distinguish from his chair, came to rest upon me, 'that the loss of certain basic courtesies among our citizens, and among our youngest citizens above all, does not, of itself, comprise the fairly innocent informality that well-intentioned liberals would have us believe. No. It is, I am convinced, a symptom of a far-reaching and truly distressing cultural collapse, one in which the individual places his own will and desire above the common good in ways we, who are now ageing, would have considered unthinkable. Rudeness is, I argue, a symptom of the profound anarchy that our culture currently faces but refuses to acknowledge, a chaos in which everyone has lost sight of his place in a natural—or rather, civilized, which is far greater a compliment than the natural, civilization being what distinguishes us from mere beasts—hierarchy. What motivates good behaviour—' he paused, and sipped his Scotch, with a slurp rendered louder by our universal silence; even Etienne, whose eyes rolled ceiling-wards and whose feet twitched, sensed that our grandfather's discourses demanded a semblance of attention. 'What motivates good behaviour and what motivates excellence are the same thing: fear. Fear of God, fear of the rod, fear of failure, fear of humiliation, fear of pain. And that is a fact. And in our society, today, nobody is afraid of anything. Shame, rebuke, imprisonment—none of it means anything to anyone. Kids need to be taught,' he said, looking now at my father, who managed to meet his gaze without apparently seeing him, 'that their actions have repercussions, real ones. Kids should be a lot more afraid than they are.'

'Not just kids,' I said, nodding and licking the salt from my lips.

'You would have me believe that *we*,' my grandfather's ire, only barely reined in, was a fierce steeliness in the quiet of his tone, 'that *we*, around you here in this living room, behave with as little regard for anyone outside ourselves as you and your little friends?'

Tempted to insist that my friends were not 'little', but wise after many years to the cost of such baiting, I adopted my most innocent and childish voice and said, 'Oh no, nothing like that. No, I meant the woman in the market today. Right, *Maman?*'

My mother, who sought only to slip invisibly through these evenings, glared at me and pressed her lips.

'What woman?' asked my grandmother.

'Yes, what happened?' My father seized on any strand that might divert his own father's discourses.

'It was nothing,' my mother insisted.

Etienne squirmed. My grandmother tilted his juice cup to his slippery lips.

'That's not true, *Maman*. You were terribly upset.'

'Carol, what happened?' My father leaned forward in his chair. My grandfather's gaze, from beneath his wild brows, burned my mother's cheeks.

'Oh, Sagesse makes a mountain out of a molehill. It was just one of the pedlars, in the market, who didn't like the look of me for some reason.'

'She spat at us,' I explained.

'Whatever for?' my grandmother asked.

My mother shrugged. 'Just rude, I suppose. She was a nasty, tough old thing.'

'She accused *Maman* of being in the National Front, in town for the funerals.'

'Probably a communist,' my grandmother said with a sniff. 'You didn't take it to heart?'

'Of course not. But she *was* very unpleasant.' My mother adjusted her skirt.

'As if,' my grandfather took a breath and spouted, 'as if our country's troubles stemmed from the National Front! As if *that* were an insult! How absurd!'

'How do you mean, *Grand-père*?'

'I don't vote for Le Pen,' my grandfather said, 'but I'd defend any man's right to. For a start, because we—you too, my little girl, although you know about as much history as a spotted dog—we, all of us in this room, owe that man a debt. To the last, he fought for our country, he believed in our people, he understood what it was, what it meant.'

'Algeria.' I whispered it.

'That's right, my girl. Algeria. And anyone who votes for him, maybe they're merely repaying that debt. I don't happen to agree with a lot of his policies, and I think it's political suicide for representatives of the FN to come down here and associate themselves with a posse of undisciplined children, children who exemplify the very anarchical destruction—in this case, self-destruction—that I've just been talking about. Left, right—the politics don't matter. It's chaos, it's entropy, and anyone with any wit should keep away. But the FN's not the problem. People who think it is are misguided.

'It's just a symptom of the problem. Of the *problems*. Plural. The problems that this nation faces, overrun with immigrants— Arabs, Africans, the English speakers, all of them, our culture assailed on all sides. Our children, for God's sake, building bombs for no reason! And our government—this decrepit, farcical liar who fancies himself emperor—our government has nothing to say about it, nothing at all!'

My father coughed and looked into his drink.

'Le Pen, at least—he says the wrong thing, I think, for our time and our moment, but at least he has something to say. At least he knows his own mind. That's what you should've said to the Pinko fishwife—'

'She was selling olives, actually,' my mother murmured.

'Olives, fish, garlic, whatever. That's what you should've said to that peasant—at least he doesn't wait for advice from Moscow on how to respond to a local crisis. At least he has an honest response— a *French* response.' My grandfather grunted, sipped his Scotch, rattling the ice cubes.

I sat deep in the back of the sofa, swinging my feet slightly, watching, as my brother, strapped in his chair opposite me, twitched and rolled his bright grey eyes and appeared, also, to be watching. I was quite impressed by the firecracker I had so nonchalantly launched in our midst: I hadn't known I would provoke so fulsome a response, so ready a distraction from the pettiness of late swims in the Bellevue pool.

At supper, my grandfather said almost nothing, as if he were spent. He seemed small and slumped over his *pissaladière*, then over his slices of lamb shoulder. He sipped indifferently at his rosé and stared, often, out to the now-dark sea, and when my father asked him about the notion of a security guard at the front gate, he seemed not even to hear. My father looked at my mother as if to say 'I told you so,' and she raised a finely arched brow.

'Who's for more potatoes?' urged my grandmother, at her end of the table. 'More peas?'

The second nocturnal bathing, a week later, took place without me. I could not have prevented it, and could only laugh when Marie-José told me. She sat outstretched on her bedroom floor with her spatula and honeyed mire of melted wax, smoothing it in even swathes on to her long brown legs and tearing, with exaggerated winces, at the invisible fair bristles. She told me the story in between the stripping sounds, and waved the sticky spatula for emphasis.

'Your grandfather—Christ, girl, he's a madman! It was earlier, you know, than last time, so I guess we thought it would be OK. It must have been before ten, nine-thirty even, and we were *trying*— we saw his lights on—trying to be quiet. But I think it was Cécile, she was screaming like a pig in the water. I think—' She paused to slather the back of her left calf. 'I think she has a thing for Thierry. Don't laugh—it's obvious. You wouldn't think *anyone* could go for him, the shrimp. But she's no *Vogue* model herself.'

'And she's short,' I said.

'And he's older than she is. And I suppose she doesn't know him very well. So anyway—she gets on my nerves, that girl—every time he swam near her, she'd start shrieking, even though the rest of us were doing our best to shut her up. He was loving it, of course.'

'You think he's interested?'

'Probably. I mean, how often can he get a look in? None of us would touch him. And at school he's a joke.'

'You're starting to make *me* feel sorry for him.'

'Wait for this, then. Because you really will. Even I felt a little sorry. It was so funny. You see, we were trying, except for those two, to be quiet. Well, *quieter*. I mean, we were talking and stuff, but most of us didn't scream. And we were in the pool for a while, you know, and he—your grandfather—he didn't come out. I think we figured that maybe they were entertaining, or something, or maybe they were out somewhere else. I mean, all he had to do was tell us to be quiet.'

'So? What happened?'

The wax was cold and petrified on Marie-José's leg, but she was too caught up in her story to attend to it.

'Well, all of a sudden there's this voice on the bridge,'—there was a walkway over the pool from the courtyard above, with steps leading down to the water—'saying, "All right, who is it?" And then,

"I know which ones you are," and "Get out of the water." So we do, I mean, what choice do we have? We didn't hear him coming, you know. It was so weird.'

'What did he do then?'

We were both leaning forward, our bodies plumped in the grubby pink shag carpet that covered Marie-José's bedroom floor.

'He turned on this monster torch. Huge, like a searchlight, and he shone it on our faces, and then when it landed on Thierry—I mean, he's never liked me, he thinks I'm badly brought up, but Thierry, he thinks of him as polite, you know, because Thierry always says "Good day, sir" in that brown-nose way. So he gets the torch on Thierry and he says "Come here," and Thierry steps forward. And then your grandfather steps back a bit, I guess, because the next thing is, he's shining the light on *all* of Thierry, you know? He's *exposing* him.'

'Geez. Jesus Christ.'

'So there's little Thierry, with his hands over his balls, twitching around and whimpering and *completely* humiliated.'

'Oh Jesus.'

'I felt for him, I really did. Even you would have, I swear. Your grandfather stood there, aiming this great beam of light on skinny Thierry, and he starts this interrogation. Like "Does your father know you're here?" and "Don't you have summer school homework and shouldn't you be doing it?" and "Is everyone here a resident, or are these little friends from town?" and "Do you have any idea what it's like to be trying to sleep or to read with this racket?" And Thierry tried to point out that we were next to the staff apartments, that the guests were hundreds of metres away and couldn't possibly have heard, but that just seemed to annoy your grandfather more.'

'And then?'

'In time he just turned off the light and left us to get dressed. I'm surprised we didn't all catch pneumonia, we were standing there naked for so long. In-sane. Thierry was pretty funny about it, considering. But I suspect Cécile lost interest, once she got a good look. I wonder whether it would've been you, if you'd been there?'

'Me?'

'With the torch. Whether your grandfather would've lit you up like a Christmas tree.'

'Naked? Don't be sick.'
We doubled with laughter, clutching our sides and gasping.
Marie-José peeled the wax off her leg with a scream and we found
that, too, unreasonably funny.
'How was your night, anyway?'

I hadn't been at the poolside because Thibaud had, at last, asked me
out. I say 'at last' because for three summers he had come with his
parents to the hotel for a month, in their fat white Mercedes, from
Paris. And for three summers, I had eyed his black curls and his
impish hazel eyes, had marvelled at the pattern of freckles on his
brown back, had preened and tried to cast interested but veiled
glances at him, my skills at twelve and thirteen fairly primitive, so
that Thibaud could not help but know of my infatuation. But at
twelve and thirteen I was still scrawny and flat-chested, and he, two
years older than me, showed no interest.

A year older than me, Marie-José, whose breasts had burst forth
by the time she was eleven, and who had also already reached her
full, impressive height at that age, she who learned early to flick the
golden brown waves of her hair in an insouciant but enticing way—
Marie-José had been flicking and winking at Thibaud for a couple
of years and she, voice of experience to my thinner, unvoluptuous
youth, had assured me several times that 'the vibe wasn't there': 'I
think he might be gay,' she'd said, pursing her lips in modest
disapproval. 'Men have a way of looking, of appreciating, even if they
aren't planning anything. I mean, your *father* looks like that at me.'

I had so long envied and feared her mysterious power that I
usually accepted her judgements—the sexual ones, that is—without
hesitation. But with Thibaud, I kept faith secretly, and continued to
brown my skin with the touch of his fingertips in mind, and to stuff
my bra, which did not seem to fill out fast enough on its own, with
carefully folded bulges of white tissue.

When, at last, that summer, he seemed to take notice of me,
when he asked—so casually, so clearly nervous—as we climbed the
cliff back from the beach one afternoon, if I would like to go for a
drink, I was not surprised, although it was so surprising. I had
imagined the moment so many times that it seemed, on the hot gravel

path, that I might have misheard. When later, in my own room, I played our brief exchange over in my head, I heard different nuances with each repeat, and felt tremors in my body that were half-delight, half-fear. He had asked if I wanted to go for a drink and I, feigning ease, had said, simply, 'Sure, whatever.'

I didn't tell my mother that I was doing anything different from usual. I didn't lie, but it didn't seem worth mentioning. Even slight sins of omission, though, have a way of tripping you up, and it was when she, upon hearing from my grandfather of the previous night's events, was expecting to have to punish me for partaking, that she discovered I hadn't been at the hotel, or at least hadn't been swimming with the others, and then sought to condemn me for dishonesty.

In fact, my evening with Thibaud had been disappointingly innocent. I don't know what I had anticipated, but I had felt my heart like a great snare drum beneath my lace-edged T-shirt. I wore my favourite one, the colour of a rosy shell, showing off my slender arms to best advantage (it was not long since they had been skinny and without advantages at all). I wore my most presentable pair of Levis, their hems fashionably clipped at the ankle, and a thick black leather belt. I wore my sandals, my newest, all straps, and I carried over my shoulder a navy cardigan I had stolen from my mother. I hesitated a while over my hair, and ultimately chose to leave it loose, knowing that although it did not have Marie-José's pre-Raphaelite wave it could nonetheless be used to play with nonchalantly. I glossed my lips and brushed my bangs over my forehead in such a way that they would hide the pimple that had sprouted there.

But all my efforts had been a waste of time: Thibaud, when we met by the hotel gates, said nothing about my appearance. He said very little at all, except to ask me whether I had managed to get hold of Marie-José's moped for the evening, and when I said I had, to ask me to drive it. He wasn't surly, just silent, and I couldn't tell whether he was nervous, or whether he regretted his blurted invitation. He was a Paris boy, and wealthy; and this was only a summer seaside town, and I the hotelier's granddaughter, a gawky girl in jeans who idled the year around in these beautiful but vacant surroundings. I was smart enough and afraid enough to recognize these facts, and the possibility that he had changed his mind.

Claire Messud

As I drove the moped down the Corniche towards town, with Thibaud's hand on my waist, so tentative, and me without a licence to drive—as we took speed on the hill, all possible interpretations of his reticence, from adoration to nervousness to distaste, visited me, bright as fireworks, each seeming wholly and uniquely true in its moment. But by the time we reached the café on the sea wall, I had run the full gamut and begun again with no certainty, while he had done no more than tighten his grip around me on the sharp turns in the road and try to keep the flailing strands of my hair out of his mouth.

The café, on the boardwalk directly above the beach, was festively lit with multicoloured lanterns and hung with bits of boats and plaster fish. Thibaud and I took a table on the terrace, in uncomfortable white plastic armchairs still gritted with the sand of day visitors in their bathing suits. He ordered beer and I a Coca-Cola, and we talked, desultorily, almost dully, about the hotel and its guests and our friends. Only at the moment when, reaching for the ashtray, his fingers brushed the back of my hand, did I feel a current snake the length of my body and erupt into tingling, and with it, that moment swelled beyond all natural proportion: that gesture, out of the whole evening, would wait patiently, and lie awake with me in bed that night, the whole evening reduced to that.

Finally, when he had drained his second beer, he leaned across and murmured a suggestion that we walk a while along the beach. Occasionally we crossed other couples or groups walking, the fireflies of their burning cigarettes the first herald of their approach. We did not touch as we walked, a failure that seemed purposeful to me: I felt my restraint because I knew the lightest brush would result, inside me, in a report as forceful as a gunshot, and I would lose the thread of the conversation that, finally, we seemed to be having. These sensations were new in being real rather than imagined (although they fluttered still only in my mind): I was actually there, along the soughing sand, with this tall and serious boy, the two of us, like other couples, walking. My brother, Etienne Parfait, would never amble on a beach at night with the moon floating in the water and the rank salt in his nostrils, wondering in every fibre, and anticipating a touch on the skin so strongly felt without its having happened that it took

186

on the quality of a waking dream. What words could convey that, even if he were to understand them? But I wanted him to know.

When Thibaud and I arrived back at the hotel, it was not late, but neither of us suggested that we seek out the others. So it was that we did not know about the swim, nor about my grandfather creeping like a burglar among our friends. We dawdled in the concrete cavern of the parking lot, beneath the flickering bleach of the fluorescent light, serenaded by the trickle of a forgotten garden hose and the occasional scurry of a lizard along the wall. I fiddled with my hair (which I knew, by now, to be a rat's nest) and he, hands in pockets, toed the ground. Eventually I said I had to go, although I didn't, particularly. He did not protest, but walked me out, along the alley of palms to the hotel gates; and stood there, shadowed by the street lamp, as I turned on to the road and started off in the direction of home.

For this catalogue of unspoken and ungrasped opportunities, my mother expressed herself gravely disappointed in me. It was a disappointment—as much about the failure of our friendship, hers and mine, an alliance that we both had long lived by, as it was about my breaking any rules—whose depths I could glimpse in her decision not only not to tell my father, but not even to threaten to do so.

'All you had to do was *ask*,' she insisted, tight-lipped, as we set the dinner table the following evening, when I had heard the story of the pool from Marie-José, and my mother had heard it from my grandmother. 'How did you get into town? And who is this boy?'

'It's nothing. He's just a friend. I don't want to talk about it.'

'I don't know which is worse—you raising havoc with those kids up at the hotel, or sneaking off with...how old is he, anyway?'

'My age. *Maman*, it's no big deal. We met some friends for coffee in a café on the Corniche, and that's all. I would've thought...'

My mother glared at me, her hooded eyes, which I had inherited, spitting light. She waved a knife in her left hand, feeling its weight. 'What would you have thought, exactly? Honestly, Sagesse, I've had just about enough. You can't imagine what...this is the last thing your father needs, to worry about you. The last thing I need. These days—

I don't know. I don't know what to do.'

The slip from rage to misery was instantaneous, a familiar melodrama. The knife sagged, suddenly so heavy in her hand that she dropped it, with a piteous (and self-pitying) clunk, upon the table. And as the script of years demanded, I was beside her in a second, with my arms around her, knowing that although I could not see her face, her chin had puckered, waffle-like, and her eyes were milky with tears. When I hugged my mother, I was always aware of how small she was, how close her bones were to the surface, her shoulder blades like spiny wings, quivering, prepared for flight.

'Don't cry,' I soothed, stroking at her perfect hair, smelling her perfume and beneath it the faint, delicate odour that was her. 'Don't cry. It isn't anything. It was nothing. There's nothing to be upset about.' I drew back and watched her features struggle into a hesitant, damp grimace, the approximation of a smile.

'I'm fine,' she said, as much to herself as to me. She dabbed her eyes with her cuffs and resumed the busyness of arranging cutlery at our places.

'I think it would be better,' she began again after a moment, 'if, for a while, you didn't go out in the evenings. You're hardly ever here. How much time have you spent, this summer, with your brother? And your father and I—well, your father's very busy, I know, but still, he'd like to feel he knew what his own daughter looked like. At your age I was—'

'You were working in the summertime. I know. You had a summer job. But that was in America, *Maman*. Things are different here. It's a different century, practically.'

'Sometimes I think you ought to be sent to summer camp, if your father won't have you going out to work.'

I snorted. 'Nobody goes to camp, *Maman*,'—I meant, only poor kids did, and not anyone at all from our town: who would leave when in front of us stretched the enticements of the open sea, when we were already in the place where the entire nation sought to come on holiday?—'And nobody I know works. Nobody.'

'You lack discipline. All of you.'

'*Papa* says there's time enough for that later, that now is for learning.'

My mother shrugged. 'And everything, as we know, is always your father's way. We live your father's life, after all.'

'Speak for yourself.'

'Believe me, you do too. You just don't know it.'

Eventually my mother came back around to what it was she wanted: I was to be grounded for a week of nights. She did not have the force to command me, so her promise was wheedlingly drawn, a pact between friends, born of guilt. But I agreed.

I had promised, and I tried. She didn't ask me to give up my daytime routines, after all. They continued to blend into one another, bathed in sunlight and the cicada song, scented with suntan oil and the dry, hot smell of the pines, interrupted only by the quiet hour of luncheon, which I generally took at my grandmother's table. Mindful for the first time of my figure, I picked miserably at lasagne, or at great slabs of steak, served by Zohra, my grandparents' aged Arab servant.

Although my grandmother had peppered my childhood with her versions of our family's history, which I thrilled to hear, she was not the sort of grandmother who crowed over my every endeavour, whose bosom offered welcome refuge. Rather, she expressed concern through criticism: 'Sit up straight,' 'Don't chew with your mouth open,' 'Don't run in the corridors.' She believed that meals should be sedate times, given to the full enjoyment of our food and to the sound of her husband's voice.

When he was there, and in good humour, my grandfather told jokes or stories, spilled over with anecdotes from his work, or from their long, exceedingly long, lives; or else he prised the details out of my days like an expert fisher for pearls. When he was angry, the table quivered with the sound of his rage, whether audible or present only in his violent thrusts at the china and silverware. When he was not there—and in that gloomy week of my grounding he was not there once, too busy in his madness to leave his desk, or if he did, then only to roam the hotel grounds and spy on his employees—then my grandmother and I would sit in near silence, serenaded by Zohra's humming and cleaning in the kitchen.

Daily there followed, in that apartment, a trough of silence as deep as death. Zohra slunk away and left the shuttered rooms to the breathy see-saw of my grandmother's snores. At weekends, my grandfather would lie beside her with a magazine until he, too, succumbed, the two of them beneath the rosary-draped crucifix on the wall like curled offerings, Christ's ever merciful eye upon their wrinkled bodies. It was fearsome, as a child, to discover that the world could be so still during daylight: I had had to endure it, when I was smaller and my mother left me in their care for the day; or in the winter holidays, even at fourteen—but at least in winter the wind cavorted angrily around the window frames and the raindrops spat against the glass, disrupting the unending rhythms of their sleep.

That summer, though, that week, the luncheon hour alone was sufficient penance: I was paroled before siesta, a criminal loosed on to the back pathways to the beach or snoozing—somehow a livelier sleep, with the breeze at our skin—on the bridge over the pool. Everyone knew that I had lost my night privileges, and they knew why. My date with Thibaud, which might otherwise have been a source of gossip and speculation only behind his back and mine, became everybody's favourite joke. Not even Marie-Jo would defend me. Thierry was the most insistent: 'Locked up for your lover boy, eh? Like Rapunzel in her tower. Thibaud, you'll have to go rescue the damsel in distress! Better hope the grandfather isn't standing guard!'

Cécile made the Rottweiler noise. It had been Thibaud's joke, but he wasn't interested, any longer, in following it up.

'Too much necking and you'll get your head chopped off!' was another of Thierry's cracks. Marie-Jo knew there hadn't been any necking at all, but she kept her own counsel, smirked. Later she said, 'Come off it, Sagesse, it's good for your reputation. Do you want people to think you're a frigid prude?' She laughed, not kindly. 'It's doing him a favour too. My God, what *is* he? He didn't even *try*? Not even a kiss? I told you, he's queer, that one. You'll see.'

The fact was, Thibaud had retreated. He didn't even seem to look at me any more, let alone try to swim near me or walk with me. And as I had no part in the night gatherings, and only Marie-José's reports of them to go on, I had no idea at all what Thibaud was thinking. More tormenting than my dreary lunches, or than my mother's heavy sighs at night over her English novels, was my mind's picture of everyone assembled on the steps under the oldest plane tree; and the accompanying soundtrack, the conversations that in my absence might—would, I was sure of it—stray to cover me, the questions Thierry or Renaud would ask of Thibaud: 'Can she kiss? Too much tongue or too little? Her tits aren't up to much, are they?' Over the years—over that very summer—I had played along in the grilling of other girls, or boys even. I knew I wasn't fanciful.

I hid one night, two, three, four, in my parents' leathered library, prone on the slippery black Danish sofa in the aquatic television light, watching old American cop shows and black-and-white Westerns dubbed clumsily into French. I stared for hours on end and saw nothing but myself, walking along the town beach at Thibaud's shoulder, or sitting, our hands just touching, in the café by the shore. Like a sorceress with a crystal ball, I saw, too, the screeching, gesticulating crowd by the pool, in their cloud of cigarette smoke, and I heard them making fun of me.

On the fifth day, I decided to take matters into my own hands. No sooner had Zohra brought in the two leaky rum babas that were our dessert (it was a stroke of luck: I was known to loathe them) than I scraped back my chair and slipped my napkin into its ring.

'Already?' asked my grandmother, blinking at my request.

'We thought we might go down to the town beach,' I lied. 'And rent pedalos. If you don't get there early, they're all gone.'

'If you'd mentioned it before, I would have moved lunch forward. But all right. Be careful. How will you get there?'

'On the bus. Don't worry.' I was already standing. I knew that if she saw us at the pool upon waking from her nap, I would have only to say that the tourists had beaten us to it, and rather than wait our turn, we had come back.

'Don't swim, dear. Not for an hour.'

'Of course not.'

As I left she was spooning the oily sponge of her baba rather sorrowfully to her mouth. I ran, the shortest way, through the shrubbery to the back path, to the hotel. It was a risk, loitering in the lobby—that my grandfather or even my father might pass through, that Cécile or Laure might come up before Thibaud did. I could see him, through the glass doors on the restaurant patio, at a large table, under a parasol, with his parents. He sat, expressionless and silent, turning from one parent to the other as they spoke, like the umpire in a tennis match, occasionally brushing his hair back from his face with an irritated hand. He kicked his sneakers idly against the legs of his chair. His mother asked him something, a fine trail of cigarette smoke wafting from each nostril just before she spoke, her cigarette clamped between lacquered vermilion claws. Underneath her hat, I knew she had eggplant-coloured hair, immovable and shiny: she was the type of woman my mother feared.

Thibaud shook his head in response to her question, and stood to leave. At the far end of the terrace, I saw Cécile and Laure winding among the tables, and I cursed my luck; but they turned into the restaurant rather than coming along as far as the lobby doors, and they did not try to catch Thibaud's attention. He came on alone, into the cool marble from the glare outside. He did not know he was being watched, but still his face gave nothing away. He was about to cross to the elevators when I called out.

'You don't often come in here,' he said.

'Too risky. Might run into my father and grandfather.'

'So what's up today?'

I had not prepared a lie. 'I never had a chance to thank you for the other evening. With all the fuss about the swimming...'

'No. And the fuss about me. Sorry about that.' He seemed almost to be laughing, so I did.

'Parents, y'know. All the same.'

'Mine don't care what I do.'

'You're a boy. And you're older. A bit.'

'I suppose.'

He fingered his room key, clacking the metal against the translucent plastic square with the number on it and 'Hotel Bellevue' in gilded capitals.

'You headed to the pool?'

'Of course. What else is there to do? I just...I wondered... I wondered if you wanted to meet up tonight.'

'Tonight? But you're under lock and key, aren't you?'

I shrugged, in conscious imitation of Marie-José's nonchalant shrugs. I was fiddling with the ends of my hair, flicking a swatch around my forefinger. 'So?'

Enjoying yourself?

Then why not subscribe to Granta? You'll SAVE UP TO £40.

(Or treat a friend? A Granta subscription makes a wonderful gift: unusual, thoughtful and lasting.)

Some of the best new fiction, memoir, reportage and photography appears first (and often only) in Granta. Subscribe today, and you will save up to £40 on the £8.99 bookshop price, and get a year's worth (or more) of writing that matters, delivered to your home.

You save £11 (30%) with a one-year subscription (4 issues) for just £24.95.

You save £25 (35%) with a two-year subscription (8 issues) for £46.50.

You save £40 (38%) with a three-year subscription (12 issues) for £67.

The order form is overleaf.

'Essential reading.'
Observer

'This is writing at its very best.'
Scotland on Sunday

'Never take Granta for granted.'
Daily Telegraph

THE MAGAZINE OF NEW WRITING

THE SEA

CHILDREN

India!
THE GOLDEN JUBILEE

LONDON
the lives of the city

AMBITION

RUSSIA
THE WILD EAST

Order form
Save up to £40!

Your details (we need these even if you're just giving a gift subscription)

Name

Address

Postcode

○ I'd like to subscribe for myself, for: ○ One year at £24.95 (£11 off)
○ Two years at £46.50 (£25 off)
○ Three years at £67 (£40 off)

Start the subscription with issue no: _____

○ I'd like to give a gift subscription for: ○ One year at £24.95
○ Two years at £46.50
○ Three years at £67

Start the subscription with issue no: _____

Details for a gift subscription

Name

Address

Postcode

Message:
(optional: we'll send a letter announcing your gift and, if you like, incorporating a brief message)

Payment details

That's____ subscriptions for a total* of £_____ , paid by: ○ cheque (to 'Granta')
○ Visa, Mastercard, AmEx

Card no: / __ / __ / __ / __ / __ / __ / __ / __ / __ / __ / __ / __ /

Expires: / __ / __ / __ / Signature: _____

* **Postage.** The prices shown include UK postage. Please add £8 per year for the rest of Europe,
£15 per year for overseas (airspeeded delivery).   F5S66

○ Please tick if you'd prefer not to receive occasional offers from other, compatible organizations.

✉ Post ('Freepost' in the UK): Granta, Freepost, 2/3 Hanover Yard, Noel Rd, London N1 8BR, UK
☎ Or phone/fax credit-card orders:
In the UK: **FreeCall 0500 004 033** (tel & fax)
Outside UK: Tel 44 171 704 0470, Fax 44 171 704 0474.
E-mail: subs@grantamag.co.uk . Website: **www.granta.com**

GRANTA

Thibaud emitted a strange blowing noise, like an attempt at a chuckle. This, I could tell, was not how he expected me to behave. 'What did you want to do?'

'It's difficult for me to go into town. I might run into somebody, it might get back to my folks... I thought we could meet here, maybe go for a walk. I don't know.'

'Why not? I'm not sure I can stand another evening with Thierry, anyhow.'

'Isn't he *such* a jerk? You almost feel sorry for him.'

'Maybe you do.'

We fixed a time, and a place—by the round bench, where the little children played; none of our group would ever wander over there—and then I left him, a shadow slipping between the mirrored jaws of the lift. I managed to duck out of the lobby just as Cécile and Laure were coming down the stairs from the first floor.

Thibaud made me wait. Even as I cowered in the shadow of a dwarf palm opposite the designated bench, wondering whether to go home, he sidled up, all darkness.

'You came.' I smiled in spite of myself.

'Of course.'

'What do you want to do?'

'To do?'

'Well, we could hang out here, or walk down to the beach, or— I'd better not go into the hotel because—'

'As if,' he said. 'Let's walk.'

He took my hand in his. It squirmed there, dry, for a second, then lay still, eliciting in me riotous palpitations. I could not speak. He did not speak. He led me, or we led each other (everything between us seemed suddenly, at last, to be understood) by the most circuitous route possible to the *chemins de la plage*, to their starting point beneath the swimming pool, where, in the pool's foundations, a porthole like a Cyclops' eye gave vista to the wavering, illuminated water. Not far above us, perhaps fifty feet, the others sprawled and chattered; phrases and whole sentences drifted down—Marie-Jo's laugh, Thierry's voice, breaking occasionally in its insistent chirrup.

There was a bench there, cut into the rock, and from it we could map the coast and the sea ahead—the same view as above, interrupted at this lower level by the spikes and billows of the trees. The porthole, at our backs, watched with us.

'We can eavesdrop,' Thibaud said, gently scraping my palm with his fingernails. 'Let's sit awhile. See if they wonder where I am. See if they guess.' We giggled, whisperingly, titillated at the possibility of discovery, at our spying communion. The voices, the whooshing rise and fall of the sea, my blood, the noiseless fingerings between us: as ever, I listened.

It was not long before he leaned into me and murmured, 'May I?' and kissed my neck. Then it was no longer a matter of the time, or of the others, or of my parents: too immediate and consuming for any of them, his tongue strayed into my ear and on to my eyelids and into my mouth (like a cat, I thought distinctly, cleaning her young). It was an intimacy novel and exciting to me, from which I felt, at the same time, observantly detached: I was in the moment and apart from it at once, able to register the sensation of his saliva, cooling and drying on my cheek, the slight roughness of his chin, the surprising coarseness of his curls to the touch, his lemony smell, anxious even as I matched his embraces with my own fervour that my kissing was too zealous, too passive, or too spitty.

By the time we heard the others tramping to the poolside— directly over our heads—we were lying flat on the bench, me beneath him, my T-shirt rucked up the better to admit his nimble fingers to my skin, and a smattering of sharp gravel to my back. The proximity of our friends alarmed me, and I tried to sit up; but Thibaud dismissed my attempt, silencing me first with his hand over my mouth and then with his lips on mine. Our adolescent fumblings fumbled onwards, but for me the sounds beyond our bodies now intruded. We could hear their shuffling feet, and the slap of their discarded clothing on the railing overhead. We could hear their whispers (might they not then hear ours?), then the cascade of splashes as they dived, with the expert timing of showgirls, one after the other. A few droplets splattered through the poolside slats and showered down upon us.

Thibaud would not be deterred. Fearing that one or other of them might slither, underwater, to the porthole to catch the view (another game of which, as swimmers, we never tired), and might there instead glimpse our entwined bodies, I advocated a remove, wanted us to tiptoe further seawards and plant ourselves invisibly in the undergrowth. But Thibaud, preoccupied with the buttons of my fly, would have none of it.

'They'll hear us if we move,' he hissed. And then again, more gently, his hand sliding from my navel, 'May I?'

'I don't know.'

'Don't know what?'

'If you may.'

'Have you never—?'

'It's not that,' I said, although it was, at least in part.

'Have you let other guys?'

'Well, I—' There was, I felt, a right answer to this query, something between prude and slut, between 'no' and 'yes'. Honesty didn't enter into it. 'That's for me to know and you to find out,' I said.

'So may I? Go on.'

'Sh.' The others, or at least a few of them, were clambering from the water, raining their drippings unpleasantly upon us, laughing aloud now and jeering at Laure, whose clothes Thierry, in a gesture of love (poor Cécile!) had thrown into the deep end. Wily Thibaud chose to take my silence as acquiescence: he slipped his hand uninvited into my underpants, and began, inexpertly, to mash his fingers in the folds of my sex, a manoeuvre he compounded by stopping my mouth with his ardent tongue.

'That's nice, isn't it?' he muttered in my ear as his finger crept, snail-like, inside me. 'You're not sorry?'

His hip bone crushed my thigh. His fingers were cold in so warm a place, and his manipulations felt exploratory, even clinical; or perhaps it was merely the unlikeliness of this boy's hand in this position—of me, of us, in this position. 'So this,' I thought, 'is what it's like.' Afraid, above all, of disclosure, I didn't utter a sound.

We couldn't, from our vantage, have seen the skirmish on my grandparents' terrace. The others could have, but didn't, or not until too late. Our first awakening was the report of the gun—a massive cracking sound that bloomed into wild screams and symphonic wailing. We later learned that the bullet had struck the wooden

Claire Messud

railing just above us, scattering both shrapnel and splinters.

I heard my grandmother shrieking, far away, 'My God, my God, Jacques!' and Cécile's voice, recognizable only by its pitch, a keening chant overlaying the others' yelps: 'Fuck, oh fuck, oh fuck.' I didn't hear my grandfather at all. His rage was concentrated entirely in the rifle blast; it had no other voice.

Thibaud was off me, and I was struggling with my jeans, still tingling and engorged. 'Jesus,' he said, and even in that moment when nobody was listening for us, I waved him silent. 'But what happened?'

I didn't go to my friends. I couldn't. Doomed on all sides: by my parents, if discovered; and, among my peers, an assassin by association. Thibaud took off at a run, but not before he promised (the quietest whisper) not to betray me. Incredibly, the black sea still glittered ahead, rising and falling unabated, and I lurked there, by the porthole, listening.

'He's crazy. Completely crazy.'

'He'll pay for this.'

'You bet he will.'

'Christ, Cécile, you OK?'

'I'm hit—on the arm'—Thierry, in tears—'I'm *bleeding*.'

'Look at Cécile's back, for Chrissakes!'

'Are you joking? Can you see anything?'

'Somebody get an ambulance! Call the police!'

'Can you walk? She can walk, I think.'

'Just about.'

'Call the fucking cops. Murderer. I'll get my mom.'

'Where'd he go?'

'Where can he go? They'll get him. We all *saw* him. Jesus fuck.'

'He's insane. He'll go to jail for this.'

'I'm *bleeding*.'

'It's a scratch, Thierry. Cécile, can you walk? Where are her clothes? Where are my clothes? We can't take her naked.'

'We shouldn't take her anywhere. Wait for the ambulance.'

'Don't be ridiculous. This is crazy. I can't believe this is happening.'

'Should we wash her off?'

'In the pool? Don't be sick. Cécile, Cécile sweetie, talk to me. Can you walk as far as the driveway, for the ambulance?'

'Who's going to tell her parents?'

'Fuck, her parents. Where are they?'

'In the hotel, you nit. Stop blubbering.'

'I think I'd better go to hospital too.'

'Whatever—look, I can't believe this. My God.'

And then the sound of Marie-Jo's mother, out of breath, almost hysterical, and close behind her other voices, men's and women's, huge torches jerking and swinging and a dawning like daybreak overhead as they inspected Cécile's blood-dripped, shrapnel-scattered back under the glare.

'There's no bullet hole. The bullet's not in her,' said a man, someone's father. 'For God's sake, get her parents.'

At which point I crept away, skirting the paths, ducking in the undergrowth at the sound of footsteps, hidden behind an oleander bush by the gate as the ambulance careened past, all red lights and honking. Once on the road, I ran. I sped the half a mile as though I were invisible, as though I or it weren't there at all, as though I were guilty, with Thibaud's spit tasting now like blood in my mouth, and a voice pounding in my head with every footfall, 'It didn't happen. It didn't happen. This never happened. It didn't happen.'

And in the door, and up the stairs, and first I crawled under my bed and cried, and then I stood up and took off my clothes and went into my bathroom and brushed my teeth furiously without running the water (it didn't happen, it didn't happen), and I put on my nightgown and lay in my bed staring out at the sinking moon, willing it all away, pretending I was asleep. But the lemony smell of Thibaud's skin was on my skin, now; and when my mother woke me the next morning (softly, softly, things were that bad), I knew it was all true. □

GRANTA

HOW PINKIE KILLED A MAN

Adewale Maja-Pearce

It was two years since I'd been in Zambia and I was looking forward to seeing Ronnie and his cousin, Pinkie. I arrived in Lusaka early in the morning and checked into the hotel before heading to their place to let them know I was around. On my way out of the hotel I ran into Leonard. He was one of the money-changers I had used on my previous visits and he was instantly recognizable by his limp. He seemed perplexed when I told him where I was going.

'So you didn't hear?' he said.

'Hear what?'

'About Ronnie,' he said in his high-pitched voice. 'He's dead. He died of AIDS.'

'I didn't know,' I said.

'Yes,' he said, nodding his head. 'More than a year now.' He frowned. 'Who was telling me?' He shook his head. 'I can't remember. Anyway, Ronnie's dead.' He paused a moment. 'Everybody is dying of AIDS,' he continued. 'Only yesterday I went to the hospital and one of the patients called out to me. I didn't recognize him until he told me his name. He was thin like this,' he said, holding up his little finger. 'And he used to be big. It's terrible.'

I tried to take in what he was telling me but all I could think about was Ronnie laughing as he explained to me that Leonard used to be a pickpocket until one day he was caught and beaten up, which was how he had got his limp. On the other hand he may have contracted polio as a child. You could never tell with Ronnie.

'Anyway, Pinkie can tell you,' he said. 'I hear he got married to a girl from Tanzania. Come, I'll give you a lift.' He pointed to a decent-looking Toyota saloon parked across the road.

'Since when?' I asked.

'Two months,' he said. 'From South Africa. They gave me a good price.' It seemed that he knew a man who was in with one of the gangs of carjackers in Johannesburg. I had heard about those gangs. They usually shoot their victims at traffic lights in broad daylight to avoid any unnecessary arguments.

'But the windscreen is broken,' I said as I got in.

'I've ordered a new one,' he said. 'It should be here any day now.'

As soon as he dropped me off I saw that everything had changed. The front gate had been fixed, there was a new zinc roof over the front porch, the extensive garden had been cleared of junk and planted with corn, tomatoes, avocados... Inside, the kitchen was a proper kitchen and not just a long table with two wooden benches on either side and a cooker in the corner you'd rather not examine too closely. There were curtains on the windows. It was now a real home, and not just a convenient shelter for passing coloureds from Harare, Gaborone and Jo'burg, which was how Ronnie had liked it.

Pinkie took me around the back and pointed to a stool under an avocado tree. He rolled a *skaaf*.

'So you heard what happened?' he said. 'I wanted to write to you but I couldn't find your address.'

Pinkie smiled—Pinkie was always smiling—and watched me in silence as I pulled on the draw.

'One morning he started complaining that he wasn't feeling well and the next thing he collapsed,' he said. 'At first I thought it was malaria. Ronnie used to suffer a lot from malaria. There were a couple of times in the past I thought I had lost him. Anyway, I took him to the hospital and they did a blood test.' He paused for a moment. 'They confirmed that he was HIV positive. From then on Ronnie was confined to his bed because his feet swelled up to twice their size and he couldn't walk.'

'How long before he died?' I asked.

'Seven months. He fell ill in April and died in November.'

Pinkie stood up and reached for an avocado, which were just then in season. He handed it to me.

'That was when I killed a man,' he said abruptly, and watched me again with his green eyes. Pinkie had the most beautiful green eyes. He once told me that he had inherited them from his mother, a coloured woman from Cape Town who had somehow ended up marrying a Zambian.

'What happened?' I asked.

'It was about three in the morning. I was fast asleep when suddenly I was woken by Ronnie calling out that somebody was trying to steal the television set through the open window. You remember we never used to have a TV? I bought it along with a video recorder so Ronnie could watch movies while he was in bed. It made a big difference to him, you know, just lying there in bed, day in, day out.' He laughed. 'By the time Ronnie died he had gone through all the videos in the shop. Anyway, when I heard Ronnie shouting that this guy was trying to steal the TV I got really mad. I ran out of the house in my shorts—no shoes even—in time to see him making for the bottom of the garden. I caught up with him just as he was about to scale the fence.'

Just then Pinkie's wife came out with a saucer of biscuits. She was slight, fair-skinned, nineteen years old. She smiled and put down the saucer and returned to the house.

'I was mad,' Pinkie repeated, clenching his fists with the recollection; 'I hardly even knew what I was doing at the time. I dragged him to the front yard and tied him to an old bedstead with some wire. And then I beat him and beat him and beat him. I swear, I was mad as hell, you know, with Ronnie dying and his mum in the house. She had come all the way from Switzerland so she could be with him when he died. They used to scream at each other all the time. Anyway, it got to me, you know. I was just hitting on the guy, bam, bam, bam, until my fists were sore and then Ronnie's mum came out and started begging me that it was enough so I left him right there and went back to bed.'

The next thing, he said, it was daybreak and he heard the neighbours in his compound. They were beating the guy.

'As soon as they saw him tied up there they decided he must have been the one who was stealing in the area over the last few months,' Pinkie said. 'But even if he wasn't the one they had decided that he would pay for it anyway as a lesson to others.'

Pinkie's wife called him from the house. While he was away I kept thinking I would soon hear Ronnie's distinctive voice coming round the corner. He had a loud voice which seemed to come from deep in the back of his throat. Pinkie returned with two mugs of tea.

'You should have seen it, man,' he continued. 'Blood everywhere. I told them to stop but by then you could see that the guy was in serious shit so we untied him and dragged him out to the road. I didn't want him in my compound, you know? And then we thought that we couldn't just leave him there like that so we decided I should go to the police station and tell them we'd found a thief. I could tell them we'd beaten him because we caught him stealing.

They couldn't blame anybody for that. So that's what I did. I told them it looked like the guy needed help so they better come and collect him but I wasn't going to sign any papers.' Pinkie smiled and shook his head. 'No man,' he said, 'I wasn't going to sign no fucking papers, I can tell you.'

It took the police a couple of hours to come, Pinkie said, because first they had to wait for the morning shift to arrive, and then when the shift eventually rocked up they couldn't find a van, and when they eventually found a van it wouldn't start so Pinkie had to fix it. Pinkie was good at fixing things. That was how he made his money. The whites preferred to use him because they couldn't trust the blacks who would say they could do something when they knew perfectly well that they couldn't. Anyway, when the police finally made it they just threw the guy in the back of the van without any ceremony so his head hit the floor with a bang but everybody could see by then that he was dead. Still, they had to take him to the hospital so they could certify that he really was dead but they didn't insist that Pinkie sign any papers. A thief who was caught stealing must expect a beating, after all. Most thieves who were caught died as a result.

Pinkie fell silent for a moment. 'He was a young man, very black with bushy hair,' he continued. 'He couldn't have been more than twenty years old. Probably he couldn't find work so he started stealing to survive. Things are tough these days.' He paused again as he sipped his tea. 'I'm sorry it happened but I guess it just got to me, Ronnie dying and all the tensions and everything.'

I still couldn't properly take in what Pinkie was telling me.

'I miss him,' Pinkie continued. 'You know what I mean because you understood him. A lot of people didn't understand him. They didn't see how gentle he was because of the way he used to behave, shouting at people and everything. The real Ronnie was very gentle, wouldn't hurt a fly.'

It was true. Where Pinkie came across as soft-spoken and courteous, Ronnie was loud and rough. If someone had told me that one of them was destined to kill a man I would have guessed Ronnie, although putting it like this might be unfair to him.

Pinkie started rolling another *skaaf*. I looked around.

'You've done a lot in the garden,' I said.

Adewale Maja-Pearce

'I decided to do something about the place on the very day that we buried Ronnie. You remember I used to talk about planting vegetables and stuff? And it helps a lot with the food bill.'

A light breeze rustled the trees and I recalled the first time I met Ronnie. It was during my second visit to Zambia about five years before. I was drinking in the half-empty bar of my hotel when this tall, stockily built coloured man came striding in like someone on an urgent mission. Ronnie never walked, even when he wasn't going anywhere in particular. He paused in the middle of the bar long enough for anybody who was around to take notice of him, then turned and nodded to me—I was the only other coloured in the bar—and went over to a black man sitting on his own at a table nearby.

'You fucking black people,' he said; 'why don't you fuck off back to the bush?' He stood over him, not frowning but not smiling either, and I knew he was doing it entirely for my benefit.

'Ronnie, I've warned you before,' the man retorted, putting down his glass.

'Fucking monkey,' Ronnie said.

'Don't let me warn you again...' the man started saying, whereupon Ronnie suddenly burst out laughing and clapped him on the shoulder. 'Hey, *mena*, relax, what the fuck's the matter with you? Why can't you black people take a joke? Always serious, serious.' He laughed again and then, without so much as a by-your-leave, he plonked himself at my table and shouted for the waiter to bring him a beer now, at once, this minute.

That was Ronnie all over, as I discovered in the course of the evening. He would push you so far and then, before you could take umbrage, he would pretend that it was all a joke. Those who knew him took it in their stride; those who didn't were quickly disarmed by the unexpected about-turn; but neither was ever quite sure whether he really meant the insult or not. Perhaps he didn't know himself, although I never saw him behave in that way to anyone he really liked. Later, I came to see his behaviour as part of his restlessness, the sense that he was living in a small place with limited possibilities but lacking the drive to try his chances elsewhere. He had only ever travelled out of Lusaka once, a couple of years before, when his mother sent him a ticket to visit her in Switzerland. He stayed a month. He didn't much like it there, he said, it was too clean and ordered. They used to hose down the streets every night, he said in disbelief, and if you played loud music after a certain time at night the police would come and tell you to turn it off. He preferred Zambia, he said, where you could do what you liked.

I used to visit Lusaka a lot in those days and we used to hang out together all the time. He never had any money because, unlike Pinkie, he never did any work, but that didn't bother me. He never tried to con me and because he knew his way around and had plenty of time on his hands he ended up saving me money in taxi fares. He was good at keeping out of the way when I was interviewing people for my own work, and afterwards we'd hit the bars. Pinkie, who didn't have any head for drink, also laid off the women because even in those days people were falling sick and dying. Not that Pinkie said anything. He never preached at anyone, just went his own way, and if we rocked up at the cabin the worse for wear and he was around he would more often than not get some graze together. Pinkie could cook, although it was always the same: mealie meal and greens. Occasionally, I'd give him money to buy a chicken and then we'd have a real feast. They were good days.

'It was only a month after you left that Ronnie fell ill,' Pinkie said, passing me the joint. 'It went on for so long that sometimes I wished he would just hurry up and die. Do you know what I mean?'

'Yes,' I said, but of course I didn't know what it was like to spend seven months watching your cousin die. 'How old was he?' I asked. It had only just struck me that I didn't know Ronnie's age. I just had the impression that he was younger than me.

'Thirty-three,' Pinkie said.

He was even younger than I had thought.

'It was dreadful,' he said. 'Sometimes he would become unconscious and we'd take him to the hospital and then he would come round and we'd take him home again. I don't know how many times that happened. And then one day the doctor said that he wouldn't last much longer and we should leave him there. From then on I used to visit him every day after work and just sit with him. We would talk about the old times. Ronnie would remember something that happened and then he would ask me if I remembered. Mostly I did and then we'd talk about it, him remembering this part, me remembering that. All kinds of shit I thought I had forgotten.'

He paused a moment.

'I was with him when he died,' he continued. 'I had just arrived at the hospital. Maybe he was even waiting for me. As soon as I sat down beside his bed he opened his eyes and whispered that he was having difficulty breathing and that he couldn't see anything, and then he just sort of went.'

Pinkie was silent for a while. I recalled that this was almost the same spot I had last been with Ronnie. It was about eleven in the morning. I was on my way to the airport and I got the taxi to stop because I figured I still had enough time before my flight. Ronnie had only just woken up. He was sitting in his shorts rolling a *skaaf*. I remember how we'd smoked in silence and then how he'd walked me to the taxi and how I'd told him that I'd be back the following year, except that I didn't make it for some reason or other. Not that it would have mattered.

'So that's how it was,' Pinkie said finally. 'It was tough watching him die and he and his mother screaming at each other all the time. I guess it just got to me. I didn't mean to kill that guy who was trying to steal the television. Nobody should die because of a TV, should they?'

'Anyway, it happened,' I said as reassuringly as I could.

'I just lost control of myself,' he said. 'If I could go back and undo it I would, but I can't. I just have to live with it, that's all.'

I stood up. The sun was overhead and I had some appointments to make.

'So when are you coming to eat with us?' he asked. 'My wife wants to cook you something from her place.'

We agreed on the following evening.

'I should show you Ronnie's grave,' he said as he drove me back to my hotel. 'One of our cousins carved the headstone. It was nice, real nice.'

In the event, we didn't make it. This was partly my doing. I generally avoid funerals and cemeteries and all the paraphernalia surrounding death. □

GRANTA

THE SNOW GEESE
William Fiennes

Two years ago I took the train to Blackpool to congratulate my brother on his engagement. We ended up spending the night in a hotel called the De Vere, a modern place on the outskirts of town, with full conference facilities. The Derby County football team had just arrived for a training weekend. The De Vere even had a library, stocked with the sort of arcane titles one finds only in such purely decorative reading rooms. These books had been salvaged from attics, boot sales and defunct institutions. They had been bought as job lots and delivered musty in tea chests. The books were desirable not for their cargo of story, image and idea but for their efficacy as features of interior design. The antique rimpling of morocco-bound spines was clearly intended to evoke a life of butlers, heirlooms and imperial progress. What the designer wished to say was, *This is a place to which gentlemen may retire with cigars.*

The conjunction of volumes was so bizarre that I jotted down some of the titles on the back of our bill the next morning: *Living Machinery* by A. V. Hill; *Quebec, Historic Seaport*; volume five of *The Works of John Ruskin*; Praeger's *Wagner as I Knew Him*; Townsend's *Biography of His Holiness Pope Pius XI*; volume eight of the *Harmsworth Self-Educator*; *Higher Mathematics for Chemical Students* by J. R. Partington; *The Factorial Analysis of Human Ability* by Godfrey Thomson; volume six of Buckle's *Life of Disraeli*; and, crucially, volumes eleven to seventeen of *The West of Scotland Agricultural College Annual Reports*.

I was to root out that list a few months later, after I went to visit my parents at a hotel near Chepstow. This hotel had a library, too, and its catalogue was more than a match for the De Vere's. In addition to a heated swimming pool and two tennis courts, guests had at their disposal a complete set of Sully's memoirs; G. Marañon's *La Evolución de la sexualidad y los estudios intersexuales*; Carl Stormer's *De L'Espace à L'Atome*; an Anglo-Burmese dictionary; the complete works of Heinrich Heine; and Louis Leprince-Ringuet's *Les Rayons Cosmiques*. One whole shelf was devoted to editions of the *Dublin Review* from the 1890s; volumes in which one might be lucky enough to find, say, a short biographical sketch of Richard Monckton Milnes, Lord Houghton, or an essay on 'English Catholics and the Social Question'.

The management were not resting on their laurels: on top of this marvellous educational resource, the hotel was hosting the Welsh Women's Open Golf Championship. I'm not much into golf, but it was no small delight to get up early in the morning and wander down to the practice tees to watch the women loosen up their swings in the breeze coming off the Brecon Beacons. By seven o'clock, six women would be lined up at the tees with a supply of balls spilling from buckets tipped on the grass behind them. Lollipop signs marked out each fifty yards down the fairway, at the end of which I could just make out the snooker baize of the green, planted, like the moon, with its single flag. Next to the buckets of balls stood two-tone leather bags emblazoned with the logos of sponsors (Ping, Wilson, Choice) and the players' names printed in a font intended to give the illusion of freehand. The women drew clubs from the bags with the nonchalance of archers.

Caddies stood next to the bags: old men with shrewd, weathered faces and spectacles hanging from their necks on braided strings. Each caddy stood ready with a towel, and when his pro complained of a dirty club head or perspiring hands he'd step forward, holding out the white cloth like a votive offering.

The women wore what amounted to a uniform: white socks, buttoned-up polo shirts, baggy shorts in tartan or gingham, and neat studded shoes that clacked on the paved walkways of the country club. The women's sleek, tanned calves resembled fresh tench attached to the backs of their shins. Their hair was streaked blonde and furled into chignons that poked through the apertures at the rear of their baseball caps. Some of them spurned the cap and wore no more than a tinted perspex visor. Sunglasses were parked on top of the visor.

There was something musical to this rehearsal: the rhythm of the swing, the thwack of woods and irons through the dimpled balls. As the women pulled the clubs back over their heads their forward knees gave in the slightest genuflection but their heads remained absolutely still, all their concentration focused on the ball as the swing unwound in a circle whose centre was the drive's sound. Only when the swing was complete did they allow their gaze to lift, to watch the trajectory they'd coined, following the arc of the ball as it fell beneath the fretwork of distant pylons.

It was after such a morning display that I discovered the library. These books, like those at the De Vere, had not been accumulated over time; they had been brought in all at once to lend the room with its comfortable chairs and oatmeal lampshades an ambience of study that was entirely spurious. Browsing the shelves, I was surprised to find myself pausing at an insubstantial-looking volume, a book that was not exotic or abstruse but that had once been part of my life, a story I remembered. The volume's slender fawn spine was barely wide enough to contain the title or the author's name: *The Snow Goose*, by Paul Gallico. I pulled out the book and settled back into one of the armchairs, as perhaps the golfers would themselves settle back after a long day out on the course, winding down with a drink and a back issue of the *Dublin Review*.

At school, aged ten or eleven, we had been read this story by a teacher called Mr Roberts. Mr Roberts was a kind, tall man with a red face who wore sunglasses indoors for genuine optometric reasons. His upper teeth pointed in many different directions, like a diagram of sunbeams. Mr Roberts loved the Arthurian novels of T. H. White, and he loved these slim novellas by the American writer Paul Gallico, and it was clear even then that in the empty lessons right at the end of term there was nothing he liked more than to forget the syllabus and read us a story. And one of the stories he read was Paul Gallico's *The Snow Goose: A Story of Dunkirk*.

Gallico's novella opens on the Essex coast, somewhere in the Great Marsh between Chelmbury and Wickaeldroth, a desolate region of half-submerged meadowlands, saltings, mudflats and tidal pools. The Great Marsh is home to wildfowlers and oystermen, and the resort of huge numbers of wild geese, gulls, teal, widgeon, mallard, redshanks, dunlins and curlews. At the end of an old sea wall, at the mouth of the River Aelder, stands an abandoned lighthouse in which, since 1930, a man called Philip Rhayader has made his home.

Rhayader is 'a painter of birds and of nature, who, for reasons, had withdrawn from all human society'. He is a hunchback; his left arm is 'crippled, thin and bent at the wrist, like the claw of a bird'. He is repellent to women. Yet his heart is 'filled with pity and understanding' and he is an artist of great talent, so 'uncompromising' that he hoards his work in the remote lighthouse, thinking it unworthy of public appraisal. His is the condition of all romantic adolescents: his beauty is not noticed by the world. So he spends his time painting, taking out his sixteen-foot sailing boat, and tending to the wild geese and ducks that flock to his lighthouse as if to a sanctuary. In the spring these migrants 'answer the call of the north' and in the autumn they return; Rhayader is comforted by the thought 'that implanted somewhere in their beings was the germ knowledge of his existence and his safe haven'.

One day in 1933, a young girl called Frith, 'as eerily beautiful as a marsh faery', brings Rhayader a snow goose that has been shot by a hunter. As Rhayader's arm is like 'the claw of a bird', so Frith is 'nervous and timid as a bird'. This is imagery's way of saying, *They are made for each other*. Frith thinks of Rhayader as an 'ogre' but knows that he has the 'magic that could heal injured things'. While the ogre bandages the bird's wing and fits a fine splint to its broken leg, he tells the marsh faery that the snow goose was born 'in a northern land far, far across the seas, a land belonging to England'. This is ogre-speak for 'Canada'. He explains that the bird had been caught up in a storm and blown across the Atlantic to the Great Marsh, where it had promptly been shot down by a poacher.

Rhayader christens the snow goose 'The Lost Princess' and cares for it through the winter at his sanctuary. Frith visits regularly. In the spring, the goose flies away with the other migrants and Frith's visits come to an end. Rhayader misses her. The goose returns in October, having 'summered in Greenland or Spitsbergen'. As the years go by, the goose returns to the lighthouse each autumn, and Frith comes to visit the sensitive hunchback with his paintings and his devoted birds.

Time passes. War breaks out across the Channel. Frith becomes a young woman. She finds herself frightened by 'the power of the unspoken things between them'. In 1940, at the end of May, she comes across Rhayader loading supplies into his sailboat. He is getting ready to join the ramshackle fleet of ferries, trawlers, yachts and pleasure craft that crossed the Channel to rescue the Allied Forces from the beaches of Dunkirk. 'Men are huddled on the beaches like hunted birds,' he tells Frith. He's like a bird, she's like a bird: all the vulnerable souls of the world are birds. To Frith, Rhayader is 'no longer ugly or misshapen or grotesque, but very beautiful'. When he sets sail for France, the snow goose flies with him.

Gallico continues the story by means of a conversation between two soldiers in a pub in London's East End. They are remembering the retreat from Dunkirk. They both recall a man in a small sailboat making repeated journeys under heavy fire, ferrying seven men at a time from the beach to an excursion scow waiting in the deeper water, the little boat accompanied at all times by 'a bloomin' goose'. To one of the soldiers, Rhayader looked like 'the good Lord...like the pictures from the Sunday-school books, wiv 'is white face and dark eyes an' beard an' all'. The goose looked like 'a bloomin' hangel of mercy'.

In an officers' club in Brook Street, a retired naval commander also recollects the events at Dunkirk. Gallico shifts to his upper-class register. The words 'dashed', 'chap', and 'queer' appear frequently. Commander Keith Brill-Oudener remembers coming across a derelict small boat in which a man lay dead, machine-gunned. A wild goose perched on the rail of the boat, as if in vigil over the body of the dead man. When the little boat was sunk by a mine, the goose circled three times overhead, 'like a plane saluting', before flying off to the West.

Frith is waiting at the lighthouse. She knows that Rhayader will not return. The sight of the snow goose approaching releases 'the surging, overwhelming truth of her love': the bird seems to her to be 'the soul of Rhayader taking farewell of her before departing for ever'. (In Plato's *Phaedo*, Socrates compares his own impending death to the departure of a swan.) Some weeks after Dunkirk, a German pilot mistakes the lighthouse for a military objective and blows Rhayader's life's work to oblivion.

I read the story in the ersatz library while the tournament got under way outside. It was almost fifteen years since Mr Roberts had read the novella in class: now I was suspicious of its sentiment and the heavy-handedness of its religious allegory. I was alert to the story's obvious debt to *Beauty and the Beast* and resistant to the easy portentousness of its abstract nouns. But I couldn't quite dismiss it altogether, drawn not by the love story or the cute healing of the bird, but by the seriousness with which the novella treats the idea of home—the geese migrating from summer home to winter home; the snow goose losing its way home and finding another home; Rhayader killed while taking part in the enterprise of bringing people home.

I should have remembered the book the previous autumn, when I'd actually *seen* the geese. I was working on a master's degree in Washington, and an article in the weekend edition of the *Post* gave me the idea of driving out to Delaware's Atlantic shore to see the flocks of snow geese. Delaware's coastal flatlands are a winter home for thousands of geese whose breeding grounds lie in the eastern Canadian tundra. They arrive from the cold north each October and settle in colonies of between 1,000 and 150,000 pairs. Their white plumage, relieved only by black wing-tips, means they cannot rely on camouflage to avoid detection when nesting and feeding: they depend on the sheer number of individuals in each colony to detect and deter predators.

The highway out of Washington was flanked with strip-malls, gas stations and motels: shabby inns with hoardings promising holiday specials, cable television and free local telephone calls. I passed through a toll gate, and the road began to rise on the suspension bridge over Chesapeake Bay, the long arc of the bridge like the parabola of a golf ball struck from shore to shore. The bridge went on and on. Cars travelled its length like beads of oil moving along a high wire. The water below glittered in the October sun. There were yachts out from Annapolis and training vessels out from the naval academy and all the sailboats were pleasingly keeling in the fall wind. I couldn't keep my eyes on the road. I wanted to look out over the bay, at the sky beyond the steel fretting of the bridge. The highway's slow, shallow descent felt like the landing of a glider. And then we were on the eastern shore, back among the real-estate developments and motel hoardings.

The land flattened to a plain as I got further east. I remember clapboard houses in their own neat plots, white church spires and telegraph wires threading the claws of crows and starlings. I had been driving for several hours by the time I reached Smyrna. I stopped at a diner for lunch, a place with booths, springy leatherette seating and an array of deep-dish pies in a cold cabinet. The waitress served a slice of cherry pie to an old man sitting alone in the booth next to

mine, a man she addressed as Mr Harris. As she put the plate down
before him she said, 'My goodness, they could be blueberries, they're
so dark, these cherries.' A boy, sitting up at the luncheon counter,
said to his friend, 'Oh man, they've run out of straws! What kind
of a life is this?'

There was another Smyrna in the Old World: the city in
southern Turkey now known as Izmir, famed as the birthplace of
Homer, who had opened book three of *The Iliad* with an image of
migrating birds:

> Now with the squadrons marshalled, captains leading each,
> the Trojans came with cries and din of war like wildfowl
> when the long hoarse cries of cranes sweep on against the sky
> and the great formations flee from winter's grim ungodly storms,
> flying in force, shrieking south to the Ocean gulfs, speeding
> blood and death to the Pygmy warriors, launching at daybreak
> savage battle down upon their heads.

Mr Harris got up from his booth. He wore a grey tweed jacket,
check shirt and charcoal slacks, and, once standing, he put on a grey
hat with a black felt band. He walked out of the diner and got into
his car, a maroon Ford Crown Victoria. Then, before driving off, he
sat very still with his head lowered, as if taking a nap or uttering a
silent prayer. He was squinting as he drove out of the lot, screwing
his face up against the sun.

I left soon afterwards. It wasn't far from Smyrna to the wildlife
reserve at Bombay Hook, a protected area of marshland right at the
edge of America. I left the car at the visitors' centre: I'd been driving
for too long and needed to walk. Other cars were cruising along the
gravel tracks that run through the reserve, circling the ponds where
the birds congregate. The cold wind tautened the skin on my face
and made my lips numb. The flat, empty landscape had the
desolation of Gallico's description of the Great Marsh: Bombay Hook
felt like the limit of the known world. Somewhere to the east,
imperceptibly, the sea began.

I found the snow geese on Raymond Pond: thousands of the
white birds in a dense flock, a drift of snow across the water. The
colony made a tremendous noise; a furious, vibrant gabble, a noise

pitched somewhere between the gossip of schoolgirls and the percussion of industrial machines. Now and again a breakaway troupe of geese rose up from the colony and flew away in loosely flexing skeins. Some of the skeins joined other skeins of geese, the black lines of birds crossing and linking to form the shapes of Chinese ideograms, the characters for *south* and *winter* and *home*.

The earth's axis is not perpendicular to the plane of the earth's orbit around the sun. We are tilted at about 23.5 degrees. The tilt means that the northern hemisphere is slanted away from the sun during the winter half of the year, and towards the sun during the summer half. The tilt gives us our seasons: annual changes in environmental conditions to which animals must adapt if they are to survive and reproduce. Migration is a response to this periodicity.

Every year, short-finned eels swim 2,000 miles from the Pacific islands of New Caledonia to the rivers of south-east Australia. For the first stage of this journey they are no more than transparent eel larvae drifting on the currents among salps, siphonophores, sea butterflies and the ghostly, phosphorescent creatures called comb jellies. Monarch butterflies leave the mountains of the Sierra Madre in Mexico to fly north across America to the Great Lakes. Grey whales, each one longer than a bus, make an annual round trip of almost ten thousand miles from the lagoons of Baja California through the Bering Straits to the Chukchi Sea. Even plankton undertake daily vertical migrations, following light and food and warmth up and down the rungs of fathoms.

These journeys are all surpassed by the scale and complexity of the migrations undertaken by birds. Each autumn thousands of turkey vultures leave North America and funnel through the Isthmus of Panama, returning north so punctually the following spring that the residents of Hinckley, Ohio, hold a festival to celebrate their arrival each 15 March. At about the same time, ospreys leave central and eastern Russia, heading south for Thailand, Malaysia, Borneo and the Philippines. After summer breeding in eastern Europe and central Siberia, red-footed falcons cross the Black and the Caspian and the Mediterranean seas on their way to the savannahs of south-eastern Africa. Demoiselle cranes pass over the Himalayas and down the valleys of Nepal en route from Siberia to their Indian winter grounds.

Bar-headed geese have been recorded flying higher than Mount Everest as they make their annual pilgrimage from the mountain lakes of central Asia to their winter homes in the Indus valley. A Rüppell's griffon vulture once got into the jet engine of a plane 37,000 feet above the Ivory Coast. Such collisions, so-called 'bird strikes', are a particular problem in Israel, a small country with a high density of migrating birds and a large number of military and civilian aircraft in a confined space. Some species keep low to slip beneath the winds, as fighter planes will underfly the cover of radar.

In the Pacific region, the lesser golden plover, the knot, the great knot and Latham's snipe have all been recorded making non-stop flights of 3,000 to 4,000 miles. The tiny ruby-throated hummingbird flies more than 600 miles across the Gulf of Mexico without a break. The record-holders are the Arctic terns. These birds nest around the fringes of the Arctic, on the most northerly lands in the world. Each autumn, after breeding, the terns fly all the way to the Antarctic, where they are reported roosting on ice floes and fishing for krill at the edge of the pack ice. They might travel an annual distance of 25,000 miles—roughly equivalent to the circumference of the earth. The terns that breed on the islands north of the Arctic Circle experience the twenty-four hours of daylight that occur there in the summer months, and then fly south to the same conditions in the Antarctic summer, enjoying more hours of daylight in a year than any other creature on earth.

Our understanding of how birds accomplish such incredible journeys—how they know when to go and where to go, and how they have the strength to get there—remains incomplete. The study of bird migration began with Aristotle in the third century BC. In *Historia Animalium VIII*, Aristotle recorded the migrations of cranes, pelicans, quail, doves, swans and geese. But he also promoted two theories that would prove to be false trails: the ideas of 'hibernation'—that swallows, starlings, storks and thrushes didn't migrate at all, just hid themselves somewhere cosy until the weather improved—and 'transmutation'—which explained the seasonal disappearance of certain species and the simultaneous appearance of others by suggesting that one had simply turned into the other. The

Roman naturalist Pliny agreed with Aristotle on both these points.

Later it would be widely held that swallows spent the winter submerged in lakes and rivers. Fishermen were said to have brought up nets full of swallows. Cuvier thought it beyond any doubt that the martin 'passes the cold season under water at the bottom of marshes'. A pamphlet published in 1703 declared that swallows flew to the moon at the end of September, 'for she is the fairest object to draw their inclination'.

The modern study of bird migration began with the First International Ornithological Congress, held in Vienna in 1884. The congress resolved to record bird migration systematically with the help of a large number of observatories and a methodical programme of ringing or banding. Observatories were established on the island of Heligoland in the North Sea; at Rossitten, on the Courish Spit in East Prussia; at Cape May, Connecticut; at Hawk Mountain, Pennsylvania; at Falsterbo in southern Sweden. The first atlas of bird migration, compiled by Schuz and Weigold, was published in 1931.

Birds today are tracked not only by ringing or banding but also by radar, with migrant swarms appearing as clouds on radar screens, each bird's echo a single point of light. Birds are monitored by radio tags, tracked across the globe by satellites. It is a huge project of observation: in North America alone, more than one and a half million birds are ringed every year. But the numbers of nocturnal migrants are still estimated by counting the silhouettes that pass across the white face of the moon.

Are these great journeys examples of learned or inherited behaviour? Migratory birds held in captivity under constant environmental conditions still display the migratory restlessness known as *Zugunruhe*. *Zugunruhe* is almost exclusively expressed by 'whirring'—the generation of high-frequency wing-beats while perching. Normally placid captive birds orientate themselves in the direction that they would head if they were free to fly. In a 1988 study of the garden warbler, *Zugunruhe* was recorded and analysed using video recordings. The researchers multiplied the total time of whirring activity by the average flight speed of the species. The resulting distance would have brought the birds right to the centre of their species-specific winter quarters. The phenomenon of *Zugunruhe* implies that migratory behaviour is triggered by endogenous annual cycles known as 'circannual rhythms': the birds have a gene for going. The knowledge of where they should go is also at least in part inherited. Even juvenile birds in captivity show spontaneous directional preferences with the onset of migration: they possess an innate directional sense, an inherited inclination probably controlled by a number of different genes. This was demonstrated in experiments conducted by the Dutch ornithologist A. C. Perdeck in the 1950s. Perdeck was studying the starlings that migrate in autumn from the Baltic region south-west through the Low Countries to northern France and the British Isles. Over several years he caught and ringed thousands of starlings as they passed through the Netherlands. More than 11,000 birds were then loaded into aeroplanes and released at airports in Switzerland, 370 miles to the south-east. The results were a revelation.

No matter if they were released individually or in flocks, adult starlings, with at least one previous migration behind them, readjusted their course and headed north-west to their normal wintering grounds. But the inexperienced starlings continued along the same south-west course they had been taking along the eastern coast of the North Sea. They ended up in the south of France, in Spain, even in Portugal. The young birds, that is, flew on a fixed heading that was presumably genetically coded. The older, experienced birds had developed a navigation system that allowed them to correct mistakes.

How birds navigate over such vast distances has still not been fully explained. Birds are certainly able to 'pilot' themselves using well-known sites or landmarks such as rivers, islands and hills. Birds may also pilot according to audible landmarks: the calls of frogs in marshy areas, the sibilance of waves, and even infrasound—the fluting of wind through mountain ranges—may all be seized upon as directional cues. Wheatears almost always depart at dusk, when the setting sun pronounces 'West'. In addition to their sun, magnetic and star compasses, Professor Floriano Papi at the University of Pisa proposed an olfactory compass: his experiments in the 1970s showed that homing pigeons can be trained to respond to winds carrying a specific scent (olive oil or turpentine). It has also been hypothesized

William Fiennes

that birds may be sensitive to the smallest shifts in gravitational pull—sensitive, that is, to the Coriolis Force, the force produced by the spinning earth.

Birds of prey, pelicans, herons, storks and cranes all migrate by day because they rely on thermals: rising columns of warm air formed only when the ground has been heated by the sun. The birds rise on each column of air until the thermal weakens, then they simply glide down to the base of the next, a method known as 'thermal soaring'. White storks have been observed using the warm air that rises from the gas burn-offs at oil-drilling points in the Sahara—flocks circling above the flames at night, long after the natural thermals have disappeared, the storks riding the night thermals across the sands.

Other migrants alternate bouts of flapping with bouts of gliding on outstretched wings, a technique known as 'undulating flight'. Small birds (warblers, finches, thrushes) travel in bounds—flapping to gain altitude then folding their wings and diving in 'ballistic flight'. Albatrosses, gannets and petrels travel by 'dynamic soaring'—they glide downwind, gathering speed, then turn sharply, climbing into the breeze, using the airflow to give them lift, then turning downwind for the next glide. These birds may also be seen 'slope soaring' on the updraught of the ocean swell, exploiting the lift created by the wind rising over the hills and ridges of the sea.

Migrants may travel in swarms, in oblique lines, in echelon or V-formations. The upwash of air from a bird's wings has a lifting effect on its neighbour. In a V-formation, every bird except for the leader is assisted by the slipstream of the bird in front. Watch such formations as they pass overhead and you may see the leading bird swing out from its position and rejoin the line further back. Small birds have been observed hitching rides on the backs of larger birds; probably cases of very tired individuals executing emergency landings on convenient flying islands.

Some individuals are bound to be weaker, or just unluckier, than others. Every year, millions of birds get lost; sent off-course by adverse conditions or faulty navigation. Contrary winds are a hazard for any bird. In 1927, a lapwing ringed in northern England was swept across the Atlantic to Newfoundland. Migratory American species are often seen in the Scilly Isles off the south-west tip of England: these have probably been caught up in the westerly winds generated by depressions in the Atlantic. Warblers and vireos from the New World are often spotted in Essex. For many years, a black-browed albatross, a native of the southern oceans, spent the summer among gannets nesting on the Shetland island of Unst. The albatross even built a nest, though its chances of finding a mate were close to zero. Such errors are the raw material of evolution.

Gallico's notion of a vagrant snow goose arriving in Essex is not unfeasible. A young snow goose ringed in Canada was found in Holland in 1980, thus proving that genuine vagrants do reach Europe on occasion. But it is more likely that snow geese spotted in Essex have escaped from captivity or originated from feral (semi-tame) populations elsewhere in Britain or Europe. Two snow geese were seen at Leigh-on-Sea on 13 and 18 April, and again on 11 May 1911. One snow goose remained at Hatfield Broad Oak from 10 to 14 January 1921. A party of four snow geese was seen flying north over Great Clacton on 16 April 1982, a sighting that coincided with an influx of the birds into East Anglia and Kent. Whether these were genuine vagrants, blown across the Atlantic by unfavourable winds, is not known. So when Rhayader tells Frith that the Lost Princess was carried by storms across the ocean from that distant northern land—well, he's guessing.

Gallico's ornithology is haphazard. He describes the Great Marsh as home to an influx of migrant pink-foot geese, barnacle geese and white-front geese, none of which are common visitors to Essex. The geese that do flock to Essex in September and October, fleeing the harsh winters of Siberia, are the brent geese, around 35,000 of which overwinter in the county. Yet Gallico does not mention them. *The Snow Goose* is a fairy story and its world is a figment: Chelmbury, Wickaeldroth and the River Aelder do not exist. No one who lives along the Essex coast has ever heard of the Great Marsh. Rhayader is a village in Wales.

Gallico is probably best known today for *The Poseidon Adventure* (1969), the story of the cruise liner tipped over by a freak tidal wave, later made into a film in which Gene Hackman repeatedly hauls Shelley Winters out of water. Gallico was born in New York on 26 July 1897. He served in the First World War as a gunner with the US Navy, returning to Manhattan to spend the next twelve years as a sports editor and columnist. He liked England: for a while he took a house on a hill above Salcombe in Devon, often fishing for bass offshore. He covered the Second World War for *Cosmopolitan*, then made his home in Europe, where his following as a novelist was assured after the success of *The Snow Goose*, which appeared in 1941. After the publication of his first book of short stories, *Confessions of a Story-Teller* (1946), Gallico produced novels at the rate of approximately one a year. Hemingway, whom Gallico encountered once in a club bar, is said to have remarked, 'I wish I had written *Snow Goose*.' He died in Monte Carlo, in 1976.

I had no particular interest in Gallico, and certainly no desire to read his collected works. But his little book had spun from itself a silkline of curiosity I could not ignore, and this was why I took the train home one Saturday in March to ask my mother and father if I could borrow the car. From home I drove south-east, towards Essex. Somewhere near Beaconsfield, a flock of seven swans flew over the motorway. Near Margaretting, I saw a pair of Canada geese flying south, their long black necks stretched out like piping. Approaching Maldon, nine brent geese flew overhead in a perfect V.

I was heading for Maldon because of its rivers, the Chelmer and the Blackwater. The Chelmer reminded me of Gallico's Chelmbury, and it's at Maldon that the Blackwater begins to flare into a wide estuary where tides pull in and out of mudbanks and saltings and numerous creeks and inlets. I could see these on the map: Thirstlet Creek, Goldhanger Creek, Lawling Creek, Maryland Creek, Cooper's Creek, Steeple Creek. It seemed that on both sides of the Blackwater were areas of marshland that might correspond to Gallico's description of the Great Marsh: 'It is one of the last of the wild places of England, a low, far-reaching expanse of grass and reeds and half-submerged meadowlands ending in the great saltings and mud flats and tidal pools near the restless sea.' I wanted to find that place, and I wanted to see the migrant geese before they departed for their distant northern home.

South of Maldon, between the estuaries of the Blackwater and the Crouch, lies a small peninsula known to its inhabitants as The

Dengie Hundreds. Much of Dengie once belonged to the English Channel; sea walls were raised in the sixteenth century, and land was reclaimed from the water to be grazing marsh for sheep and cattle. I drove from Maldon through the Dengie villages of Latchingdon, Steeple and St Lawrence. Clumps of tall pampas grass grow outside the suburban homes. The road runs through parks of holiday chalets, the cream and beige prefabricated cabins laid out in rows down to the waterside. I left the car at Bradwell Marina, on the northern tip of the peninsula. The wind was strong; halliards ticked quickly against metal masts. The twin grey blocks of the Bradwell nuclear power station rose from the marshes like tombs. I walked along the grassy sea wall towards the station. The massive structure was emitting a high-pitched mechanical whirr which became more and more sinister as I approached. Above this nuclear music all I could hear were the oboe caws of gulls.

I followed the sea wall out to the mouth of the Blackwater, right out to the English Channel. Just inside the wall runs the borrowdyke—the trench made during the raising of the wall and now filled with water. Beyond this neat canal the farmland begins. Two tractors were ploughing. Saltings and short patches of shingle beach lie between the wall and the sea, and concrete pillboxes, bunkers left over from the Second World War, are embedded in the rampart at regular intervals.

After a while I came to a line of eleven rusting barges grounded on sandbanks. Birdwatchers sat on folding stools along the sea wall, training binoculars and telescopic lenses on to the sands around the useless hulls. To the north, the imposing bulk of the nuclear station loomed over the marshes and the water. To the south, another structure dominates the flat land. St Peter's Chapel was founded by Saint Cedd, a monk who sailed down the coast from Lindisfarne in 653. Cedd established a Christian community here, and built a chapel using the stones and foundations of the Roman fort of Othona. The chapel was restored in 1920, and is still a centre for 'Celtic Spirituality'—words that are printed in a fussy 'Celtic' font whenever they appear in the chapel's literature. The chapel looks like a barn, and for a time it *was* a barn: you can see, bricked-in, the holes in the side walls that once allowed the entrance of farm wagons. It's cool inside, and, in the visitors' book, children have left their verdicts on the place: 'Quiet. Lonely. Very Old. Quiet. Spooky quiet. Quiet. Quiet. Quiet.'

Standing on the sea wall near the rusting hulls, these two structures on opposing horizons made for a clamantly symbolic tableau, a topography that would not be out of place in Bunyan. To the north, the power station, the fortress of technology, monument to all the potency of the physical world. To the south, the ancient chapel, the house of God, a place for contemplation and prayer. I stood there for a while, equidistant between these two. I listened to the birdwatchers identify the black-backed gulls, redshanks and dunlins that were picking their way around the hulls of the barges.

But Dengie was not the place: the marshes here were not sufficiently riven with inlets and creeks; there needed to be a real maze of waterways for Rhayader to navigate in his sixteen-foot sailboat. So I drove to the north side of the Blackwater, and found a room in a bed-and-breakfast in Tolleshunt d'Arcy. In my room, next to the mirror on the dresser, there was a little row of books: Wilbur Smith's *A Time to Die*, Harold Robbins's *A Stone for Danny Fisher*, and, sandwiched between these two, Westergaard and Resler's *Class in a Capitalist Society*.

It was a short drive the next morning to Tollesbury and Old Hall Marshes, a wildlife reserve managed by the Royal Society for the Protection of Birds. I drove up a dirt track, across two cattle grids, through an iron gate to some farm buildings and the tiny RSPB office. The two wardens, Chris and Paul, were getting ready for a bird count later that morning. They had a computer in the office, a fax machine and shelves of files and reference books. Big windows gave the wardens a panorama of the green marshes. Chris and Paul frequently leave off what they're doing to reach for hefty binoculars and scan the flatlands beyond the glass.

'Sounds like Old Hall to me,' Chris said when I showed them the opening pages of *The Snow Goose*. 'When you mentioned *The Snow Goose*,' said Paul, 'I thought you meant the album by Camel.' I must have looked confused, for Paul immediately explained that Camel, a pop group of the 1970s, had recorded an album of music 'inspired by *The Snow Goose*'—an album that included tracks called 'Great Marsh' and 'Rhayader'. 'So it was a kind of concept album,' I said. 'Yes.' 'Like Pink Floyd?' 'Not really. Well, I won't say they're on another planet. Let's just say that Camel have a *very distinctive sound.*'

I left the office and walked out on the farm track that leads across the marshes to the sea wall. Swarms of birds lifted from the marsh as I walked, black against the grey sky, like shreds of charred paper rising from a fire. I walked up on to the grassy dyke. Beyond the wall, to the north of the reserve, saltings and mudbanks gave way to the mud of the Salcott Channel at low tide. On the southern horizon, beyond Tollesbury, the silhouette of Bradwell Power Station was stamped like a monstrous imprimatur. Clouds of lapwings were rising from the grass, flying a short distance, then settling, watched by a pert hare. Dunlins were tottering through the mud at the edge of the water, and so were curlews with their long, down-curved beaks like surgical scissors. Little mounds, the long-established hills of meadow ants, pimpled the marshes. Four brent geese flew north just a few metres above me, heading for Mersea and Brightlingsea.

I'd walked for about half an hour when I found the flock—more than a thousand brent geese gathered on the marsh around a shallow pool. Brent geese have black necks and charcoal bodies and a distinct patch of white on the tail, and the noise they made was not the raucous gabble I remembered from Bombay Hook but a low, civilized murmur, the voice of Edwardian gentlemen in a panelled library. I thought of how a snow goose would stand out in such company, its snow-white livery bright amidst the dark grey bodies of the brents. I watched as more geese flew down to join the flock, gliding down, then tilting their bodies backwards, then flapping hard in a kind of reverse thrust as the feet drop and the bird settles on the water.

This was no longer 'one of the last of the wild places of England': the power station, the post-war housing of Tollesbury and the yacht masts in Tollesbury marina all contradicted the marsh's claim to be wilderness. But so much was right—the channels and pools in the marshes, the tidal creeks, inlets and estuaries, the saltings, the dunlins and wigeon and teal and lapwings and redshanks, the oystermen still working in the nearby village of Goldhanger: all these were present in *The Snow Goose* and present here, around me. A wind blew hard from the North Sea across the bare ground. Following the sea wall round to my right, from the Salcott Channel to Tollesbury Fleet, I found a small boat moored to an orange buoy in one of the pools in the middle of the saltings. I had an idea of the skill it would take to navigate the creeks and channels to the open sea.

I drove back through Maldon and Chelmsford and round the northern suburbs of London. The motorway cuts through the Chiltern Hills into the Thames Valley, and then there was Oxford, Deddington, Milton, Bloxham, a journey I have made a thousand times. In the last few miles, my landmarks begin. I pass the dairy buildings, the almshouses, the toll cottage. Things appear in inevitable sequence. I recognize a particular arrangement of fields: the Brake, the Pike, the Bretch, the Chaddle, the Shoulder of Mutton, the Great Ground. A line of trees, the gradient of a hill, even the character of the road's turning are sources of comfort, enough to set off a glow or quickening of blood somewhere on the far edge of my noticing: a gut feeling of where I am, how close to home. □

GRANTA

BIG BOY SPORTS
Jayne Anne Phillips

K ate won the boat at Big Boy Sports' July Super Sale, where she'd gone to buy Sam a birthday present. Big Boy Sports was famous for the apple-cheeked boy-faced balloon that floated above the oversized marquee of the store. Big Boy's extremely friendly clerks and clerkettes all wore the same red baseball cap as the boy-faced balloon, and red shirts with name tags sewn above the right top pocket, like gas station attendants. A mixed metaphor of some sort, Kate concluded, baseball and gas stations, all very American, but still, baseball was not gasoline. Baseball wasn't merchandising, or it shouldn't be. She thought of buying Sam a baseball glove, supple brown leather; he would be nine years old; he should have a glove at their house, Matt's house, even if he already had one at home, his house, his mother's house. But no.

'Nerf,' she said to Alexander as she strolled him toward the store, across the parking lot.

'Bye,' he said back, 'bye bye bye.'

He was too young to say words, of course he was; they were sounds listeners heard as words, sounds he liked, sounds as sensical as the sounds he heard, sounds hands, mouth, skin that touched him were pleased to make. Kate paused once they made the sidewalk to let down the back of the stroller. Alexander, seven months old and full of milk, lay back in drowsy mid-swoon. Kate had nursed him the moment she found a parking space, motor running, air conditioning on full-tilt. 'Something Nerf,' Kate told him, 'something new and just invented.' All things Nerf were Sam's desire, plastic accoutrements and big spongy bullet/missiles; they were just the ticket, just what the doctor ordered. Kate followed doctor's orders frequently but she drew the line at guns.

'Get him what he wants,' Kate's mother had told her.

Kate and her mother often held opposing opinions. In such instances, Katherine signalled to Kate with small silences or fondly directive remarks that she, Katherine, was still senior partner in their mother/daughter enterprise.

'I can't buy him a gun,' Kate told her. 'I don't plan to buy my own son guns.'

Her mother looked up with a faint smile, eyes tired behind her glasses. 'Boys like their guns,' she counselled.

229

'I'll find some other Nerf thing,' Kate assured her, 'a big sports toy.'

And she went off to Big Boy Sports, where she'd never been, having helped her mother into bed, turned on the window fan, and filled the styrofoam pitcher with ice water. Katherine had good days, good weeks, but this week was not one of them. She'd had lunch, she would stay in bed, she would call their neighbour if she needed anything before Kate got back. She would be fine. 'Get something good,' she'd told Kate, as though stepmothering were an enviable task. Not task, Kate thought, challenge: enviable challenge, rife with spiritual surrender, preparation for anything, certainly preparation enough for Big Boy Sports.

Driving while Alexander gurgled, car seat fastened backward on the passenger seat, Kate had considered her destination; generally she avoided consumer megastores, places located miles out on four-lane highways whose sites involved vast acreage, whose products were saturation-advertised on network television she never watched and pictured on day-glo boxes of sugar cereals she wouldn't let anyone eat. Already, in addition to being the stepmother, she found herself the bad guy, censor of Twix and Kix and Twinkles and Sugar Pops. At the health food store, she bought the brightest boxes she could find, but the boys ate bagels. That was all right. Bagels were good for them, she told Matt, especially with cream cheese or (natural) peanut butter. They wanted to bring their own Jif and Sonic Booms from home. After three discussions with Matt, Kate prevailed; they left behind their rations and guns with sound effects; they brought their sponge ammunition and Nerf weapons, as long as they shot them outside. Inside, Jonah roller skated from room to room, cradling his RotoRetro-Launcher. What did RotoRetro *mean*, Kate wondered? Did the gun shoot forwards and backwards, exist in simultaneous time, create a vortex of motion or emotion? Yes, absolutely.

Sam would have none of it. He brought his gun in his father's car, then left it strategically placed across the front passenger seat, as though to reserve the best seat for the ride home. It was one more detail that wrung Kate out, as though it were about Matt; no matter how much the boys had of Matt, it wasn't enough—until she remembered how her own brothers had fought over shotgun, the shotgun seat, singular even before bucket seats, when the broad front seats of Mercurys and Chevrolets were like big couches, indestructible and bed-like, with no seat belts, as though there were no wrecks, or big curved windshields to fly through. Wrecks. She'd reached over to check the belt threaded through Alexander's car seat and nearly missed the exit, though the Big Boy balloon was clearly visible from the highway, wafting moored and bright in sunlit air over hundreds of cars whose baked rooftops shone like glinting knives.

Chimes rang as Kate walked through one of numerous sets of double doors; she wondered for a moment if some metal on the stroller had set off an alarm. But no, the chime, melodious, detached, mechanical, rang at every entry, rang now, as others entered, as a girl in a red baseball hat approached Kate and Alexander. The baby stirred. 'Shhh,' Kate murmured, moving the stroller back and forth, back and forth in place. She put her finger to her lips as the clerk reached them.

The girl smiled. Red lipstick. Beautiful teeth. Aquamarine contacts; decidedly unnatural, but attractive. 'Raffle ticket?' she whispered. 'Just fill it out and drop it in the barrel. Part of our July Super Savings. Lots of sports articles. Beach and playing field.'

They both looked down at Alexander, who closed his eyes and sighed. Kate shot the clerk a glance of grateful collusion, then asked, 'All toys for boys?'

'Oh, I get it,' the clerk said, lifting an expertly shaded brow. 'You mean, do we have toys for *girls*. Well, you know, girls *love* buying toys for boys. It's *just* about their favourite pastime.' She leaned a little closer and dropped her voice. 'You wouldn't believe the groups of girls we get in here. They rove around and try to lift things—tennis balls, water pistols.'

'All for boys, no doubt.'

'No doubt,' the clerk said.

Kate frowned dramatically. 'Or maybe they're feminist guerrillas, protesting the whole enterprise.'

The girl looked at her blankly, but Kate caught a whiff of patchouli oil, which was odd. Perhaps the make-up and perfect hair were a disguise. Kate herself had gone back to wearing her long hair in a ponytail, the better to keep it out of Alexander's mouth. 'I'm

Kelly,' the clerk said now, as though to get them back on track. She touched her name tag with bright red nails, then, practised as a stewardess, performed an ever extending, fluid gesture to indicate the barrels beside every register, the alphabetized aisles, the entire world of Big Boy Sports. The vast ceiling provided its own arc of horizon, a world aglow with fluorescent light and banners. 'Here's your form,' Kelly said musically, 'keep your stub. Next drawing in twenty minutes. You must be present to win!' She leaned closer, still sounding rehearsed. 'I'm not supposed to tell which barrel we draw from next, but it's fifteen—my station.'

'Oh, sorry,' Kate said, 'I'm in a rush. I won't be here for twenty minutes.'

'Really? You never know.' Kelly extended her perfect manicure, a form, and a tiny pencil. 'He's asleep. Take you a minute.' She turned. 'Use my shoulder.'

Kate did, writing. 'You're good at this. Do you get a commission?'

'We're supposed to pass out every ticket of every book we're assigned, but nobody checks. A lot of them,' she wrinkled her nose, 'don't bother, they toss the tickets at the end of the shift. But I figure, why not get in the spirit? Somebody's gotta win.'

'Not me,' Kate said, 'I absolutely never win anything. Born on a Saturday.'

Kelly looked perplexed.

'Works hard for a living. Remember the rhyme? Which day are you?'

'Tuesday, I think.'

'Tuesday's child is fair of face. There you go. Who needs astrology when we've got nursery rhymes?' Kate returned the pencil and resumed motion, calling back over her shoulder, 'Drop it in fifteen for me. By the way, where would I find Nerf sports things, big things? I need exact directions—I'm new here.'

'Nerf? All of Aisle Twenty-one. We've got everything! Balls, blocks, bowling sets, parachute men, sports, small weapons, big weapons—'

Kelly's voice faded. Strolling quickly, Kate reflected that she'd come to the right place. Sam's present did need to be big. Stupendous. Impressive. Compensatory, said her shadow voice. Yes, all right.

Something he would fasten on, revel in. Something to completely seduce him and blur the boundaries of the transition he and Jonah were always making, here to there, there to here, even on their birthdays. Perhaps Kate had more trouble with the coming and going than they did. Then again, how would she know? They didn't exactly talk to her. She talked to herself, or to Matt; lately she just tried to be helpful, like an assistant. Helpfulness was her new mode on Wednesdays, Fridays and Saturdays: cooking, making beds, picking up, doing all the Alexander and Katherine work so Matt could be with the boys. Mondays he took them to dinner in their suburb and came home late. He said divorced dad was a full-time career, in that he thought about it even when he wasn't doing it. Second wife, by contrast, now that she was one, seemed to Kate a rather murky situation, not quite legitimate, at least in her case. Matt couldn't relate. After all, he'd been a first husband twice. There were stepfamily counsellors, Kate knew, and an actual Stepfamily Association, with an 800 number. Kate wasn't quite ready to call. They were newly-weds, she reminded herself, all of them, she and Matt and the three kids. Even the dogs were suffering. Kate's mutt, Luna, liked Matt's boys but visibly drooped in Alexander's presence, venting her distress on Katrina, Kate's mother's toy poodle, who was constantly distressed and distressed everyone. Sweet sixteen, Matt joked of Katrina. When truly exasperated, he referred to her under his breath as a three-pound deaf mute. Katrina, whose haphazard incontinence seemed to worsen by the day, suffered her exile in the barricaded kitchen rather stoically except at night, when there was no one to carry her back and forth to Katherine's bed. Big Boy Sports was miles of back and forth; Kate found herself in Pool Appliances, which seemed limitless. Were there really so many swimming pools in stony New England? Where was Nerf? She kept going.

Suddenly, at last, the twenty-one sign was directly overhead and they were enveloped in spongy forms as far as Kate could see. 'IT'S A NERF, NERF, NERF, NERF WORLD!!!' proclaimed arched banners in red, white and blue, and 'HAVE A NERF FOURTH OF JULY!' They would spend tomorrow, the Fourth, at Matt's uncle's house, north of the city. It was a beautiful house with a private beach. Her mother would love to see the ocean. Somehow, Kate had to include her, though the ride was nearly an hour. She perused the weapons, thinking. There was Jonah's RotoRetro-Launcher amid SubAtomic Uzis and rows of something called a Mack-Ack-Ack; Kate had to admit the guns were fabulous, in the sense that they were full-fledged fantasies. Perhaps Matt was right—time for Kate to join the mainstream. He pointed out that her brothers had played with guns, guns Kate cherished now that they were cast aside. Didn't she display, in the room she called her office, a leather Roy Rogers holster with metal studs and fake rubies? The two six-guns had once held metal bullets in cylinders that really turned, but nothing came through the barrel, and the only sound effect was a jewel-like click when the trigger was pulled or the hammer cocked.

Cock the hammer. There was an interesting phrase.

Guns were different now, Kate told Matt. There were toy sub-machine guns and missile launchers and Gatling Grinders. Why not a weapons detonation computer board, she suggested, on which a child pressed one red button to detonate a simulation loud enough to level the house, the city, even the state and the eastern seaboard? Now, now, Matt would say, there were bombs when we were kids. Back in the placid Fifties, the early Sixties, bombs had seemed closer to home. So close, Kate agreed, that toys had to do with cowboys and detectives. Radioactivity was not a selling point when people were building bomb shelters and schools held drills. Everyone into the bathroom! Crouch by the toilets! There sat the third-grade girls with their arms over their heads, amazed at their first sight of a urinal, a whole wall of urinals: the windowless boys' room was most centrally located, and big enough for all three primary grades. Ah, me. The men on the Nerf gun boxes still dressed in battle fatigues, like old-fashioned warriors buffed up on steroids. As though to compensate for their silence, the relatively safe Nerf projectiles were ridiculously oversized circles, spheres and tubes in the shout-it-out colours of psychedelic sherbets. How satisfying to blast away with them, running and jumping and bouncing off walls, and how deluding, as though people could simply blow apart whatever didn't work. A therapist had once told Kate to close her eyes, visualize the problems she'd mentioned, mark them with visual Xs and explode them. Kate refused. I'm just trying to get you to clear your mind, he'd explained patiently. Kate told him she didn't want to clear her mind; she wanted to figure it out. So typical, commented her then boyfriend, a computer whiz social activist. Typical? Sure, you poets like to be up against it, he said, permanently grinding away. Hmmmm, Kate had murmured, pulling him toward her by his jeans pockets. Leaving Nerf weapons behind, she heard his breathy voice admit into the past the deep benefit of her personal flaws.

Here were sports at last. She and Matt had different games, more like play than combat. Daily life was already so full of demands and schedules, many of them negotiated between Matt and his ex when Kate was not present. Matt tried to be accommodating; his ex was alone with the kids; she had them more often than he; he said she was moody and emotional. Not like Kate, was the implication; despite her 'artistic temperament' and present vocation as a stay-at-home sometimes writer/editor, Matt considered Kate self-contained and calm, someone to whom he could turn for talk and advice, a really equal partner. Rephrase, Kate said. When a man talks about equality, it usually means a woman is getting the raw end of a deal. Matt protested that he meant it, it was true; regardless, he couldn't imagine Kate and a raw deal occupying the same planet. Kate tried to warn him that she seldom wept or ranted, but got quiet when she was hurt or angry. Or, Matt reminded her, she could be funny, ironic, even, horrors, sarcastic.

Matt told Kate that his ex had said she still loved him when they went to get their divorce papers. She didn't want to, she said, but she did. Good move on her part to say that, Kate observed. You don't believe her? Matt asked impishly. Kate shrugged. If she loved him so much, why had she treated him so badly? What was all that with her boyfriend, in the year before Matt met Kate? Why did she only get clingy when she realized Matt had met someone, namely Kate? Matt paraphrased, mock-dramatic: she *just* couldn't decide, she needed *space*. So now she has some, Kate had quipped. Afterward she castigated herself for her lack of empathy. Of course it was hard, with the kids, but hard too to be sympathetic, when Matt's ex made it so hard on Kate. The kids weren't allowed to take home anything Kate gave them. If they brought things from their house to Matt's, they weren't allowed to take them home again unless the transport back and forth occurred that same visit. If an object was left behind to exist in Kate's sphere a while, it had to stay, as though it were tainted. Maybe that was why Jonah held on to his Launcher and wore his roller skates; he was afraid he might forget some important thing that would have to remain behind for ever, along with his father.

'Ma,' Alexander said, awake now. 'Bye.' He gazed in seeming wonderment at the red, white and blue balloons wafting in clusters in the highest twenty feet of the arched ceiling.

'That was a brief nap.' Kate adjusted him into sitting position. 'You were due to wake up as we checked out. Now you can help shop.' She wondered if she would have to worry about Alexander mouthing and sucking and inhaling filaments of Nerf, or perhaps Nerf was scientifically engineered never to break down, even under the warm assault of human saliva.

Time was of the essence. Essence of what, Kate thought idly, and for whom? Alexander would be content another fifteen minutes. Kate moved along. Here were Nerf bowling kits, very strange; candlepins that fell over silently, with no thwack when the ball hit them. Then she saw the archery set, which was big and boisterous looking, with a regular bow and a crossbow, a medley of Nerf arrows in various shapes and sizes, some tipped with Velcro. There was a bright nylon target, silk-screened in a surprisingly thoughtful way—figures meant to represent various ages of weaponry stood to the side of each target ring, frozen in the act of letting fly: a barbarian at the outermost ring, a medieval-looking figure, a Robin Hood era hunter with a falcon on his arm, and so on, until the bull's eye featured a modern Olympic archer. Sam would like shooting for points, adding up his score.

'Eureka,' she said to Alexander. 'Two bows, so Jonah can play, but one crossbow just for Sam, the target, and an extra set of Velcro arrows.' She was piling big, lightweight boxes atop the stroller and its fabric sunshade, negotiating a turnaround, peering from behind to steer back up the long, long aisle to check out.

Perfect, she thought, lots of boxes, lots of presents with big ribbons. Archery combined sport and weapons, and maybe she could find an age-appropriate book—*Weapons of Antiquity*, say, with pictures, or a story book. There might be time to stop by a bookstore before picking up the cake. She'd already strung streamers and set the table—today was Sam's actual birthday. At this very moment his mother was presiding over a party for his class. Cupcakes, probably. It was Friday; tonight Matt was in charge of a cook-out. Kate was in charge of the party and beach preparations for tomorrow. 'Are you down there, Mr Boo? I'm up here. Don't worry. We're nearing the finish line.'

Alexander crowed in response to their increased speed. Kate imagined the sunshade collapsing under its stacked cargo. Explain that one: I buried my baby in Nerf boxes. Thankfully, the Perego was nearly indestructible. Kate sailed toward the checkout. *We have a winner!* proclaimed loudspeakers from every direction. *Proceed to Aisle Fifteen!* continued a perky female voice, *Claim your prize, displayed in our Rafters of Prizes!* There was distortion, a loud squeak. Fine. Kate headed for Checkout One, which was deserted but for the clerk. Kate stacked the boxes on the counter and fell to surveying packages of plastic figures displayed beside the register. Boys loved bands of little men to set up and take down. She might find archers, to put on the cake—

'Got a raffle ticket, Ma'am?' The clerk addressed her as the register hummed and pinged.

Kate frowned. Where had she put it? 'Do I have to have one?'

'You get a ten per cent discount if you turn in a raffle ticket.' *Everyone's a winner!* insisted the loudspeakers.

'Never mind the discount.' Kate folded back the stroller sunshade, got her wallet from the Babytote.

The clerk pointed to Alexander. 'Is that it? It's bright red, like what he's got.'

'Oh, God!' Kate bent down to pull a soggy scrap from Alexander's fist. Actually, it was soggy on one end and his chin was smeared red. She dropped the ticket on the counter and put her finger in his mouth, checking for detached bits, rubbing the red from his gums. Red dye no. 2, and her mother always said thick paper was made from filthy rags.

'You won,' said the clerk.

'Won what?' Hurriedly, Kate handed over her credit card.

'The numbers match.' She pointed to a number bleeping red on her register. 'You get your discount, and you win. Just let me have

Jayne Anne Phillips

you sign—' Already, she was handing back the slip, along with the ragged raffle stub. 'Go right over to Fifteen to claim your prize. I'll bag your purchases. You'll need help out to the parking lot, anyway.'

Alexander shouted as though he were responsible. They'd probably won batteries, or a set of golf balls. Kate pushed the stroller to Checkout Fifteen. There stood Kelly, enunciating into a microphone, her register line roped off. '*Big Boy July Super Savings!*' said her now eminently recognizable voice. She saw Kate with the stub in her hand and reached for the scrap of red. '*Oh my gosh!*' she called out, still broadcasting, '*Is it you? Did you win?*' Then she put down the mike and checked the stub. 'You did! You did win!'

'Kelly,' Kate asked, suspicious, 'did you pick the ticket?'

'Nope, a machine picks them. You won, fair and square. Let's see. You won prize nine—there it is! You won the boat!' She flung both arms up, unrehearsed now, pointing directly above them.

Kate saw a lantern, skates, a portable basketball hoop, wading pools, bicycles, a pup tent suspended in perfect form, all labelled with big black numbers, dangling from red, white and blue bungee cord. The objects swayed a bit in a barely discernible breeze of air-conditioning. It was clever, and Kate had entered beneath all this without even looking up. There was the boat, a bright yellow inflated rowboat banded in black, like a bumblebee.

'Gaaaaa,' continued Alexander, 'duh!'

Kate suddenly heard him. Wonderful. He was swearing before he talked. 'How will I ever get it home?' she said aloud.

'Comes with a pump, silly, folded up. And oars! That's just the display model.' Kelly had a shopping cart all packed: black plastic oars, a heavy-duty pump that looked like a slim oxygen tank, and a square, plastic-encased bundle the size of a respectable suitcase. 'Very heavy-duty, and big enough for two,' she added. 'Want to buy the baby a life jacket? We have them in all sizes.'

'I wouldn't let him in that, life jacket or not, unless it was in the backyard. But his dad will like it, if he ever has time to inflate it.'

'Takes a minute,' Kelly assured her. 'This pump is great—bike tyres, air mattresses, whatever. The boat is the very best prize. You're lucky!'

Kate laughed. She supposed she was.

There were no archers at *Party Cakes* but Kate bought a packet of tiny plastic baseball players—it was summer, after all—and they looked very engaged, turned toward one another, their miniature pedestals set in white icing on Sam's cake. His name was all done up in red and blue; at home Kate had got the whole confection out of the box on to a cut-glass platter, where it truly reigned supreme. Matt always said kids didn't care whether they ate their cake off cardboard or china, but surely anyone saw, over time, how care was taken for them, and things done specially. Until they drop the glass plates and they break, Matt pointed out. Well, of course. For tonight there were paper plates and cups, all birthday embossed with red 9s and exclamation points. The *Party Cakes* sale bin supplied hats and a paper tablecloth to match; modern parenthood was full of thematic opportunity. Alexander was happy in his Play-yard, mouthing teething rings, so Kate wrapped one of the high-backed plastic lawn chairs in crêpe paper and made Sam a crown. Surely kid's birthdays should always involve crowns. She'd thought of inviting one or two of Sam's friends for supper and cake, to see him open his presents, but it seemed too invasive. Unless, someday, Sam suggested it, which he might. Their only piece of Sam now was when he appeared, before he disappeared. If the kids were going to have one real home, which they certainly needed, wasn't the other relegated to a kind of limbo in which special occasions took place a second time? Kate decided against glitter. Glitter would be all over everything and Alexander would be glad to ingest it. She went with the tinsel pipe-cleaners she found in the bottom of the art drawer she'd made for the kids: paper, crayons, play dough, coloured pencils, all pretty much under-utilized, except by Kate.

'You certainly are having fun.' Kate's mother stood in the dining room doorway. She'd dressed up in her white linen skirt and blouse.

'Mom, you look great. Did you see the cake? And how does this look?' Kate held up the crown, still unfastened. 'I'd better wait until he gets here to tape it, so it'll fit.'

'I wish I could have made you a cake. I always think it's a shame to buy one.'

'Remember the train you did one year, with all the different cars, and the Raggedy Ann cake you made me—icing pinafore and Mary

Jane's, and red hair? I can cook, but I could never decorate a cake that way, or make a fluted pie crust. Or sew, come to think of it, which always seemed so tedious. My fine motor skills are probably lacking.'

'You compensated by developing other talents,' her mother said sagely. 'Dinner all set?'

'I made a salad, and the baked beans, and the rest Matt will do. Now, let's see.' Kate stood over Alexander, looking down at him as Katherine joined her. He liked to throw everything to the net sides of the Play-yard, then demand someone pile it all in front of him again. 'Mr Boo, will you have a hot dog, or a hamburger?'

'Wouldn't he love that. Enough with the soft mushy stuff.'

'Let's move him to the porch. Can you hold him, while I move this contraption? I've got the swing out there already. Let me lift him to you—' She bent down to swing him a time or two, a ritual he'd come to expect and greeted with squeals of delight. '—but sit down, because it'll take me a minute, and he's so heavy.'

'I feel better, really. But I'll sit if you insist. You're really going to move that big thing?'

'Sure.' Kate gave her the baby, then unsnapped the metal hinges of the Play-yard, moved the fabric pad aside to grasp holes in the centre of the fibreboard bottom. The sides came down, creaking as various Alexander implements fell into the netting. 'It may be used,' Kate said, 'but it works. And no bars, I'd like to point out.'

'Is that what you got at the Ladies' Auxiliary? Actually, babies like bars. They chew them and pull up on them. And play peek-a-boo behind them—'

'OK, Mom.'

'But I'm sure you're right. Play-yards are probably an advance.'

Kate fastened open the screen doors to the patio. The dogs, taking their ease in the fenced yard, began barking at various decibels, providing one another with competitive motivation. Katrina stood over her tiny chain, having stretched it to the limit, while Luna bounded in and out, showing off. Kate set up the Play-yard and went back to get Alexander. 'Mom, come outside and try the recliner. Another second-hand find, and it has a cushion.'

'My goodness, you got a recliner?'

'Yesterday, same source. It's nothing fancy, just one of those plastic ones.' Kate situated Alexander.

'It's nice you have this for me,' her mother answered, 'but don't buy any more porch furniture down there. Someday you'll have the money to buy things that match. Then what will you do with these?'

Kate turned to see Katherine already in position against the dark green cushion, feet propped up, arms on armrests. 'Well, look at that,' Kate said, 'a perfect fit, after you bad-mouth my eclectic style.' She hadn't realized the recliner was exactly the right height; her mother could get up and down without help, and the cushion, which had come from some more exalted incarnation, was thick and comfortable. The whole thing was, yes, a stroke of luck—Katherine would spend more time on the patio, for the rest of the summer, instead of lying on the downstairs daybed, indoors. So simple and so important. What else had Kate not considered, what else should she do?

'You know, I'm just realizing,' she told Katherine. 'You look so comfortable. Tomorrow, we'll take you to the ocean just like that. We'll take one of the seats out of the van and load the recliner in the back. You can rest all the way there.'

Her mother looked doubtful. 'And what will you do with me when we get there?'

'Matt says they have a beautiful enclosed porch, with a big window that looks right out on the ocean. I'm sure there's a chaise. Or we could walk on the beach, and I'll put the recliner just where the sand begins to be wet, so you can look at the waves. Wouldn't you like that?'

'It seems so much trouble for you.' She looked down at her dog then, who yipped frantically in response. 'Katrina, you simpleton,' she said, 'you've managed to wind your chain in and out of that dogwood tree forty times. Now you're in a fix. No, I'm not coming over there to get you.'

'I'll get her,' Kate said, 'if she'll stick with you and not run away.'

'I know you worry about her taking off between the rungs of the fence, but really, she can't see a thing. Why would she run away?'

'Adventure. Excitement. How can you be so sure the raging passions of her youth are quelled? Katrina, it's me,' Kate told the dog.

'I'm just coming to unhook you. Why do all poodles have rhinestones on their collars?'

'It's a law.' Katherine took the dog in her hands. Katrina nestled beside her, emitting the satisfied groan of the long put-upon. 'I can assure you,' Katherine said, 'she won't move until someone moves her. As for youth, well. Youth is so much of life, when you don't grow old.' She lay her head back on the cushion. 'I think of my mother; she was barely middle-aged.'

'But Mom,' Kate said quietly, 'they didn't know how to care for her, then, in that place. If she'd had a hysterectomy, she probably would have recovered.'

'A spot the size of a dime. They said they could cure her with radium. She went to Baltimore—it was really the best they had, at the time. She was fifty-six. I'll be sixty this summer. Katie, you'd better get to living.'

The baby began to fuss. Kate picked him up. She was living, wasn't she? Then why did she find it so hard, momentarily, to breathe? Her former 'adult' existence—college, grad school, single life, thinking, writing, travelling, working—in which she'd interacted solely with adults, now seemed so luxurious in the vast time and space given over to consideration, thought, large and small decisions. It was a world in which no one was dying, no one was being born; a half-life, floating world, a bubble from which she observed and recorded and made of her observations an alternate world of association and image, a world as real to her, as present, as the food she ate. She was too busy now, too tired, too occupied with taking care and keeping up, too drenched in sensation, to think about living, to draw conclusions; she ate to keep going, to stay awake, to stay competent, to be healthy, to feed her baby, to get everything done. The interior world had receded, replaced by other lives and their attendant mysteries. She was the caretaker; she *took care*, waking every day within her own flat-out evolution. The events she lived inside shifted moment to moment over packed hours filled with detail and camouflage: meals and laundry, toys and shopping and baths, naps, doctor's appointments, conferences with doctors, and the double row of plastic pill containers with childproof caps her mother could barely manage to open. The diminutive bottles were the amber colour of some transparent, primeval sap, identical but for their staggered heights and dosage schedules, and the complex content of their neatly typed labels.

Her mother asked, 'Did you get the book you wanted for Sam?'

'Oh no,' Kate said, 'I forgot. I totally forgot about the books. Anyway, there wasn't time.'

Books. Who was she without them? She called herself a freelance editor, but she hadn't actually accepted a project since Alexander was born. Life seemed work enough. As for her own work, if she were a writer, she would be writing, despite everything. She was no longer a poet; she didn't try now; she was a coward. Somewhere, on the other side of a terrible expanse, she would begin again. She had to think so. She read poems, other people's poems, the same ones again and again, as though she couldn't comprehend them but was focused and comforted by their very cadences and sounds, their voices in her mind, voices she could not hear unless she was staring at the words themselves. As though a door opened and shut, or a light went on and off; there was brilliance or darkness, and nothing in between but the free-fall of time, its disappearance. There was so much to do, and there was not time. Kate walked the width of the flagstone patio and back, keeping Alexander in motion as he fussed against her. She'd fed him; he shouldn't be hungry. He rubbed his face and yawned, but he'd already napped. She should be tired, not he. In the garden, which seemed far away across the compact lawn, mounds of blue salvia were in rampant bloom, clusters and spears of blue against a pale textured green of ground cover her mother called rabbit's ear. The velvety, overgrown leaves had climbed the fence; along the front of the bed, they spilled on to the grass. Kate heard voices, then a run of song from a car radio; Matt had pulled into the driveway. Alexander began to cry in earnest. 'They're here,' Kate whispered into his hair. 'I'll check on things in the kitchen,' she told her mother.

She sat at the table, nursing, as Matt came in. 'Hey,' she said, and lifted her face for his kiss.

'How's the boy?' He stroked Alexander's downy head.

'Fussy. He could be patented as a stress-absorber, but he expresses what he absorbs almost immediately. You might say there's

Jayne Anne Phillips

a catch in the dynamic.'

'There's certainly a catch somewhere.' Matt loosened his tie.

'You don't look pleased. What's wrong?'

'He's in such a bad mood.'

'Sam, you mean? Sometimes birthdays are too much. Maybe I did too much.'

Matt looked around him, appearing truly puzzled. 'He hasn't even seen what you did—they're still in the car, arguing over whose launcher is whose. The guns are exactly alike, but Sam is convinced Jonah switched them. The dining room looks great, by the way, and the presents. Sometimes, no matter what we do, it's not right. There's no way to anticipate.'

'Transition,' Kate told him. 'Sam will settle down in an hour or two.'

'But will I?'

'Yes, you will. You're hungry. They're hungry. You'll feel better after you fire up the grill and throw the meat on it. Isn't barbecuing the modern equivalent of clubbing a mastodon?'

'I would like to club a mastodon.'

'And you have to be satisfied with wielding a spatula. This is what we mean by modern distortion of basic urges.'

'We're walking distortions, all of us but Alexander here.'

They heard Jonah's quick step—footsteps today, no roller skates—and his piping voice. 'Sam! Sam! There's presents in here!'

'See? They've made it inside.' Kate stood to burp the baby.

'Dad!' Jonah stood in the doorway, wearing sunglasses and a Jonah outfit—shorts, T-shirt, bat-cape, unmatched socks and sandals, baseball hat. He held up the pump that went with the boat. 'What's this, and the big present with no wrapping? Is it for me, since Sam gets all the others?'

'You sure did get a present,' Kate said, 'but not that one. The boat is for all you men, and your dad's in charge of it.'

Matt turned to look at her. 'What boat?'

'I won a boat, a blow-up boat, at Big Boy Sports. Can you believe—'

'Wow!' Jonah shouted. 'It blows up! Let's blow it up! My friend has a race car that does that when you hit it with another race car.'

'Not that way, hon,' Kate told him gently. 'You blow it up with air, inflate it, like a balloon. That's the pump you're holding.'

His face fell. 'Oh.'

'I know it doesn't look very interesting right now, all folded—' Kate followed him back into the dining room, worried the boat would steal the thunder from Sam's presents, from Sam. Kate had left the oars outside and piled the rest in a corner; she should have put it all out of sight. But Jonah appeared to have lost interest. He was in the yard, throwing a tennis ball for Luna. He'd put Katrina, who looked alarmed, in the Play-yard, and Kate's mother was getting up to retrieve her. 'But Katrina is a baby,' he was saying. 'She's my baby,' Katherine was telling him, 'but in dog years she's an old lady. That's why she has accidents sometimes.' Not now, Kate hoped. Alexander could swing until she'd had time to inspect the Play-yard; she wanted to get supper started; Matt could take over once he changed his clothes. She heard him walking up the stairs, his step less buoyant than usual. There was Sam, standing by the fence in his jeans and sneakers and black T-shirt. He looked sombre in his wire-rim glasses, watching Jonah. Maybe something had happened. Picking up the kids on holidays, Matt was always running into groups of former in-laws gathered in the big house his ex and he had shared. Matt had told Kate how numerous little cousins had set up a chorus last Christmas: Matt should come back home. 'Well, he's not going to,' Sam had announced flatly. Kate supposed Matt told her these things because they were hard for him to bear, and Kate was meant to help him bear them. She settled Alexander on one hip and picked up the plate of meat Matt had left on the table.

'Kate?' her mother called.

'Coming.' She backed through the screen door to the patio and gave Katherine the plate. 'Just let me get him in the swing. It's a perfect moment for swinging. Hello, Sam. Are you hungry for a hamburger?'

'Sort of,' Sam said.

'Is it French fries too?' Jonah asked.

Was there time to make French fries? She'd need a full bottle of canola oil. 'I'll make those for you tomorrow night.'

'There's corn and baked beans for tonight,' her mother said, 'but wait until you taste Kate's French fries.'

Jayne Anne Phillips

'We like the frozen ones,' Jonah said.
'Then you haven't had the home-made kind.' Katherine held the plate high, out of Katrina's reach.
'I like MacDonald's. I get my mom to go there every night.'
'You're a liar,' Sam said.
'Am not,' Jonah said.
'Jonah,' Kate said, 'you like playing with the swing. Can you wind it up for me?' Jonah flew toward her, pleased to show how fast he could wind the lever, as Kate reflected on the several mistakes built into a godsend device. 'Winding it requires two hands,' she told her mother. 'Isn't that a design flaw?'

It was true; the unassisted mom used both hands to put the baby into the swing, where he might begin crying before she could set the thing in motion. Said baby eventually drowsed, but the resulting pause that refreshed was limited to the life of the wind-up; the winding itself was a loud continuous ratcheting guaranteed to startle any baby within earshot into instinctual, terrified sobs, if the cessation of motion hadn't wakened him already. The thing was obviously manufactured by people who hadn't used it.

'Beggars can't be choosers,' her mother responded predictably. 'Why don't I put the meat on the grill? I'm not helpless, you know.'

'Hang on, Mom. Watch over the troops.' Kate took the plate from her.

'I can do the music box? Sam is too far away.' Jonah was already winding the smaller key, mounted on the side of the mechanism. Strains of 'Rock-a-Bye Baby' sounded, oddly pure and plaintive. Jonah liked to hold the key as it turned, and make the notes sound one by one.

'It does sound better that way, Jonah. You can make the music box go at any speed you want, but don't change the speed of the swing, OK? It's just right for Alexander.'

'The swing ticks like a clock,' Jonah called over to Sam, but Sam ignored him and stayed outside the fence, like a wayfarer. Kate thought Jonah astute; the swing was a clock; she often measured time by its clicking, and she had ten minutes to get the food on the table. Jonah's perceptiveness could be wearying in a younger brother; Sam turned his back. Soon Jonah would be seriously opportuning him, and cross if Sam didn't respond.

'I bet Sam wants to count his birthday presents.' Kate stood at the grill. There. Underway. 'You stay out here, Jonah. I bet Sam wants to go in and take a look.'

'Take a look at these, you mean?' Matt was carrying all the presents on to the patio in a big pile.

'That's it.' Kate's mother got up to help. 'Bring the mountain to Mohammed. Can you see where you're going?'

'All those?' Sam watched through the fence.

'Come take a look, big guy. And guess whose chair this is, all streamers, and whose crown, on the chair?'

Sam opened the gate and came into the yard to stand by his chair. 'My crown?'

'Have a seat.' Katherine looked meaningfully at Kate. 'Someone wants to fix that crown to fit you just right.'

Kate left her post and flew inside for the tape. Where had she left it? Jonah stood by the swing, watching Alexander. Kate heard him say to Katherine, 'Could I get in here?' 'Oh, you're too big for that,' came Katherine's voice. The kitchen. Kate checked the counters and the drawer before she found the tape in the sink. It was mostly dry. Through the open kitchen window, she saw Jonah at the Play-yard, fixing her mother with his sidelong, charming look. 'Can I get in *here* then? This has a lot of room.' 'It does,' Katherine agreed, 'but it's not strong enough for a big boy like you. Sit here, by me. There's just room, if you hold Katrina.' 'I'll hold Katrina!' he exclaimed. Kate ripped away the wet tape. How and why had she dropped it in the sink? She was hands and glands, no brain; it was probably better that way. Turning, she observed Luna, prized tennis ball in her mouth, slinking away into the garden.

Sam waited on the patio, holding the crown. 'Luna is growling,' he told Kate.

'Luna has to learn to share,' Katherine said.

'I'll play with her next.' Jonah was ensconced in the recliner with the trembling Katrina and a watchful Katherine.

Kate taped the crown to fit, careful not to catch Sam's long brown hair. For next time, she would find a dress-up cape. 'Have a seat, Sir Sam.'

Jayne Anne Phillips

'King Sam,' her mother corrected her.

'I'm going to open all my presents right now!' Sam reached out with open arms.

'The hamburgers!' Kate said.

'This won't take long, believe me.' Matt looked genuinely delighted.

It wasn't food he'd needed, obviously. Kate watched them from the grill as she warmed rolls, cooked the meat. 'Wow,' Sam kept saying, his voice drifting off as he applied himself studiously to each new parcel. Paper and ribbon fell away, piling up in sheets on the grass. Jonah had abandoned Katrina and dragged the boat outside in its plastic bundle; now he sat himself atop its folded bulk and waited. It was too late to give him the extra bow. Sam had already opened everything and was meticulously arranging each object around his chair, minus cardboard trappings and packaging, in a kind of ready order, poised for use. He stood still, satisfied, then raised his eyes to his father. There was a lag of a few seconds in which Kate felt a tense apprehension; she heard the slow, occasional click of the nearly motionless swing in which her baby slept.

Then Sam threw himself against Matt and hugged him hard.

In the silence, Kate's eyes met her mother's. Katherine winked at her, and nodded.

Later, when Kate walked outside with the cake, it was dusk, and the little flames shone. The plastic baseball men had sunk into the icing just enough; their miniature feet appeared poised on a sweet, snowy field. 'Dad, it's a night game,' Sam said, and blew out the candles.

They were en route, crossing the bridge above the naval yard, the city skyline behind them.

'Does your uncle have life preservers?' Kate asked Matt. She sat just behind him on the middle seat, Alexander's car seat buckled beside her.

'Of course he does, and yes, the kids will wear them if that boat actually inflates, and yes, I promise I'll take them one at a time.'

'I still think I should have ridden in the back of the van with Mom,' Kate answered. 'The kids should all be belted. Traffic, holiday weekend.'

'No, I'm way in the back. I don't need a belt. I'm on the boat.'
Jonah sat atop its bright yellow length, which he'd unfolded beside
the recliner, roller skates in his lap. 'Anyway, your mom doesn't have
a seat belt. She's even lying down where a seat used to be.'

'She's a grown-up,' Sam asserted. He'd claimed the passenger
seat beside his dad, but couldn't conceal his intense interest in Jonah's
progress with the pump. Sigh and squeak, sigh and squeak; in the back
with Katherine, Jonah had managed to affix the air tube; he held the
cylinder of the pump between his feet and pumped air into the boat
even as he sat inside it. Kate turned to see the boat swelling perceptibly,
then alarmingly, murmurously inhaling as it grew. She'd once told
Matt, back when they were first falling for one another, how she
hoped she might 'contribute something' to his boys' lives, something
they wouldn't have had if they'd never known her. This wasn't exactly
what she'd envisioned. The big yellow boat, taking form before her
eyes in the elongated back of the van, suddenly struck her as funny.

Katherine was laughing as well. 'Poor little thing,' she called up
to Matt. 'He's really expending some energy back here.'

'The boat is getting big,' Sam said.

'It's going to be bigger than the recliner,' Jonah claimed, 'bigger
than the van.'

'You might have to climb out,' Katherine advised him, 'and turn
it sideways, so we'll still have room to breathe.'

Sam asked, 'Can I pump now, Dad?'

'No,' came Jonah's voice, 'the boat is mine. The bows and
arrows are yours.'

'Kate said the boat is everyone's.' Sam looked to Matt for
arbitration.

'But we said he could take care of the boat for today,' Matt
answered, 'since you brought your archery set with you.'

'Today's *my* boat day,' Jonah asserted.

'Who puts it in the water, Jonah?' his father asked sternly.

'You do, Dad. But I'm getting it ready, and I'm the one that pulls
it to the beach. You said.'

'Yes, I said. Kate, you're quiet. Still mourning your Baby
Bouncer?'

'I can't believe he's outgrown it. I liked holding him in front, just next to me.' Kate watched the shore beside them. She loved this vista, the sea wall and the flats below, though the beach looked dirty, the water too polluted for swimming. There were no big houses here, only vinyl-sided bungalows and apartment complexes with metal awnings. Older pensioners watched the surf across a four-lane highway and walked their dogs along emptied sand barred with deep black streaks. 'The backpack is for big kids,' she said aloud. 'It's so restraining, with the metal frame and the straps.'

'He is a big kid. He's almost crawling. We need something big enough to hold him still, don't we? The frame makes him feel secure enough to stay put and just look around.'

'You're right; I'm glad you suggested it. And he does want to see, don't you Boo, all Mom walks through. We'll stroll on the beach and see the gulls and the shore birds. I promise we will.' She reached over to Alexander with his plastic book, his chiming rattle, and he grabbed her wrist with both chubby hands. 'Bye,' he told her, mischievous, holding on, not waving.

'Ten thousand byes,' Kate said. 'Monkey, you know what "bye" means. Like this.' She made the hand motion, opening palm and fingers. He watched her, smiling.

Sam sang with the radio, Jonah applied himself to his boat. Katherine closed her eyes. Kate sat up, leaning near to Matt. 'What does your uncle do, living in this big house on his beach?'

'He's the one that owns the leisurewear company. You see his clothes in department stores, sweaters mostly.'

'Handmade?'

'Factory made, I think, in the Philippines, and Argentina.'

She leaned up closer. 'Where labour is cheap, and people disappear.'

Matt threw her a glance. 'I doubt he had anything to do with *that*, Kate.'

'I'm sure not,' Kate said quietly. 'I mean, no more than we do, by not trying to stop it.'

He looked at her in the rear-view mirror. 'Kate, we can't stop everything.'

She sighed. 'Ah, but can we stop anything?'

'We can stop thinking in those terms—' he looked at his watch, '—for the next four hours, until we drive back from the ocean. Enjoy the day, the sea, everyone out of the house, your mother being well enough to come along.' He fixed her with an enquiring look in the rear-view mirror. 'How's that? How's happiness for a big boy sport? Temporary, undeniable happiness.'

She nodded back. 'Yes, and tonight we'll see fireworks.'

Jonah had paused in his labours. 'It sounds like no more air is going in.'

Katherine was holding the boat up with both hands. She'd helped Jonah turn it sideways; now she gave it a little shove, shifting its yellow bulk to rest against the opposite side of the van. 'That's what determination will do for you,' she told Jonah. 'It's as hard as a rock. Sit tight now and maybe we'll keep it from falling on you.'

'Won't hurt me,' Jonah said. 'It's *my* boat.'

The moment they arrived, Jonah headed down around the house toward the beach, clutching his skates in one hand and the rope in the other, dragging the boat along behind him. Family members called out greetings as Kate and Matt unloaded; beach bags, a cooler of pasta and fruit salad Kate had made for the buffet, the backpack. Sam ran indoors as Matt's relatives milled around, commenting on the baby, on how big the boys had grown. Matt's aunt took Katherine's arm; she must come in and see 'our view of the ocean', so wonderful Kate's mother could visit, would she like some lemonade while the food was set out, Matt was so fond...

Kate and Matt found themselves standing alone on the circular drive with Alexander. Katherine had disappeared inside.

'See?' Matt said. 'I told you they'd take good care of her.'

'And I *am* happy. I'm going to change Alexander over there on the grass, and go down to see the beach. We'll try out the backpack. They'll all be busy with the food, they won't miss me for a few minutes. Why is it July and we haven't been to the beach?'

Matt was taking the food inside. 'You may not realize this yet, but infants and sandcastles don't necessarily mix. And we have been, well, busy.'

'Busy, he says.' Kate knelt down with the baby and put him on the grass. The lush front yard had the look of a serviced garden, the grass cool in the shade, thick and tufted. Alexander kicked and squirmed. Free of clothes, he wanted to turn over and go. Kate leaned close and spoke to him; he stopped moving to watch the words. 'Smell the air,' she told him, her face close. She brushed his forehead with her lashes. 'Salt air. You'll live by the sea, Mr Boo, I can tell by looking at you.' She felt the expressions move across her face, reflections of his surprise, his attention, his laughter, interpretative back-and-forth between them to keep him interested, to keep her talking, only to him. 'You'll know why waves run one way and not another, you'll see it all, the tides and the storms and the sea glass.' She snapped his clothes back on, put the wet diaper in a bag, tucked it in the Babytote. She'd leave the bag until later; they were going walking, after all.

Now, into the backpack. They'd practised this morning. Kate slipped him in, belted him tight, fit the straps to her shoulders, and stood. She felt almost guiltily independent, despite his considerable weight; no stroller before her, no head at her chin, nothing in her line of vision but the path she followed along the side of the house, then down, through beach grass and gorse, past broad rocks; a path as broad as Jonah's boat, and steeply descending. Kate kept her eyes on the ground, not wanting to look or see the beach until it lay before her. She heard the waves, then saw them, lapping foam along a broad beautiful sweep. The empty sand sparkled as though pearlized. Sunlight hit her eyes at a slant, nearly blinding her. Jonah must have gone back up to the house, but where had he left the boat? Absently, she looked at the ocean. There, on a gentle roll of surf perhaps fifty feet out, bobbed the yellow boat. Jonah was in it. He waved to her. One foot was propped up; Kate realized he'd put on his roller skates. In the bright sun, she felt a profound chill. The tide was going out. She ran far back on the sand, back to where the water wouldn't reach for hours, yelling toward the house, which sat silently above them on the cliff, betraying no sign. She couldn't wait. He would get too far away. She was calling Matt's name; she would have to leave Alexander here, strapped into the pack, upright and immobilized. 'Mommy will be right back,' she said to him, 'right back.' Her voice sounded calm, as though someone else were speaking. She slipped off the pack and jammed the metal frame deeply into sand to keep it still, even if he fussed, even if he screamed, and checked the belt restraint. There, by her foot on the sand, were the castaway oars.

She let them lie; she couldn't get to him in time and carry them. She pulled Alexander's hat more forward on his head and turned, stepping out of her shoes and skirt, running. The boat didn't appear to have moved; it seemed stationary but for its rise and fall on the waves. She was in water to her knees, to her hips. How had he done this, wearing skates? She'd hoped the water was shallow but it deepened immediately. She would have to swim; the distance was deceptive. She dove in as the shelf of sand beneath her feet suddenly gave way. A shock of cold, salt in her mouth. When she was a child and travelled to Carolina beaches with her mother, the water had been warm as bathwater, the strand beyond the boardwalk glittering with lights. *Our view of the ocean*. Katherine might be watching now, might see them from the window and send the men, send Matt. Alexander's swing ticked in her head, each slow click distinct. She heard Jonah call to her, his voice little and calm. 'I got in,' he was calling, 'to wait for Dad, and the water came up.' Of course, he'd sat in the boat, too near the waves, and put on his skates; he liked taking them on and off; he liked how they fit over his sneakers. Kate swam harder; he was farther away, ever farther than he seemed. 'I know,' she called back, 'I'll pull you in.' The water seemed turgid, intent on separation, but she was moving closer. She could pace herself. She could see the rope now, still tied to the front of the boat, bright yellow, trailing in the water. Swallowed up, appearing again. She was not a strong swimmer, but she would only need to get close enough to grab the rope and get back to shore. The boat was fully inflated. It could even hold them both, if she got tired. As long as he stayed in it, as long as he didn't fall out. It was a perfect day. The sky was absolutely blue. □

'The crackle of flames and the screech of shellfire; Darko and the Jokers; an old woman with her broken teeth falling bloodily down her chest; a girl's severed ear; Hamdu, the Tigers and the final attack; frightened soldiers; the reek of smoke and the clatter of a gunship.

My war gone by, I miss it so.'

by
ANTHONY LOYD

NOTES ON CONTRIBUTORS

Jillian Edelstein is a member of Network Photographers. She moved to London from South Africa in 1985 and has worked for many international publications including the London *Sunday Times*, the *New York Times* and the *New Yorker*. She has been following the work of the Truth and Reconciliation Commission for more than two years and is currently working on a book on the subject.

William Fiennes has written for the *London Review of Books* and the *Times Literary Supplement*. His first book will be published next year by Picador.

Elena Lappin was born in Moscow, grew up in Prague and Hamburg, and has lived in Israel, Canada and the United States. She moved to London in 1993 and edited the *Jewish Quarterly* from 1994 to 1997. Her short story collection, *Foreign Brides*, is published by Picador in Britain and Farrar, Straus & Giroux in the United States. She is currently working on a novel, *The Nose*.

Adewale Maja-Pearce has written and reported extensively on Africa for many periodicals in Africa, Britain and the United States, including the *London Review of Books* and *Index*. He has published a collection of short stories, *Loyalties*, and several books of travel writing and essays, all published by Heinemann. At present, he is writing a report on the transition of power in Nigeria.

Javier Marías's novel *A Heart So White* (Harvill/New Directions) was awarded the Dublin IMPAC Award as the best novel published in English in 1996. His most recent book, *Dark Back of Time*, will be published by New Directions in the United States. He lives in Madrid.

Claire Messud's first novel, *When the World was Steady*, is published by Granta Books and was shortlisted for the PEN/Faulkner award. Her story, 'The Professor's History', appeared in *Granta* 51. 'Adults' is taken from her new novel, *The Last Life*, which will be published this year by Picador in Britain and Harcourt Brace in the United States. She lives in Washington DC.

Jayne Anne Phillips is the author of *Black Tickets, Machine Dreams, Fast Lanes* and *Shelter*. 'Big Boy Sports' is taken from her new novel, *Mother Care*, which will be published by Jonathan Cape in Britain and Knopf in the United States.

Stacey Richter lives in Tucson, Arizona. Her collection of stories, *My Date with Satan*, will be published by Scribner.

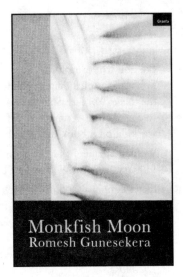
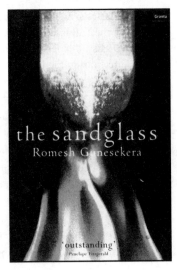